AF738697

Corporate Governance of Chinese Multinational Corporations

Runhui Lin · Jean Jinghan Chen · Li Xie

Corporate Governance of Chinese Multinational Corporations

Case Studies

palgrave
macmillan

Runhui Lin
Business School
Nankai University
Tianjin, China

Jean Jinghan Chen
Faculty of Business Administration
University of Macau
Macau, China

Li Xie
International Business School
Xi'an Jiaotong-Liverpool University
Suzhou, Jiangsu, China

ISBN 978-981-15-7404-7 ISBN 978-981-15-7405-4 (eBook)
https://doi.org/10.1007/978-981-15-7405-4

© The Editor(s) (if applicable) and The Author(s), under exclusive license to Springer Nature Singapore Pte Ltd. 2020
This work is subject to copyright. All rights are solely and exclusively licensed by the Publisher, whether the whole or part of the material is concerned, specifically the rights of translation, reprinting, reuse of illustrations, recitation, broadcasting, reproduction on microfilms or in any other physical way, and transmission or information storage and retrieval, electronic adaptation, computer software, or by similar or dissimilar methodology now known or hereafter developed.
The use of general descriptive names, registered names, trademarks, service marks, etc. in this publication does not imply, even in the absence of a specific statement, that such names are exempt from the relevant protective laws and regulations and therefore free for general use.
The publisher, the authors and the editors are safe to assume that the advice and information in this book are believed to be true and accurate at the date of publication. Neither the publisher nor the authors or the editors give a warranty, expressed or implied, with respect to the material contained herein or for any errors or omissions that may have been made. The publisher remains neutral with regard to jurisdictional claims in published maps and institutional affiliations.

Cover credit: © Alex Linch shutterstock.com

This Palgrave Macmillan imprint is published by the registered company Springer Nature Singapore Pte Ltd.
The registered company address is: 152 Beach Road, #21-01/04 Gateway East, Singapore 189721, Singapore

Foreword

Multinational corporations (MNEs) have presumably become the significant driving force behind globalization. Through hundreds of years of development, it has experienced the climax of the development of three waves of multinational companies in Europe, America, Japan, South Korea, and China. Especially after the global financial crisis in 2008, Chinese companies have continuously established their footprints and expanded their business scale internationally, which has been gaining worldwide attention. According to the Fortune Global 500 list in 2019, there were 129 Chinese companies on the list, surpassing the United States for the first time. The collective rise of Chinese multinational companies has a significant impact on the development of the world economy and technological progress.

With the increase of foreign direct investment of Chinese MNEs, operational risks due to weak corporate governance mechanism in the process of internationalization have become increasingly prominent. In this vein, governance of MNEs has become a critical research area as well as a practical issue in recent years. Upon the firm's internationalization process, the first challenge would be the difference in institutional settings, since the multinational governance needs to adequately address the adaptability of regulatory environment, social and cultural institution, and local corporate governance mode. In addition, the diversification of governance system and operational practice which caused by the geographical boundary expansion with entrusted principal-agent chain extension and information asymmetry not only enhance the multinational coordination costs, but also lead to high business costs. Therefore, the study of how to integrate multinational corporate governance and to construct a system firewall for transnational operational risks are crucial to improve the company's transnational operational capabilities and leverage the product and capital markets.

With more Chinese enterprises establish business globally, they have gradually developed their paths with Chinese characteristics while integrating into the world business stage. Some of them have grown into the league of world-renowned multinational groups. However, the majority of Chinese MNEs have been puzzled by the problem of corporate governance and institutional gaps which have hampered their development. At this stage, there is no comprehensive review of Chinese MNEs' experience and their business model on corporate governance. This book is intended to fill this void.

Based on in-depth studies of Chinese MNEs, this book is the first empirical study of Chinese MNEs supported by primary real-life cases. It has provided valuable empirical evidence to support the arguments surrounding theoretical research of MNEs governance. It is an excellent example of collaborative work between China Academy of Corporate Governance Research in Nankai University and the Faculty of Business Administration in the University of Macao. It has provided valuable managerial, policy insights and implications for business executives as well as policy-makers.

Professor Weian Li
President of China Academy of Corporate Governance Research
Nankai University
Tianjin, China

Acknowledgments

We are extremely grateful to all our contributors who have made the publication of this book a reality. We specifically thank Professor Runhui Lin, Professor Jean Jinghan Chen, and Dr. Li Xie for their valuable guidance and comments about case selection, theoretical framework construction, and book structuring.

We would like to thank Dr. Hongjuan Zhang, Dr. Chunyan Wang, Mr. Qing Huang, Dr. Jingli Song, Dr. Changbao Zhou, Dr. Kanghong Li, and Dr. Fei Li for their contributions of initial draft of the book. There are also others who are not featured directly in the book as contributors but have played some equally active parts in ensuring the publication of the book, including Dr. Ya Li, Dr. Na Li, Dr. Jun Wu, Dr. Jie Mi, Dr. Yuan Gui, and Zaiyang Xie. We would also like to show our gratitude to them.

We are grateful for the financial support provided by the Natural Science Foundation of China (NSFC: 71772096, 71533002, 71672123), the Ministry of Education's Key Research Base of Humanities and Social sciences (16JJD630002), and the Ministry of Education's Project of China (18YJC630233). We also thank for the support provided by China Group Companies Association and a number of business people.

We are equally grateful to the publishing team at Palgrave Macmillan headed by the Senior Editor Jacob Dreyer and other members of the publishing team who have supported this publication. We are deeply grateful to our respective families for their support. Thanks to our colleagues and friends who have supported us in seeing through this publication.

Contents

Notes on Contributors

Jean Jinghan Chen joined the University of Macau in 2018 as a Chair Professor in Accounting and Finance and the Dean of Faculty of Business Administration. Prior to joining the University of Macau, Professor Chen worked in the United Kingdom's higher education sector for almost 30 years. She was the founding Head of Southampton Business School and a Chair Professor in Accounting and Finance at the University of Southampton in 2014. Professor Chen also worked as the Associate Dean of Faculty of Business, Economics and Law, the Vice President and Chief Executive of Surrey International Institute, and a Chair Professor in Financial Management at the University of Surrey, as well as the Executive Dean of the International Business School and Chair Professor of Accounting and Finance at the Xian Jiaotong branch of Liverpool University.

Professor Chen was elected by UK Business Schools and held two senior roles as a Council Member and the Chair of the Council's International Committee in the UK Royal Chartered Association of Business Schools (ABS) during 2014 and 2015. She was also elected by the China Management Academy in November 2015 to serve as an Executive Director of the China Academy of Management has been in that position since then. To recognize Professor Chen's outstanding contribution to High Education, the Ministry of Education of China presented her with the prestigious national "Outstanding Overseas Scholar" award in 2012.

Professor Chen has been recognized internationally as an expert of accounting and finance in general and more specifically in the field of corporate governance. This recognition has been reflected by serving as an editor on the editorial board of some of the world's leading academic journals, delivering international conference keynote speeches and seminars and participating in advisory and review bodies. She has published over 100 articles in leading international academic journals and conferences, including *Strategic Management Journal, Journal of Management Studies, Journal of World Business, Journal of Business Research, European Financial Management, European Accounting Review* and *British Accounting Review*. Professor Chen is a Fellow of CPA (Australia) and a fellow of the Higher Education Academy (UK).

Qing Huang is a lecturer with Nankai University's College of Tourism and Service Management. He has published articles in the *Journal of Hospitality and Tourism Management*. His research area is hotel management. He is especially interested in exploring how the country's social environments continuously affect the hotel's business performance.

Kanghong Li is a lecturer at Business School of Yangzhou University in Yangzhou, China. Since completing her Ph.D. in management in 2015, Kanghong Li has maintained her research focus on corporate governance and organization innovation.

Fei Li is a lecturer in the School of Business, Zhengzhou University, Zhengzhou, China. Since completing his Ph.D. in Management in 2019, Li Fei has maintained his research focus on corporate governance and finance and innovation. He is especially interested exploring how the power and psychological feature of top executives affect the corporate innovation and performance.

Runhui Lin is a Professor in organization and management of the Business School at Nankai University, as well as the director of the Network Governance Center of the China Academy of Corporate Governance (CACG). He was also a visiting scholar at Harvard University (2004–2005) and a member of several academic associations both domestic and abroad, such as the Academy of Management (AOM). He serves as the peer reviewer of the National Natural Science Foundation of China (NSFC), AOM annual meetings and some top management journals in China. He received his Ph.D. in Management Sciences. His research focuses on *corporate governance of Chinese MNCs, network governance*

and innovation, data and information governance, and ***network analysis methodology***. He has published over 120 papers in international academic journals and conferences, such as the *International Journal of Information Management, Journal of Asia Business Studies, Asia Pacific Journal of Management, Enterprise Information Systems*, and *Asian Business & Management* in addition to top Chinese academic journals, such as *Management World* and *Nankai Business Review*. He has also authored or co-authored 13 books in Chinese and English in the above fields.

He has taught M.B.A., EMBA, and graduate students *"Information technology management", "E-business in China," and "Internationalization and corporate governance of Chinese enterprises"* in Chinese and English to Chinese students as well as international students from Minnesota University (U.S.), Bryant University (U.S.), Flinders University (Australia), Rouen Business School (France), Moscow International Higher Business School (MIRBIS; Russia), and EMLYON Business School (France). The *Information Technology Management* course, which is taught in English, has been awarded "Brand Course of English Teaching for Overseas Students in China" by China's Ministry of Education.

Dr. Lin has been the principal investigator (PI) of 10 research projects supported by the National Natural Science Foundation of China (NSFC), China's Ministry of Education (MOE), and provincial-level research grants, participating in 15 research and consulting projects from NSFC, MOE, China's Ministry of Science and Technology, SASAC, and other government agencies, including the World Bank, ADB, and big firms. Currently, he is leading a team on a key project from the NSFC on "*Transnational corporate governance and evaluation of business groups from China*," and based on this, the study of corporate governance has been expanded to business group governance and transnational governance from the perspectives of multilevel analysis and network analysis of the Chinese multinational corporations.

Dr. Lin is the deputy dean of the Business School of Nankai University, China, and he also served as the Deputy Director in the Office for International Academic Exchanges, Nankai University, China from 2007 to 2016. He is an expert on international mobility of college students and international collaboration among universities and higher education institutions.

Jingli Song is a Doctor of management who has graduated from business school of Nankai University. She works in Tianjin branch of Agricultural Bank of China, and engages in the position of risk manager. She is especially interested in exploring risk management, business strategy, and business performance of commercial banks.

Chunyan Wang is a lecturer in the School of Tianjin University of Finance and Economics in Tianjin, China. Since completing her Ph.D. in human resource management in 2013, Wang has maintained her research focus on corporate governance and human capital, building on her work on employee mobility issues, and extending it to network governance.

Li Xie is an assistant professor in Finance in International Business School Suzhou (IBSS) at Xi'an Jiaotong-Liverpool University (XJTLU) in China. Prior to joining IBSS, Dr. Li Xie worked as a research fellow at the Southampton Business School at the University of Southampton after he obtained his Ph.D. in Durham Business School at the University of Durham in the United Kingdom.

Dr. Li Xie's primary research interests lie in the field of Corporate Governance (e.g., voluntary disclosure, impression management, board of directors, andearnings management); Innovation and Entrepreneurship (e.g., Patent, SMEs, and R&D subsidies), Corporate Social Responsibility (CSR), and Behavioral Finance (e.g., Behavioral Asset Pricing and Behavioral Portfolio Management). He has published academic papers in highly ranked journals, such as *Journal of Corporate Finance, Small Business Economics*, *Contemporary Economic Policy*, and *Asian Economic Papers*.

Hongjuan Zhang is an associate professor at the College of Management and Economics, Tianjin University, in Tianjin China. She received her Ph.D. from the Business School at Nankai University. She teaches courses in strategic management. Her main research interests include strategic management, network organization and innovation, and international business. Her articles have been published in international management journals, such as *Journal of World Business, Entrepreneurship Theory and Practice, Asia Pacific Journal of Management (APJM)*, and Chinese management journals, including *Management World, Journal of Management Science*, and *Nankai Management Review*, among others. She has also presented papers at several national and international conferences on the subject of management. She also joined the Academy of Management

(AOM), International Association for Chinese Management Research, (IACMR) and other international management societies, and served as reviewers for *Academy of International Business*, *Journal of Management Science*, *APJM*, *AOM*, and *IACMR*.

Changbao Zhou is a lecturer in the School of Business, Zhengzhou University of Aeronautics, Henan province, China. Since completing his Ph.D. in management science and engineering in 2016, Changbao Zhou has maintained his research focus on Corporate Governance and Internationalization, building on his work on Internal governance structure and governance mechanism of multinational corporations.

List of Figures

Fig. 2.4 Equity and voting rights evolution of Jack Ma and his management team from Alibaba (*Notes* (1) VR refers to voting rights; and CFR refers to cash flow rights or ownership; (2) if CFR = VR, the value in brackets is VR or CFR; if CFR ≠ VR, the value in brackets is VR/CFR; and (3) 20 or 10% of voting rights refers to the lower limit of the proportion of shares held by the founder for maintaining authority. (1)→(2)→(3) During 1999 to 2004, three rounds of financing occurred. The investors were mainly venture capitals (VCs) and the shareholders proportion of Ma and his team diluted to 47%. (2)–(4): In 2005, the industrial capital, Yahoo, acquired 40% of shares and 35% of voting rights by investment and became the largest shareholder of Alibaba. After other VCs existed in 2009, Ma and his team held 31.7% of shares and acquired 4% of voting rights by an agreement with Yahoo. (4)–(5): Due to the expiry of agreement with Yahoo in 2010, Ma and his team faced the risk of losing authority. (4)–(5): During 2010 to 2014, Ma and his team maintained their authority and established partnership by restarting PE financing through separating Alipay, repurchasing shares and other means. In 2012, after repurchasing half of the shares from Yahoo in 2012, they largely held 51.43% of shares. (5)–(6): After Alibaba was listed in 2014, the prospectus showed that Ma Yan and his management held 13.1% of shares but occupied over one half of board seats thanks to partnership) 27
Fig. 3.1 Volvo sales from 2006 to 2009 (unit: 10,000 cars) 48
Fig. 4.1 Organizational structure of Jin Jiang International Hotel Management Co. Ltd (*Note* Shanghai Jin Jiang International Hotels Development Co. Ltd., mainly operates Jin Jiang Inn Co. Ltd. budget hotel business and catering and transportation business) 59
Fig. 4.2 Structure of Shanghai Jin Jiang International Hotels (Group) Co. Ltd 59
Fig. 4.3 Shanghai Jin Jiang International Hotel Group's Executive Organization Chart, Board of Directors, and Board of Supervisors 61
Fig. 4.4 Statistics of hotels in operation (*Source* Jin Jiang Hotels [2009]. *Annual Report*. Retrieved from https://www1.hkexnews.hk/listedco/listconews/sehk/2010/0428/ltn20100428426.pdf) 62

List of Tables

CHAPTER 1

Introduction

Economic globalization has become one of the most fundamental characteristics associated with the evolving world economy, in which multinational corporations (MNCs) are viewed as an important driving force of global economic integration by their overseas investment and strategic adjustment. In China, with the deepening of its "Going Out" and "Belt and Road" national strategies,[1] an increasing number of Chinese MNCs have been stepping onto the world stage and participating in global competition.

Since it joined to the World Trade Organization (WTO) in 2001, China and Chinese corporations have been gradually participating in multinational business operations and global competition, which has accelerated the progress of internationalization of Chinese corporations and the development and implementation of the national strategies mentioned above. According to the Statistical Bulletin of China's Foreign Direct Investment by the Ministry of Commerce, China's total outward direct foreign investment in 2003 was only 2.9 billion US dollars, which

[1] The "Going Out" strategy (also referred to as the Going Global Strategy) was an effort initiated in 1999 by the Chinese government to promote Chinese investments abroad. The Government, together with the China Council for the Promotion of International Trade (CCPIT), has introduced several schemes to assist domestic companies in developing a global strategy to exploit opportunities in the expanding local and international markets.

The Belt and Road Initiative is a global development strategy adopted by the Chinese government in 2013, which involves infrastructure development and investments in nearly 70 countries and international organizations in Asia, Europe, and Africa.

© The Author(s), under exclusive license to Springer Nature Singapore Pte Ltd. 2020
R. Lin et al. *Corporate Governance of Chinese Multinational Corporations*,
https://doi.org/10.1007/978-981-15-7405-4_1

has since risen sharply to 143.04 billion US dollars in 2018, a 48-fold increase over 15 years. Chinese corporations have therefore made tremendous progress in the magnitude of transnational investment.

However, compared with MNCs in developed countries, which have been running their business for a long period of time, Chinese MNCs are relatively newer players in operating international businesses and participating in global competition. Due to the complexity of the stakeholder relationships involved among home countries and host countries, Chinese MNCs have faced many unprecedented challenges in multinational business operation and governance. The institutional differences caused by the regulatory systems in different countries further expose Chinese MNCs to a variety of institutional constraints, which exacerbates the uncertainty of operating their international business and conducting multinational governance.

Over the last few decades, many leading Chinese companies have gradually developed international business operations, using a "learning by doing" approach based on their understanding of transnational governance. Given the importance that firms' governance structure can have on their implementation of corporate strategic decisions, including outward foreign direct investment, the entry mode and location of overseas ventures, corporate governance has been viewed as a system of interrelated general and institutional elements of multinational corporations. Thus, most of the existing Chinese MNCs have a urgent need to know about what efficient and effective governance structures and mechanisms of multinational corporations should be, and how to improve their current governance structures to facilitate multinational business operations and enhance the quality of multinational governance, thereby gaining certain types of competitive advantages in the long run.

In this regard, it is important and worthwhile to sort out and explore current typical problems faced by Chinese MNCs in their international business operations and transnational governance, and to analyze whether and how corporate governance as an important institutional element of MNCs affects different stages of their internationalization process. Such exploration and analysis can improve their ability to conduct transnational governance, thereby facilitating the implementation of the "Going Out" national strategy. However, based on research conducted to date, little is known about these important issues related to Chinese MNCs.

Thus, the aims and objectives of this book are to identify various difficulties encountered by Chinese MNCs when they employ "going out" strategies, such as misunderstanding of institutional differences between home countries and host countries and inefficient or inappropriate entry mode and location of overseas investments. Moreover, this foundational knowledge is used to investigate the effect of their corporate governance practices and adjustments that take the form of corresponding countermeasures in international business operations and transnational governance, which is all considered in the context of globalization.

Specifically, this book provides a review of eight typical cases and examples selected from current practices of Chinese MNCs across various industries by using a case study approach. The book identifies and analyzes the deficiencies and challenges faced by a number of Chinese MNCs associated with their involvement in the internationalization process, and it also explores how Chinese MNCs deal with issues, such as ownership control, board of directors, governance mechanisms, and performance incentives in transnational governance. The book also describes the characteristics, experiences, and lessons of these Chinese MNCs when they operate internationally and conduct transnational governance, thereby providing valuable practical insights and implications to facilitate both the development of Chinese MNCs and the implementation of "Going Out" strategies. For example, by analyzing eight Chinese case studies, the book is the first to identify and suggest three important governance mechanisms implemented by Chinese MNCs, namely stakeholder governance, board of director's governance and executive governance. The book also suggests a typical evolutionary process of corporate internationalization, which includes the following four stages: (1) the basic stage; (2) the transition stage; (3) the conflict stage; and (4) the formation stage. These important revelations and suggestions detailed in this book provide new insights and guidelines for how to improve practices and the implementation of business operations by existing and potential multinational corporations.

This book consists of eight case study chapters. The second chapter analyzes the multinational governance of Alibaba Group, an E-commerce giant, and its strategies of overseas investment and governance. This case study not only explores the evolution of Alibaba Group's parent company's equity, board structure, corporate control rights, but it also sorts out and summarizes the strategies and challenges of Alibaba's transnational governance and overseas entry mode.

The third chapter analyzes the transnational governance of Geely Group's acquisition of Volvo. From the perspectives of Geely Group's stakeholder governance, executive management, board governance, and parent–subsidiary relationship governance, this case study explores how Geely can achieve the successful acquisition and integration of Volvo by strengthening transnational governance.

The fourth chapter analyzes Jinjiang Group's acquisition of the American Intercontinental Hotel. By analyzing Jinjiang Group's cross-border merger and acquisition (M&A) process, it systematically explores the characteristics of cross-border governance before and after corporate mergers and acquisitions, while also highlighting the successful M&A experience.

Chapter 5 analyzes the construction and evolution of Lenovo group's transnational governance framework. Based on the process of Lenovo group's transnational operations, this case study divides the transnational governance framework into the four stages mentioned previously. It also discusses the formation mechanism and theoretical model of transnational governance of the corporation in emerging markets.

Chapter 6 explores the equity governance model based on WISCO's overseas investment projects. By analyzing seven cases of Wuhan Iron and Steel's investment projects in five countries, the mechanism for setting up equity governance models when enterprises enter overseas markets are discussed along with the "WISCO model," which is based on identifying the relationship between equity structure and national institutions.

Chapter 7 analyzes the governance issues of the PingAn Group's acquisition of Fortis Belgium. By systematically reviewing the entire process of this overseas acquisition by the PingAn Group the main reasons for the failure of such acquisitions and the problems and challenges faced by PingAn Group's transnational governance are explained.

Chapter 8 delves into the cross-border governance of Zoomlion's acquisition of Italian CIFA. This case mainly explores the stakeholder governance during Zoomlion's acquisition of CIFA and the multinational governance mechanism after the acquisition. From the perspective of the relationship governance between Zoomlion and CIFA and the governance structure adjustment, it provides practical implications for the implementation of corporate mergers and acquisitions synergy.

Chapter 9 is a case study of Sany's transnational acquisition of Putzmeister. It explores various multinational governance mechanisms such as stakeholder governance, subsidiary governance, parent company governance, and parent–subsidiary relationship governance in the Sany's acquisition process. It finally provides experience and lessons for improving and enhancing the company's transnational governance capabilities.

CHAPTER 2

Alibaba Group—The Evolution of Transnational Governance

2.1 Introduction

2.1.1 About Alibaba Group

In 1999, a group of 18 individuals, headed by Ma Yun (known as Jack Ma internationally), founded Alibaba in Hangzhou, China. These entrepreneurs accumulated experience gained while worked at the China Yellow Pages and the Ministry of Foreign Trade and Economic Cooperation, which they employed to set up the new company. They decided to position themselves as a "China SME Trade Service Provider," offering site design and promotional services to China's new cohort of small producers and manufacturers. Since the launch of its first website, the company has allowed small Chinese exporters, manufacturers, and entrepreneurs to reach global buyers, and it grew into an ecosystem of 16,000 employees with a service network of more than 100 million people. Alibaba Group is now a veritable global leader in online and mobile commerce. Together with its affiliates, Alibaba operates leading wholesale and retail platforms, while providing online advertising, marketing, electronic payments, cloud computing, web services, and mobile solutions.

2.1.1.1 Alibaba's Business Scope

As an internet company, Alibaba started out as a single B2B platform. It has evolved into an e-commerce ecosystem that combines B2B, Taobao (C2C), Tmall (B2C), and Yitao, Juhuasuan, Alipay, Alibabasoft, and

© The Author(s), under exclusive license to Springer Nature Singapore Pte Ltd. 2020
R. Lin et al. *Corporate Governance of Chinese Multinational Corporations*,
https://doi.org/10.1007/978-981-15-7405-4_2

Yahoo! Moreover, Alibaba's organizational structure has been adjusted accordingly along the way, including minor and major changes and from concentration to division. Since 2011, Alibaba Group's Taobao has been split into three independent companies: C2C Taobao, B2C Taobao Mall (Tmall), and the Yitao search engine. By July 2012, this ecosystem comprised seven business groups: Taobao, Yitao, Tmall, Juhuasuan, Alibaba International Business, Alibaba Small Business, and Alibaba Cloud Computing. In January 2013, Alibaba was restructured into 25 business divisions.

2.1.1.2 Alibaba Group's Public Listing

On November 6, 2007, Alibaba B2B (1688.HK) was listed on the Hong Kong Stock Exchange, setting the record for the largest-ever listing of a Chinese internet company. In June 2012, Alibaba.com officially delisted from the Hong Kong Stock Exchange. On the evening of September 19, 2014, Alibaba officially listed on the New York Stock Exchange (NYSE), with the stock code BABA and a price per share of USD 68. The stock market opened with Alibaba priced at USD 92.7 on the same day, Alibaba raised USD 25 billion, as the IPO was set to be the biggest ever.

2.1.2 Alibaba Group Development Strategy and Structural Evolution

Since its establishment in 1999, Alibaba's strategic objectives were adjusted with the expansion of the company's business scope. From its establishment, its business scope has been limited to B2B e-commerce companies. The following three goals were set: establish a company that could survive for 80 years; build a company to serve Chinese SMEs; and build the world's largest e-commerce company and become a top-10 global website.

By 2000, Alibaba had expanded around the world. However, as the internet bubble ruptured, Alibaba decided to switch strategies. In October, Alibaba retreated "Back to China, back to the Coast, and back to the Center," which was Hangzhou. Based on the reality of the company's development, returning to rationality, stopping expansion, shrinking the front line, reducing costs, global layoffs, "returning to China," focusing on providing "Chinese suppliers" for B2B trading business for SMEs and clarifying the company's own business development led to the business model returning to profitability in 2002. Although internationalization was adopted, the implementation did not go smoothly. In these early days, Alibaba's transnational governance reach was out of touch with its operational capacity.

In 2003, international e-commerce giant eBay (C2C) entered China. To avoid future threats in the B2B field, Alibaba adopted a competitive strategy, secretly launched the C2C website (Taobao), and adopted a free strategy. Between 2003 and 2006, Alibaba and eBay competed in the market. By 2006, Taobao had beaten eBay and held 70% of China's market share. The competition with world-class rivals has prompted Alibaba to grow faster. In the process of e-commerce development, Alibaba launched an "Integrity Pass" that could be used as a credit rating on Alipay, its online payment system.

In 2008, Alibaba changed its position from "one of the world's three largest internet companies" to "the world's largest e-commerce service provider." Alibaba has experienced rapid expansion, developing Alibaba Cloud and China Smart Logistic Network, and with these developments, the Alibaba e-commerce ecosystem has begun to emerge.

Since 2009, Alibaba has promoted its annual consumer discount day, "Double Eleventh" on November 11, with its registered trademark "Double Eleven." By focusing on consumer demand, this transformed production and manufacturing along with the supply chains, which cemented the "C2B" model.

In 2010, to cope with a policy crisis, Alipay turned to capital. That year, Alibaba Group began trial operations of its new Alibaba Partnership to compensate for the "the pressure from the public markets to focus on short-term results instead of long-term value creation."[1]

From June 2011 to 2013, Alibaba made a three-point change to Taobao, splitting three divisions into seven. In January 2013, Alibaba was further split into 25 business divisions. As Alibaba became huge beyond all recognition, it developed an essential organizational and structural change strategy, splitting and reorganizing its organizational structure, and laying out plans for e-commerce. A new finance and logistical system were the foundations of this online business ecosystem.

Alibaba.com was listed on the NYSE in September 2014. Before the IPO, Alibaba laid out its internationalization concept, based on which the

[1] SEC Registration Statement, 6 May 2014, page 22, https://www.sec.gov/Archives/edgar/data/1577552/000119312514184994/d709111df1.htm.

internationalization team had clearly done its homework in terms of goals and methods.

As can be seen from the Alibaba Group website, its future goals have been continuously improved and developed along with business development, and methods to achieve these goals have gradually become clear with the improvement of the e-commerce ecosystem: to develop continuously for at least 102 years.

2.1.3 Overview of Corporate Governance at Alibaba Group's Parent Company

As the world's largest e-commerce platform, Alibaba's development has experienced initial exploration, domestic market competition, M&A expansion, rapid development, and organizational transformation. Alibaba's establishment has become inherently internationalized. Established in 1999, its shareholder and executive team consist of internationalized components, providing strong foundations for its growing multinational set up. In Alibaba's development process, due to the continuous expansion of its business scope, the adjustment of strategic positioning and the corresponding organizational structure have been continuously improved and changed. Similarly, Alibaba's corporate governance structure is constantly changing. Table 2.1 provides a list of key events since Alibaba Group was established, including business changes, strategic positioning, shareholder composition, and control rights in different development periods.

2.2 Transnational Governance Evolution

The evolution of Alibaba Group's corporate governance is complementary to changes to the organizational structure and the evolution of corporate strategy. To better understand Alibaba's corporate governance model choice, it should be analyzed in combination with Alibaba's strategic choice and the development and organizational structure changes. In the analysis, Alibaba's corporate governance will be the focus, combined with Alibaba's development strategy and organizational structure evolution.

Table 2.1 Key events in the history of Alibaba Group

Period *Developmental phase*	*1999–2002* *Start-up*	*2003–2004* *Development*	*2005–2009* *Expansion*	*2010–2014* *Accelerated development*
Key event	February 1999—Alibaba launched 2000—Hong Kong corporate headquarters established UK office, US Silicon Valley R&D center, joint ventures in Korea, Japan, Taiwan October 2000—"West Lake Conference," B2C strategic turn: Back To China, Back To The Coast, Back To The Center 2002—B2B market matures	2003—Taobao, Alipay, online real-time communication software tradelink (now called Wangwang) December 2004—Established Alibaba Company, Alibaba online website, operating independently 2004—Alibaba (China) Software R&D Center was established	August 2005—Acquisition of China Yahoo 2006—Spin-off of Alibaba, Taobao, Alipay, Ali Software, Yahoo China October 2006—Acquisition of Koubei Company 2007—Established Alimama, Alibaba Software Company June 2007—Launched SME loans (mainly online operator facing) 2007—B2B business listed on Hong Kong Stock Exchange April 2008—Launched Taobao Mall (B2C) September 2008—"Big Taobao" strategy September 2008 Taobao merged with Alimama—August 2009 Koubei assimulated into Taobao September 2009 Alibaba software management software business assimilated into Alibaba B2B business company September 2009 Alibaba Cloud established June 2010 Established micro-loan company and obtained micro-loan company business license	June 2010—Established "Taobao Grand Logistics Plan" that covered the entire country by January 2011 July 2010 Launched partner system April 2010—Officially launched global Ali Express October 2010—Launched independent shopping search engine Etao.com June 2011 "Big Taobao" strategy upgraded to "Big Alibaba" strategy June 2011—Taobao three points → July 2012 Alibaba adjusted to seven business group system →January 2013—Established 25 business divisions September 2011—Taobao Mall Open B2C Platform Strategy February 2012—Alibaba Hong Kong suspended, September 2012—Repurchased Yahoo shares for USD 7.6 billion June 2013 Yu'e Bao was born September 2014 US listing (maintains leadership team voting power)

(continued)

Table 2.1 (continued)

Period *Developmental phase*	*1999–2002* *Start-up*	*2003–2004* *Development*	*2005–2009* *Expansion*	*2010–2014* *Accelerated development*
Business scope	*B2B*	B2B, C2C, Alipay	Focusing on the diversification of core business, the layout of e-commerce ecosystem	Business ecosystem, O2O
Strategic positioning	"Network Yiwu" Profit model exploration	Competitive strategy: Taobao free mode	More diversified expansion strategy, M&A strategy, big Taobao strategy	Organizational structure strategy adjustment, Greater Alibaba strategy Platformization
Overseas strategy	From overseas expansion to strategic retreat		Hong Kong delisting	Internationalization of Alibaba, global e-commerce eco-chain layout, overseas investment mergers, and acquisitions, US listing
Shareholder composition	Jack Ma and leadership team, Softbank, other VC/PE		VC/PE exited, Jack Ma and leadership team 31.7%, Yahoo 39%, Softbank 29.3%	Jack Ma and leadership group 13.1%, Yahoo 16.3%, Softbank 32.4%, others
Actual controller	Jack Ma and leadership team		Jack Ma and leadership team	Jack Ma and leadership team
Board of Directors			Four seats: Alibaba 2, Softbank 1, Yahoo 1	After the IPO: Alibaba 4, Softbank 1, Independent Directors 5
Control basis	Equity		Equity, voting rights, and Yahoo agreement, after the dispute between Jack Ma and Yahoo	Alibaba partner system

2.2.1 Changes in Shareholding Structure

Since Alibaba was founded in 1999, Jack Ma's leadership team has always been the mastermind of Alibaba's decision-making. Its shareholder composition has mainly experienced the following three stages:

2.2.1.1 1999–2005: Initiation Period, VC/PE Entry

In January 1999, Jack Ma and his founding partners jointly invested RMB 500,000 to establish Alibaba. Due to rapid development and enterprises facing resource constraints, Alibaba introduced external investment institutions, securing support from the United States during the first round of financing. The funds of investment institutions in Singapore, Sweden, and other countries resulted in the first equity dilution. In 2000, it obtained the second capital injection from several investment institutions. This is the decision that teams of founders often face in the development and expansion of their enterprises, based on the balances among the acquisition of external resources, the dilution of corporate equity, and the weakening of corporate control. The following three rounds of financing occurred during this period:

First, in October 1999, Alibaba received the first USD 5 million in investment, led by Goldman Sachs, to unite investment institutions in the United States, Asia, and Europe, including Singapore's Transpac Capital, Sweden's Investor AB, and Singapore's government technology development fund. With the USD 5 million investment, Alibaba's equity was diluted.

Second, in 2000, SoftBank joined forces with Fidelity, Huiya Capital, Japan Asia Investment, Swedish Investment, and TDF to invest USD 25 million in Alibaba, of which SoftBank invested the largest portion (USD 20 million), while Fidelity, Huiya Capital, TDF, Investor AB, and Japan Asia Investment collectively invested the remaining USD 5 million.

Third, in 2004, Alibaba's third round of financing totaled USD 82 million, with SoftBank again leading the investment with USD 60 million, while the remaining USD 22 million was funded by Fidelity, TDF, and GGV. Notably, Jack Ma's and other founders' shares fell to 47%.

2.2.1.2 2005–2010: Venture Capital/Private (VC/PE) Equity Exit, Yahoo Buys in

In 2005, at the crucial moment of Alibaba's dispute with eBay, Alibaba's need for funds prompted investment agreement between Alibaba and Yahoo. Yahoo took shares in Alibaba, and proposed an exit opportunity for the previous VC/PE funding groups. Yahoo infused 10 billion US dollars in cash, Yahoo China's business and Yahoo branding and technology in China in exchange for a 40% stake in Alibaba Group and 35% of the voting rights to become Alibaba's largest shareholder. SoftBank made a profit of USD 360 million by selling Taobao shares, then repurchased Alibaba shares for USD 150 million, and finally cashing in USD 210 million, while Alibaba management and other shareholders cashed in USD 540 million.

In 2007, Alibaba Group's B2B business was listed on the Hong Kong Stock Exchange, and the remaining VC shareholders were given the opportunity to withdraw. Before Alibaba reopened the door to PE financing in 2011, all other VC funds except SoftBank had withdrawn from Alibaba. In September 2009, Yahoo sold a 1% stake and cashed in USD 150 million. At this point, Alibaba Group had three major shareholders, Yahoo, the largest shareholder, with 39%, Jack Ma and his leadership team as the second largest shareholder with 31.7%, followed by SoftBank, with 29.3%. Alibaba's shareholding structure is shown in Fig. 2.1.

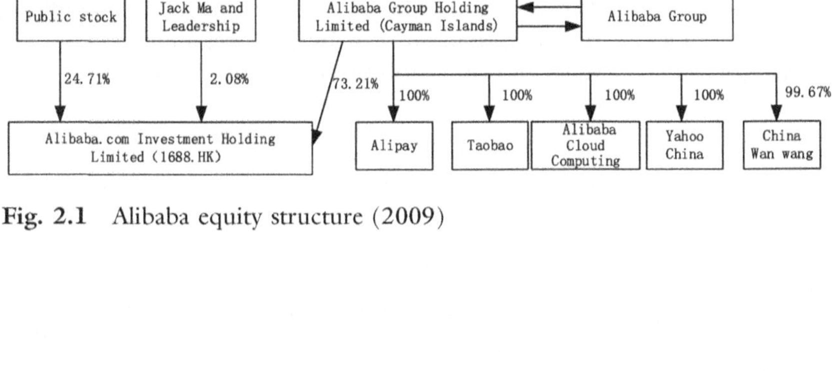

Fig. 2.1 Alibaba equity structure (2009)

2.2.1.3 2010—Present: Reopening the Door to PE Financing, Public Share Issue

According to the agreement with Yahoo, from October 2010, Yahoo, with its 39% stake in Alibaba, increased its voting rights from 35 to 39%, while Alibaba's leadership team reduced its voting power from 35.7 to 31.7%. The leadership team went from having 0.7% more votes than Yahoo to having 7.3% less. Yahoo was given two board seats in Alibaba, the same number as Jack Ma and his leadership team. Jack Ma and the founding team lost their positions as the primary shareholders, which changed the relationship among board seats. This had a profound impact on control by the founders of the Alibaba Group. To avoid losing control, Alibaba repeatedly requested to buy back shares, committing to a "Long March" prepurchase plan.

In 2011, Alibaba restarted the PE financing process. In September 2011, Alibàba sold about 5% of its management and employee stocks to equity investors Yunfeng Fund, the Russian venture capital firm DST, and Silver Lake for USD 35 billion, and obtained approximately USD 1.7 billion in financing. In February 2012, Alibaba received a USD 3 billion loan from the syndicate and a three-year loan at around 4% interest. A total of six banks and institutions participated, including Australia and New Zealand Banking Group (ANZ), Credit Suisse Group, Development Bank of Singapore Limited (DBS Bank), Deutsche Bank, HSBC Holdings Limited, and Mizuho Financial Group. In September 2012, CIC and CITIC Capital, China Development Finance, and other investors weighed in with USD 2 billion.

In September 2012, Alibaba and Yahoo reached a repurchase agreement. Alibaba Group repurchased Yahoo's holdings of Alibaba Group's shares of 50% and 523 million shares for $6.3 billion in cash and A$100 million in Alibaba Group's preferred stock. As part of the deal, Yahoo gave up its power to appoint a second board member and also gave up a series of vetoes related to Alibaba Group's strategic and operational decisions. After the repurchase program was completed, Alibaba Group's board of directors maintained "Alibaba Group" in a ratio of 2:1:1 among Yahoo and SoftBank, Jack Ma and his management team, who reemerged as the company's largest shareholders, regaining control of the board. The repurchase agreement stipulated that Yahoo would contribute 261.5 million shares when listed, to be distributed by Alibaba. Thereafter, Yahoo and Alibaba negotiated a reduction to 208 million shares. In July 2014, Yahoo and Alibaba reached a new share repurchase agreement.

According to the new agreement, Yahoo would sell 140 million shares at Alibaba's IPO, though they actually ended up selling 122 million shares. In September 2014, Alibaba Group was listed on the NYSE, and its corresponding shareholding structure is shown in Fig. 2.2 and Table 2.2.

As shown in Table 2.3, in the latest version of the prospectus submitted to the US Securities and Exchange Commission (SEC), Alibaba Group announced circulation, issue price range and financing, and for the first time, declared 17 hidden institutional shareholders aside from SoftBank, Yahoo, Jack Ma, and Joseph C. Tsai.

After the IPO, Alibaba Group's shareholder structure shifted to the following scenario: SoftBank (32.4%), Yahoo (16.3%), Jack Ma and the leadership team (13.1%), which meant the three largest shareholders held a 61.8% stake in Alibaba Group. The largest of the other shareholders included Silver Lake and affiliated entities (2.2%), Fengmao Investment Company (2.1%), Yunfeng and affiliated (1.1%), and CITIC

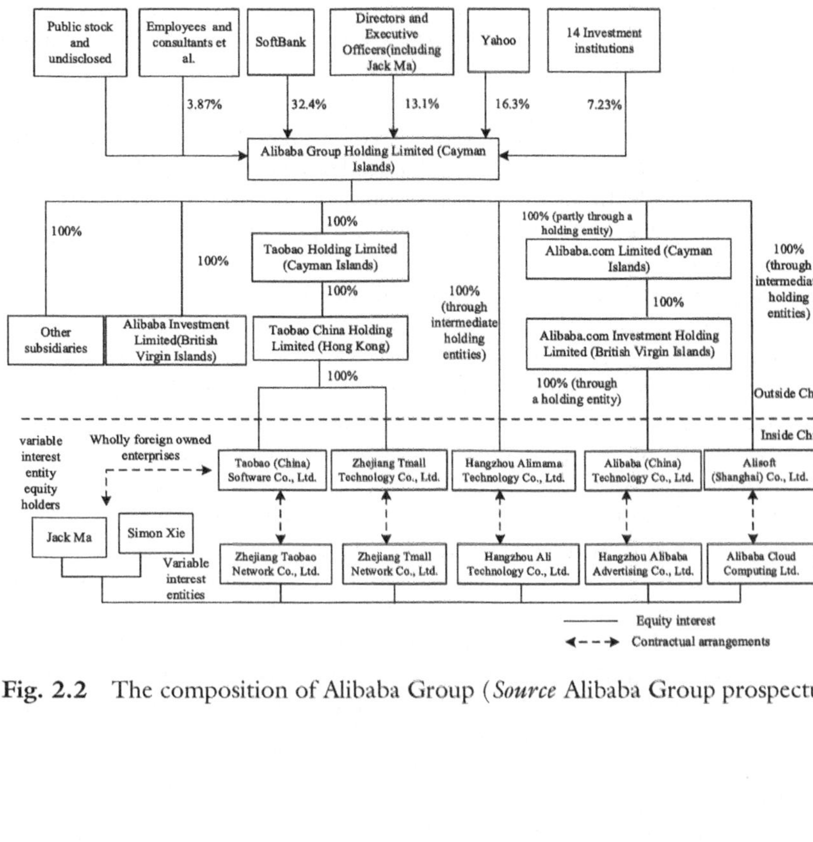

Fig. 2.2 The composition of Alibaba Group (*Source* Alibaba Group prospectus)

Table 2.2 Alibaba Group's equity structure before and after 2014 NYSE listing

Name	*Shares held before issue*		*Shares held after issue*	
	Quantity	*%*	*Quantity*	*%*
Directors and executives officers				
Jack Yun Ma	206,100,673	8.8%	193,350,673	7.8%
Joseph C. TSAI	83,499,896	3.6%	79,249,896	3.2%
Jonathan Zhaoxi LU et al.	*	*	*	*
All directors and executive officers as a group	341,920,826	14.6%	323,220,826	13.1%
Principal and/or selling shareholders				
SoftBank	797,742,980	34.1%	797,742,980	32.4%
Yahoo	523,565,416	22.4%	401,826,286	16.3%
Jack Ma	206,100,673	8.8%	193,350,673	7.8%
Fengmao Investment	66,451,613	2.8%	52,165,913	2.1%
Silver Lake affiliated entities	58,929,509	2.5%	54,829,509	2.2%
Yunfeng affiliated entities	34,814,817	1.5%	28,287,039	1.1%
CITIC Capital Excel Wisdom Fund, L.P.	25,806,451	1.1%	20,896,155	0.8%
Broad Sino Developments Limited	10,967,742	0.5%	5,483,871	0.2%
Prosperous Wintersweet (BVI) Limited	10,516,129	0.5%	9,464,517	0.4%
Ever Green Growth Limited	2,258,064	0.1%	2,032,258	0.1%
Entities affiliated with Asia Alternatives Management LLC	1,935,484	0.1%	1,645,163	0.1%
Pavilion Capital Fund Holdings Pte. Ltd	1,935,484	0.1%	1,290,484	0.1%
Li Ka Shing (Canada) Foundation	1,290,323	0.1%	967,743	0.0%
Crescent Holding GmbH	967,742	0.0%	467,742	0.0%
Siguler Guff BRIC Opportunities Fund III, L.P.	645,161	0.0%	322,580	0.0%
Siguler Guff HP China Opportunities Fund, LP	322,581	0.0%	161,290	0.0%
Arctic Capital Holdings Limited	129,032	0.0%	64,516	0.0%
4000-plus current employees as a group	79,596,549	3.4%	67,137,267	2.7%
1000-plus former employees as a group	21,407,092	0.9%	18,293,699	0.7%
Consultants and employees of affiliates as a group	12,039,883	0.5%	9,913,871	0.4%

Source Alibaba Prospectus (2014). Retrieved from https://www.sec.gov/Archives/edgar/data/1577552/000119312514347620/d709111d424b4.htm#toc709111_1, pp. 250–251

Table 2.3 Shareholder backgrounds

Shareholder	*Background*	*Headquarters or locations*
SoftBank (Masayoshi SON)	Founded in 1981, listed on the Tokyo Stock Exchange, invests in broadband, mobile and fixed-line telecommunications; e-commerce; internet; technology services; and media and marketing	Japan
Yahoo	Global internet communications, commerce, and media company	United States
Jack Ma and leadership team	Alibaba directors and executive officers: Jack Yun Ma, Joseph C. TSAI, Jonathan Zhaoxi LU, Yong Zhang, Wei Wu, Jian Wang, etc.	China
Fengmao Investment	Central enterprise CIC's wholly owned subsidiary	China
Silver Lake affiliated entities	Private equity investment company established in 1999, focusing on leveraged buyouts and growth capital investments, technology, and related industries	United States
Yunfeng affiliated entities	Founded in 2010, a private equity fund created by successful entrepreneurs, entrepreneurs, and industry leaders was named after Alibaba Ma Yun and founder Qi Feng, and Ma Yun indirectly holds 40% of the shares	China
CITIC Capital Excel Wisdom Fund (L.P.)	Founded in 2002, it focuses on investment management and consulting firms in the Chinese market	China
Broad Sino Developments Limited	A state-owned commercial bank, the National Development Bank (CDB)	China

(continued)

Table 2.3 (continued)

Shareholder	*Background*	*Headquarters or locations*
Prosperous Wintersweet (BVI) Limited EverGreen Growth Limited	Founded in September 2010, Boyu Capital, a private equity fund owned by Boyu Capital, is an investment fund focused on private equity investment in Greater China	Hong Kong
Entities affiliated with Asia Alternatives Management LLC	Founded in 2006 and based in Hong Kong, it is dedicated to providing institutional investors with a platform for private equity investments across Asia	Hong Kong
Pavilion Capital Fund Holdings Pte. Ltd.	Temasek's wholly owned investment subsidiary focuses on investing in North Asia markets such as China	Singapore
Li Ka Shing (Canada) Foundation	Founded by Li Ka-shing, the richest man in Hong Kong in 2005	Canada
Crescent Holding GmbH	An investment company established in 1994	Australia
Siguler Guff BRIC Opportunities Fund III, LP Siguler Guff HP China Opportunities Fund, LP	Funds of Shanggao Capital, established in 1991 by Shanggao Capital, individually or jointly manage multiple private equity direct investment funds and funds in funds, each fund focuses on specific areas under high-efficiency markets	United States
Arctic Capital Holdings Limited	An investment company focused on Southeast Asia, a wholly owned investment subsidiary of Consolidated Press Holdings Limited (CPH)	Australia
Consultant, employee collection	Alibaba employees, former employees, consultants, affiliate employees	China

Capital Excel Wisdom Fund (0.8%). Siguler Guff invested in two related fund companies, namely Siguler Guff BRIC Opportunities Fund III, LP and Siguler Guff HP China Opportunities Fund, LP, which held 322,580 shares and 161,290 shares of Alibaba, respectively. In addition to the above-mentioned institutional shareholders, Alibaba Group established three shareholding entities (about 3.8%) for current regular employees, former Alibaba employees, as well as consultants, and affiliated employees. Table 2.3 summarizes information regarding the identity and whereabouts of these shareholders. This table shows that after Yahoo, Alibaba has chosen investment in the form of financial capital rather than industrial capital. Investment institutions comprise an international list of China, Japan, the United States, Australia, and Singapore, among others.

2.2.2 *Board of Directors*

As shown in Table 2.4, after Yahoo's shareholding in Alibaba in 2005, Alibaba's board of directors consisted of four directors, including two representatives from Alibaba Group, one from Yahoo and one from Softbank. In 2010, due to the agreement between Yahoo and Alibaba Group, Yahoo's board of directors increased by one, becoming two from Alibaba, two from Yahoo, and one from Softbank. Jack Ma and his team of partners may lose control of the Alibaba Group. In 2012, Alibaba repurchased Yahoo's shares. After the repurchase, Alibaba Group's board of directors consisted of two members from Alibaba, one from Softbank and one from Yahoo. Jack Ma and his partners retained the right to nominate board directors, thus maintaining actual control over the company.

Before the listing of Alibaba on the NYSE, according to its prospectus (June 16, 2014), the 10-member board of directors included Jack Ma,

Table 2.4 Board structure of Alibaba Group (post-2005 agreement)

Jack Ma (Chairman)	*Joseph C. TSAI*	*Masayoshi SON, CEO of SoftBank*	*Jerry Yang, Yahoo Director (2005–2012)* *Tim Morse, Yahoo CFO (2012–2013)*
Alibaba appointment		Softbank appointment	Yahoo appointment

Source Compilation from media reports

Joseph C. Tsai, Zhaoxi Lu and Yong Zhang from Alibaba, Masayoshi Son from SoftBank, and Jacqueline D. Reses from Yahoo, Jerry Yang, Tung Chee-hwa, Walter Teh Ming Kwaukc, and Michael Evans, who were independent nonexecutive directors. However, according to the agreement between Alibaba and Yahoo, Yahoo would withdraw from the board of directors after Alibaba's official listing on the NYSE. As shown in Fig. 2.3, the Alibaba Group's board of directors consists of ten members (July 2015).

Under the Alibaba Partner System, partners have the exclusive right to nominate a majority of board members, rather than board seats being allocated by the number of shares. Although the directors nominate candidates, they must obtain the majority of votes at the annual general meeting to become a member of the board of directors. The partnership system enables Jack Ma and his leadership team to guarantee their shareholding ratio and control of the Alibaba Group. According to the

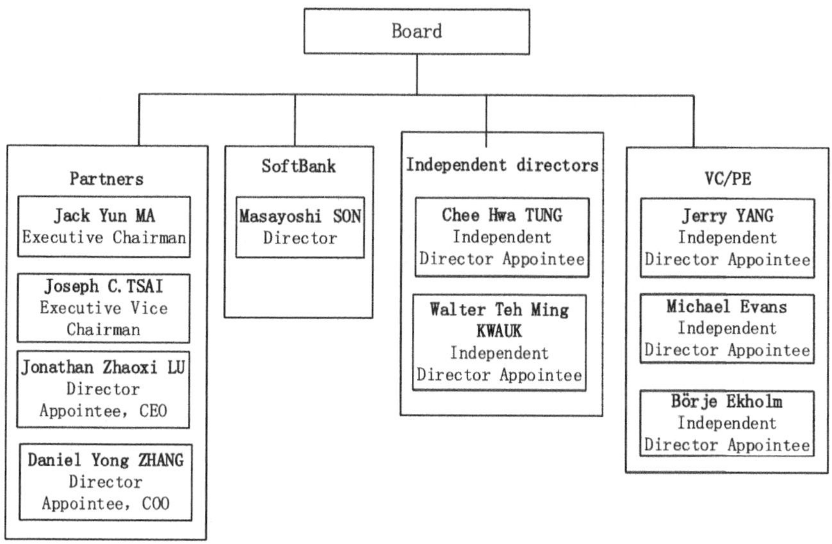

Fig. 2.3 Alibaba Group Board of Directors (July 2015) (*Note* Michael Evans has served as President and Executive Director of Alibaba Group since August 2015. *Source* Alibaba Group [n.d.]. Corporate governance, board of directors. A: Members of the board. Retrieved from https://www.alibabagroup.com/en/ir/governance_6#member)

composition of the board of directors, Alibaba partners did not fully exercise their "exclusive nomination of majority board members," but only appointed four partners to enter the board of directors. The four partners include Jack Ma, Executive Chairman of Alibaba Group's Board of Directors, Joseph C. Tsai, Executive Vice-Chairman of Alibaba Group, Zhaoxi Lu, CEO of Alibaba Group, and Yong Zhang, Chief Operating Officer (COO) of Alibaba Group.

SoftBank's nominee representative was Masayoshi Son (Japan), who had been a director of Alibaba Group since 2000, founder and then chairman and CEO of SoftBank. He was also chairman of several subsidiaries and affiliates of SoftBank, including SoftBank Broadband, SoftBank Telecommunications and SoftBank Mobile. In addition, he had been Chairman of Yahoo Japan since 1996 and has served as Chairman of Sprint since 2013. Son received a bachelor's degree in Economics from the University of California, Berkeley.

Four independent nonexecutive directors were also listed in Yahoo's prospectus, namely Yahoo founder Jerry Yang (United States), former Hong Kong Special Administrative Region (SAR)'s first chief executive, Tung Chee-hwa (Hong Kong, China), former Alibaba Group's Hong Kong Stock Exchange independent nonexecutive director and chairman of the audit committee of the listed B2B subsidiary, Walter Kwauk, and Michael Evans, former vice-chairman of Goldman Sachs. On August 4, 2015, Alibaba Group announced that it had appointed Evans as president and executive director of Alibaba Group, responsible for global business and reporting to Zhang Yong, CEO of Alibaba Group.

Walter Teh Ming Kwaukc was an independent nonexecutive director of the board of directors of Alibaba.com and the chairman of the audit committee under the board of directors. Alibaba.com was listed on the Hong Kong Stock Exchange in October 2007 and was delisted in July 2012. Kwaukc's role in Alibaba was the same as it was at the beginning. Like Wu Wei, Kwaukc was also from KPMG. He had 25 years of experience and was a partner in Hong Kong. After the Enron incident, the SEC required the board of directors of the listed company to have an audit committee, and at least one director could be identified as a "financial expert," which was a role in Alibaba's board of directors played by Kwaukc.

In June 2015, Börje E. Ekholm, head of Patricia Industries, a new division of Swedish investment company Investor AB, also became an independent nonexecutive director.

2.3 Analysis of Transnational Governance Evolution

2.3.1 *Changes in Shareholder Composition*

2.3.1.1 *1999–2005: Start-up VC/PE Entry Period, Shareholder Structure and Impact*

As an internet company, Alibaba's demand for funds forced it to continue to raise funds, though, in the process, Jack Ma held fast to the idea of maintaining control over Alibaba. This is related to the experience of Jack Ma's previous engagement with investors when he founded China Yellow Pages. His previous embedding experience shaped his logic and affected his subsequent decisions, which impacted other aspects too [40]. In addition to Jack Ma's experience, the addition of Joseph C. Tsai, a professional familiar with capital operation, also provided valuable advice on Alibaba's financing issues. Alibaba was already wary of control when considering financing options. At this stage, Alibaba's shareholding structure was characterized by an attractive equity ratio and a two-party shareholder structure.

In the first three rounds of financing, compared with the second largest shareholder, Jack Ma and the founding team had greater financial resources, but with the dilution of equity, its controlling role has changed from absolute to relative controlling shareholder. Before the acquisition of Yahoo in 2005, Jack Ma and the founding team held 47%, Softbank held about 20%, Fidelity held around 18%, and other shareholders held around 15%.

Shareholding structure. This consisted mainly of two parties: the Alibaba founding team and international VC/PE investment institutions. The primary impact of the shareholding composition on the development of Alibaba during this period is reflected in the following aspects:

- Access to external resources. The international investment institutions have given Alibaba a natural international property, providing a channel for Alibaba to obtain financial capital, as well as international joint and overseas information. This channel effect also provides an opportunity for Alibaba to "go out."
- Prism effect. Alibaba obtained investment from many famous overseas investment institutions, reflecting or symbolizing the international recognition of "Alibaba," adding brand effect and enhancing

influence, which did also generate certain returns and affect the development and performance of the company.

- Decline in equity concentration. The introduction of external capital is inevitable, and the concentration of equity decreases with the expansion of asset size, which may affect the decision-making speed of enterprises. However, in the early stages of Alibaba's development, these introduced shareholders were mainly capital investment institutions. Although the equity was dispersed, appropriate equity separation should be beneficial to the development of the enterprise, and the founding team headed by Jack Ma is the first controlling shareholder of Alibaba and remains the true controller of Alibaba.

2.3.1.2 *2005–2010: VC/PE Exit, Yahoo Shares Result in Shareholder Structural Change*

In 2005, Alibaba introduced Yahoo and its B2B business went public. Unlike other investment institutions, Yahoo acquired a 40% share (after selling 1%) of Alibaba Group, which made it the first shareholder of Alibaba Group. Based on the agreement with Yahoo, Jack Ma, and other founders, although owning less stock than Yahoo and Softbank, still has primary voting rights, and actual control over the group. With the launch of Alibaba financing and an overseas listing, the founding team's shares were further diluted, though prior to the experience, to maintain control of Alibaba, the group implemented a partnership system to achieve shareholder power and control separation, and in the case of reduced shareholding, to secure control of Alibaba. At this stage, the shareholding structure and shareholder composition of Alibaba Group was as follows:

- The shareholder structure shifted from earlier diversity to the tripartite control of industrial capitalist Yahoo, venture capital SoftBank and Alibaba's leadership group, including Jack Ma.
- No one had an advantage in the equity ratio. After 2005, when industrial capital (i.e., Yahoo) bought shares, Jack Ma and his leadership team were at a financial resource disadvantage. According to institutional arrangements contained in the agreement with Yahoo, partial voting rights guaranteed control by Jack Ma and his team. The shares owned by Jack Ma and his team were further reduced until they lost their first shareholder position. Yahoo's shareholding

exceeded the shareholding of Jack Ma and the founding team, and this shareholding composition threatened the founder's actual control of the Alibaba Group. After Alibaba Group's agreement with Yahoo expired, Alibaba Group's control and decision-making power would have been limited, which would have had a significant impact on the founding team's control over the Alibaba Group.

2.3.1.3 *2010–Present: Reopening the Door to PE Financing, Public Share Offering*

In a case in which no one party has a dominant shareholding ratio, Jack Ma and his team's control was derived from equity and voting rights as stipulated in the agreement with Yahoo. This was the transfer of power based on the interdependence between the shareholders. However, this kind of inter-shareholder relationship resource was not stable. According to the agreement with Yahoo, Yahoo would have two board seats in Alibaba in 2010, and its number of members on the board of directors would be at least the same as those held by Jack Ma and his team. Jack Ma and others took a series of actions to obtain the absolute advantage of financial resources and maintain their control over Alibaba. Alibaba's internationalization after 2010 also accelerated the implementation of overseas mergers and acquisitions, and it still has high demand for capital. The financial resources of the founders and their teams are difficult to maintain for a long time. This process has made it possible for the implementation of the partnership system created by Jack Ma and his team to maintain control, and the implementation of the partnership system has reduced their dependence on financial resources. In this stage, Alibaba's shareholding structure and shareholder characteristics were as follows:

- Yahoo dispute. To avoid losing control, Jack Ma and his team began trying to maintain their control in 2010 by establishing a partnership system. During the Yahoo control dispute, Ma took the Alipay split, additional preference shares, financing, equity repurchase and other action strategies, and first obtained an absolute advantage in the equity ratio, then disclosed the partnership system in the 2014 prospectus.
- Changes in shareholder structure. Alibaba redeveloped PE financing and introduced a number of venture capital firms, including shareholders from Japan, China, Hong Kong, China, Singapore, Canada,

Australia, and the United States. It is also worth noting that Alibaba's Chinese investment institutions included China's state-owned investment institutions. Alibaba's shareholder composition was further diversified. However, from the perspective of shareholders, Alibaba Group's shareholders mainly include Jack Ma and his team, venture capital institutions, Yahoo, employees, and consultants.

- Exploration of the partnership system. In the face of the possibility of losing control due to equity dilution, Alibaba began exploring the implementation of the partnership system in 2010. The system has been in place since 2010, and every year, new partners are selected for appointment until the time of separation or retirement. The Alibaba "Partnership" is "the operator of the company, the builder of the business, the inheritor of the culture, and the shareholder." The selection criteria is "Alibaba has worked for more than five years, has excellent leadership skills, highly recognizes the company culture, and has a positive contribution to the company's development, and is willing to do its best for the company culture and mission." The Alibaba Group Partner System gives partners the right to nominate most of Alibaba's directors. This ensures that management can retain control of the board with a small shareholding.
- The proportion of industrial capital Yahoo's equity decreased. In this stage of development, as major shareholders, Yahoo and Alibaba engaged in several rounds of negotiations, and finally, Alibaba repurchased half of the shares held by Yahoo. They then reached a relevant agreement, and after the listing of Alibaba, Yahoo sold some stock, while exiting the Alibaba board of directors.

Usually the concentration of equity is reduced with the expansion of asset size (Demsetz and Lehn 1985), and the same is true for Alibaba Group's equity concentration. From the composition of the shareholding structure in Table 2.5, the Herfindahl-Hirschman Index (HHI) of the top three shareholders' shareholdings showed a downward trend, and the concentration of Alibaba Group showed a downward trend. After listing on the NYSE in 2014, the shareholding ratio of the top three shareholders fell below 0.25. As the scale of the company's assets expands, the financing behavior (investing in investment institutions or listing) due to the increase in the demand for financial capital usually bring

Table 2.5 Shifts in Alibaba's share concentration

	First financing in 1999	*Before 2005*	*After Yahoo's shareholding in 2005*	*After NYSE listing in 2014*
Jack Ma and other founders or partners' shareholding ratio	60%	47%	31.7%	13.1%
The top three shareholders' shares	100%	85%	100%	56%
Herfindahl-Hirschman Index of the shareholding ratio of the top three shareholders	0.52	0.29	0.34	0.14

Note It is generally considered that 0.25 is the demarcation point of the Herfindahl-Hirschman Index (HHI). The closer to 1, the greater the difference in the shareholding ratio of the top three shareholders, the more concentrated the equity

the equity dilution of the original shareholders. The diversification of corporate equity is something most enterprises face. The development of Alibaba Group's equity is also a microcosm of the development of many enterprises.

2.3.2 *Changes in the Composition of the Board of Directors*

Since the establishment of Alibaba in 1999, Alibaba's shareholders, board of directors and senior management team has consisted of many countries and regions, including China, Japan, the United States, Singapore, Sweden, among others, which are characterized by naturalization. Alibaba Group has maintained a relatively small board size, with 4 people between 2005 and 2012 and 10 after being listed in the US market. According to the theory of resource dependence, "a relatively large-scale board of directors may lead to higher levels of company performance." The size of the board of directors can serve as a measure of the ability of an organization to access key resources through linkages with the external environment, reflecting the company's contraction.

Referring to the existing research on the board of directors, the size of the Alibaba board of directors (i.e., 10 members) provides Alibaba Group with access to external key resources (including funds from the external environment, external funds, etc.) compared to when there were four member, which was increased to respond to the external environment. At the same time, from the perspective of the composition of the board of directors, Walter Teh Ming kwaukc and Jerry Yang of the five executive directors and nonexecutive directors have many years of experience in the Alibaba board of directors or Alibaba, which keeps the board stable and has had a positive impact on the board.

2.3.3 *Evolution of Control*

Figure 2.4 shows the evolution of equity and control rights of the founders of Alibaba Group's corporate governance using two dimensions of control and voting rights.

2.3.3.1 1999–2004: Jack Ma and Other Founders Are the First Shareholder, Equity Control

From 1999 to 2004, although Alibaba accepted a number of VC/PE investments, its shareholding ratio has always put it in an advantageous position and has always been in control. Alibaba was led by Goldman Sachs in 1999 to unite investment institutions in the United States, Asia, and Europe, including Singapore's Transpac Capital, Sweden's Investor AB, and Singapore's government technology development fund, investing 5 million US dollars, Alibaba's equity. It has also been diluted since then; in 2000, the second round of financing was 25 million US dollars, Softbank led the investment of 20 million US dollars, Fidelity, Huiya Capital, TDF, Investor AB, Japan Asian Investment Company, and other investments of 5 million US dollars; in 2004, Alibaba's third round of financing of 82 million US dollars, Softbank led the capital of 60 million US dollars, the remaining 22 million US dollars by Fidelity, TDF, and GGV funded, after the founder team such as Jack Ma shares fell to 47%.

2.3.3.2 2005–2010: Same Shareholding, Based on the Same Proportion of the Voting Rights of Founders, Such as Jack Ma, as Well as Yahoo

In 2005, in competition with eBay, Alibaba accepted Yahoo China's investment for financial support at the cost of Alibaba's 40% economic income and 35% of voting rights. At this time, although Alibaba's share is lower than Investor Yahoo, Alibaba's voting rights still ranked first based

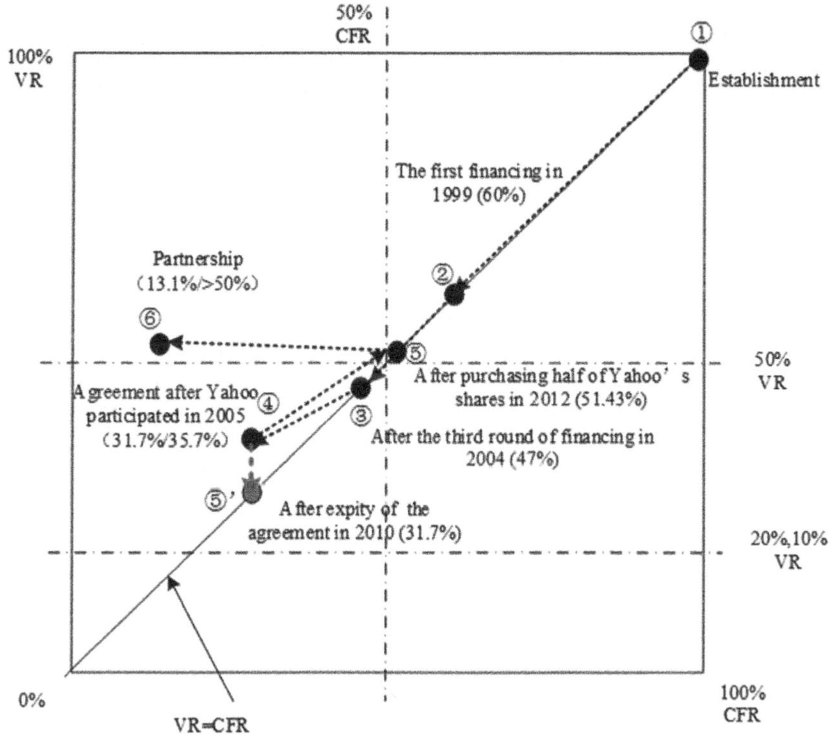

Fig. 2.4 Equity and voting rights evolution of Jack Ma and his management team from Alibaba (*Notes* (1) VR refers to voting rights; and CFR refers to cash flow rights or ownership; (2) if CFR = VR, the value in brackets is VR or CFR; if CFR ≠ VR, the value in brackets is VR/CFR; and (3) 20 or 10% of voting rights refers to the lower limit of the proportion of shares held by the founder for maintaining authority. (1)→(2)→(3) During 1999 to 2004, three rounds of financing occurred. The investors were mainly venture capitals (VCs) and the shareholders proportion of Ma and his team diluted to 47%. (2)–(4): In 2005, the industrial capital, Yahoo, acquired 40% of shares and 35% of voting rights by investment and became the largest shareholder of Alibaba. After other VCs existed in 2009, Ma and his team held 31.7% of shares and acquired 4% of voting rights by an agreement with Yahoo. (4)–(5): Due to the expiry of agreement with Yahoo in 2010, Ma and his team faced the risk of losing authority. (4)–(5): During 2010 to 2014, Ma and his team maintained their authority and established partnership by restarting PE financing through separating Alipay, repurchasing shares and other means. In 2012, after repurchasing half of the shares from Yahoo in 2012, they largely held 51.43% of shares. (5)–(6): After Alibaba was listed in 2014, the prospectus showed that Ma Yan and his management held 13.1% of shares but occupied over one half of board seats thanks to partnership)

on the agreement. As can be seen from the relevant content of the agreement, the team of founders, such as Jack Ma is threatened by Alibaba's control and is likely to lose control of Alibaba in 2010. To avoid this possible risk, before the arrival of October 2010, Alibaba adopted open financing, equity repurchase, and other measures to repurchase shares held by Yahoo to ensure control of Alibaba.

2.3.3.3 2010–Present: Partnership System, Outside the Equity Logic

Alibaba began implementing the partnership system in 2010 after experiencing a possible loss of control due to equity dilution. Alibaba's partner system, called "Lakeside Partners" (15 years ago, Jack Ma and partners founded Alibaba in a compound called Lakeside Garden). The system has been in place since 2010 and every year new partners are selected for appointment until they part or retire. A "partner" of Alibaba, as defined by Jack Ma, is the operator of the company, the builder of the business, the inheritor of the culture, and the shareholder at the same time. Selection criteria include having worked at Alibaba for more than five years, have excellent leadership skills, recognizes company culture, makes a positive contribution to the company's development, and is willing to do their best for the company culture and mission.

The Alibaba Group partnership system gives partners the right to nominate most of Alibaba's directors. This ensures that management can still control the board with limited shareholding. Alibaba founder Jack Ma once explained that Alibaba's partnership system is different from most existing partner systems, and we are not building an interest group, but to ensure that Alibaba is more flexible and competitive in any future market.

The current actual control chain of Alibaba Group: Ma Cai-30 Alibaba Partners (Table 2.6)—Board of Directors—SoftBank—Shareholders' Meeting. By the time of listing in 2014, the partnership team consisted of 21 men (70%) and nine women (30%), with an average age of 42.5 years and three aged over 50 (the oldest, Timothy A. Steinert, born in 1960), seven aged under 40 (the youngest Yijie Peng, Alibaba small and micro financial services group VP was born in 1978). The 30 partners each have a minimum of six and a maximum of 15 years of experience at the company, of which seven have been there since 1999. Among the partners, Yongming Wu, Li Cheng, Zhenfei Liu, Jian Wang, Peng Jiang,

Table 2.6 Partners in Alibaba Group in 2014

Name	*Gender*	*Year of birth*	*Entry time*	*Position*
Jingxian Cai	Male	1977	2000	Principal Engineer
Li Cheng	Male	1975	2005	Chief Architect, Small and Micro Financial Services Company
Trudy Shan Dai	Female	1976	1999	Chief Customer Officer
Luyuan Fan	Male	1973	2007	President, China Business, Small and Micro Financial Services Company
Yongxin Fang	Male	1974	2000	Alibaba Group Human Resources Director
Xiaoming Hu	Male	1970	2005	Risk Manager, SME Loan Business; Chief Risk Officer, Small and Micro Financial Services Company
Fang Jiang	Female	1974	1999	Vice President, Corporate Integrity and Human Resources
Peng Jiang	Male	1973	2000	President, Alibaba Cloud Computing, YunOS and Digital Entertainment; Deputy Chief Technology Officer
Jianhang Jin	Male	1970	1999	President
Eric Xiandong Jing	Male	1973	2007	Chief Financial Officer, Small and Micro Financial Services Company
Zhenfei Liu	Male	1972	2006	Vice President, Infrastructure Operations
Zhaoxi Lu	Male	1970	2000	Alibaba Group CEO (CEO)
Jack Yun Ma	Male	1964	1999	Executive Chairman
Xingjun Ni	Male	1977	2003	Principal Engineer, Small and Micro Financial Services Company

(continued)

Table 2.6 (continued)

Name	*Gender*	*Year of birth*	*Entry time*	*Position*
Lucy Lei Peng	Female	1973	1999	Chief People Officer, Alibaba Group; Chief Executive Officer, Small and Micro Financial Services Company
Sabrina Yijie Peng	Female	1978	2000	Vice President, International, Small and Micro Financial Services Company
Xiaofeng Shao	Male	1966	2005	Alibaba Group Chief Risk Officer (CRO)
Timothy A. Steinert	Male	1960	2007	General Counsel and Corporate Secretary
Wenhong Tong	Female	1971	2000	Chief Operating Officer, China Smart Logistics
Joseph C. Tsai	Male	1964	1999	Executive Vice-Chairman
Jian Wang	Male	1963	2008	Alibaba Group Chief Technology Officer (CTO)
Shuai Wang	Male	1974	2003	Senior Vice President, China Corporate Communications and Marketing
Minzhi Wu	Female	1976	2000	President, Alibaba.com and 1688.com
Wei Wu	Female	1968	2007	Alibaba Group Chief Financial Officer (CFO)
Yongming Wu	Male	1975	1999	Senior Vice President, Corporate Development
Siying Yu	Female	1974	2005	Associate General Counsel, China
Ming Zeng	Male	1970	2006	Senior Vice President, Corporate Strategy
Jianfeng Zhang	Male	1973	2004	President, Taobao Marketplace
Yong Zhang	Male	1972	2007	Alibaba Group Chief Operating Officer (COO)

(continued)

Table 2.6 (continued)

Name	*Gender*	*Year of birth*	*Entry time*	*Position*
Yu Zhang	Female	1970	2004	Vice President, Corporate Development

Source Alibaba Prospectus (2014). Retrieved from https://www.sec.gov/Archives/edgar/data/1577552/000119312514347620/d709111d424b4.htm#toc709111_1, pp. 232

Jianfeng Zhang, Xingjun Ni, and Jingxian Cai are all "programmers," accounting for 25% of the total number of partners (to 2014).

In fact, Alibaba's partnership system is an institutional design, and institutionalization is an organizational phenomenon. The rules and procedures of an organization, as the social construction, are independent from any individual (though the individual and his act may be influenced). The current holder of power can form an organization by institutionalizing itself. When coming into power, the dominating coalition can establish charters, rules, procedures, and information system to limit the potential power of others and keep its own. The key of power institutionalization is to legitimatize own power and reduce the legitimacy of others by certain strategy. The partnership of Alibaba is a new institution established by Jack Ma and his team to secure their absolute authority over the company. Due to the previous fight with Yahoo for authority, Ma and his team expected a kind of logic beyond other existing rules.

Edwards pointed out that the simple control system mainly depending on individuals may be replaced by a more complicated one, which is not based on individuals, and even technical and bureaucratic structure as time goes by. The strength of such bureaucratic settings (such as acting rules, company policies, and so on) lies in their impersonal appearance. Meanwhile, the control structure created by Alibaba's partnership as an institutional arrangement structuralized the personal or group control of Jack Ma and others. To Ma and his team, its advantages include: (1) power advantage is partially covered and is seemingly subject to company norms rather than personal prestige and (2) those who possess structuralized power can advance their interests without other mobilizing means. People may automatically believe that they "are qualified" to say on any occasion related to their interests. Power is pursued by institutions developed based on the advantage of resources, and the realization of such institutional arrangement weakens the dependence of power on resources.

In general, to some extent, things that are institutionalized within the organization are consistently recognized among members of the influential organization. Before any formal institutions or framework of the organization is determined or changed, such change needs to generally go through a process of meditation. Once institutionalized, it may last for a period of time. As the social structure emphasized in the Giddens structural discussion is constantly produced and reproduced by the actors, the partnership system is constructed by the founder team of actors, and the formal or informal new rules of execution change the original rules. It is a reconfiguration of resources. These social structures are both the product of past actions and the background of current behavior. The system represents a firmly defined social structure that can give the social structure a "reliability" that does not change with time. Alibaba's partner system power is more structured, and on the surface, the degree of reliance on the shareholding structure after the implementation of the system is reduced, so that Ma Yun and his partner team can maintain the control advantage when the shareholding ratio is relatively inferior.

2.4 Impact of Transnational Governance Evolution

2.4.1 *Shareholders, Board of Directors, Senior Management Team Building and Business Development*

When Alibaba was first created, it showed the genes of naturalization. It was the internationalization of shareholders and members of the executive team that shifted its orientation in an international direction. In 2000, Alibaba expanded its overseas expansion, established its corporate headquarters in Hong Kong, set up an office in the United Kingdom, set up a research and development center in Silicon Valley, and established joint ventures in South Korea, Japan, and Taiwan, and introduced talents with high salaries; Alibaba had not yet established a foothold in China. Its development direction and profit model were still unclear, and internationalization had failed.

In 2000, after Alibaba formulated its strategy of returning to China, its business was concentrated in China during 2010. During this period, the composition of shareholders changed, from the internationalization of the initial creation to the transformation of Jack Ma and his team, Softbank, and Yahoo. In the form of shareholders, other international venture capital institutions withdraw from the cash, which is also related to the concentration of their business in China. In 2010, Alibaba officially launched AlibabaExpress. In the same year, Alibaba began to deploy big data and its partnership system. In 2011, Alibaba began to implement major adjustment and transform its organizational structure. This shifted it from the previous big Taobao strategy to the big Alibaba strategy. Since 2010, Alibaba has invested in M&A for the first time in the United States. Alibaba's international business expansion and demand for capital attracted many international investors. Before listing in 2014, its shareholder composition included China, the United States, Japan, Russia, and other multicountry investment institutions, a highly international grouping.

The development of overseas business has further promoted the construction of the senior management team and the board of directors, and this construction has promoted the expansion of Alibaba's international business. In October 2013, Alibaba's overseas investment team was established by Michael Zeisser leadership of Vice Chairman of the Board of Directors Joseph C. Tsai Alibaba hired Liberty Media is responsible for digital business sector, after adding Alibaba, Zeisser report to Joseph C. Tsai. In 2014, the Alibaba overseas investment team led by Zeisser has invested in dozens of start-ups, mainly in North America, including many well-known Silicon Valley start-ups, such as Lyft for car applications, Tango for online video communication applications, and mobile citation search engine Quixey, TV content sharing application Peel and heavy mobile gaming maker Kabam. Before the global listing of Alibaba Group in 2014, the board of directors was designed. The members of the board of directors were expanded from 4 to 10 members. Experts with international relations processing experience and international relations resources were introduced and investment was introduced. As a member of the board of directors, institutional personnel are further adapted to the requirements of environmental factors in overseas systems. In 2015, Alibaba appointed Michael Evans, former vice-chairman of Goldman Sachs, as the president and executive director of Alibaba Group, responsible for the global business of Alibaba Group and reported to Zhang Yong, CEO of Alibaba Group. The interaction between business development and board building evolves, and business development drives the construction of the board of directors.

2.4.2 *Parent and Subsidiary Governance Model Choices*

In the governance relationship between parent and overseas subsidiaries, Alibaba chose its overseas entry mode according to the core level of the business, and the business content determines the choice of the governance mode of the parent–subsidiary relationship.

Alibaba is the world's largest e-commerce platform. As a core component, Alibaba has adopted different entry modes for different parts of the e-commerce ecosystem. For the e-commerce platform, Alibaba has rich operational experience and competitive advantages. Therefore, through the creation of an e-commerce platform for many countries (the internationalized B2B e-commerce platform Alibaba International), the wholly owned acquisition of the US e-commerce platform and fine market segment (Auctiva and Vendio in the US B2B website), and some mergers and acquisitions (Fanatics and 1Stdibs website). It can be seen that the expansion of Alibaba's overseas market is mainly carried out through the construction of an international e-commerce platform. The overseas investment in e-commerce is currently targeting the market. Unlike Taobao's mass market strategy in China, Alibaba's e-commerce website, which is invested or established in the United States, including Fanatics, which was invested in 2013, is targeted at market segments. For the key financial payment link of e-commerce—payment system, Alibaba chose M&A investment (Indian one97 mobile payment platform) or the establishment of cooperation agreement (Russian payment platform Qiwi wallet), and the international exploration of its own Alipay business, develop on the basis of already having a certain market. On the mobile internet side, betting on potential mobile internet companies, focusing on communications applications, content sharing and online and offline life, hopes to seize the next outbreak of mobile applications and play an important role in the global expansion process. For the downstream industry logistics system of e-commerce, Alibaba tries to establish its own logistics capabilities on a global scale. The main entry modes include partial mergers (US logistics company ShopRunner, Singapore Post) and cooperation agreements with Australia Post, Brazil Post, and China Post (Table 2.7).

Through the above analysis, we can see that Alibaba's overseas investment governance follows the following rules: building an Alibaba ecosystem and taking the advantages of Alibaba's e-commerce platform overseas. The corresponding parent–subsidiary governance methods, in

Table 2.7 Alibaba overseas investment

Year	*Company*	*Country*	*Disclosure of investment (100 million US dollars)*	*Equity ratio*	*Entry mode*	*Market choice*	*Field*
2015	One97	IND	5.75	30%	Partial M&A	Mobile payment platform	financial
2012	Qiwi wallet	RUS	–	–	Strategic CA	Payment platform	
2014	Kabam	USA	1.2	12%	Partial M&A, strategic CA	Mobile game	Mobile apps, wireless
2014		USA	2.5 (with Coatue Management, Third Point)	–	Partial M&A	Carpooling application	apps
2014	TangoMe	USA	2.15	20-25%	Partial M&A	Social application	
2013	UCWeb	CHN	Complete control	100%	Wholly owned	Mobile browser	
2013	Quixey	USA	0.50		Partial M&A	Application search engine	
2014	Amap		11	100%	Wholly owned	map	
2014	Singapore Post	SIN	2.49	10.35%	Partial M&A	postal	Logistics System:
2014 2014 2014	Australia Post Brazil Post China Post	AUS BRA CHN	–	–	CA	postal	Global Post
2013 2013	ShopRunner	USA	0.75 2.06	39%	Partial M&A	express delivery	
2010	Alibaba International Station	–		100%	Founding	B2B	E-commerce Market segments

(continued)

Table 2.7 (continued)

Year	*Company*	*Country*	*Disclosure of investment (100 million US dollars)*	*Equity ratio*	*Entry mode*	*Market choice*	*Field*
2010	Auctiva	USA		100%	Wholly-owned	B2B e-commerce service provider	
2010	Vendio	USA		100%	Wholly-owned	B2B e-commerce SAAS provider	
2013	Fanatics	USA	1.7 (with Temasek)		Partial M&A	B2C sports products	
2014	11main	USA		100%	Founding	B2C e-commerce	
2014	1Stdibs	USA	0.15		Partial M&A	B2C luxury goods	
2013 2014	Peel	USA	0.05		Partial M&A	TV remote control application developer	other

(continued)

Note M&A = Merger and Acquisition, CA = Cooperation Agreement, SAAS = Software as a Service basic terms, for the underlying data services in the e-commerce ecological chain, cloud computing, etc., Alibaba through its own cloud computing and other data R&D centers, continue to enhance their own competitive advantages and superior capabilities. In terms of e-commerce, Alibaba has entered the market through mergers and acquisitions in addition to company establishment, based on its judgment and ability, adopting controlled and autonomous governance to manage subsidiaries. For businesses, such as finance and logistics, which may be restricted by system control and barriers to entry, Alibaba enters in a cooperative and collaborative manner, through joint governance or just participation in governance. For public post-related businesses, which are not suitable for investment, they enter through the establishment of cooperation agreements, through partnership governance to expand related business.

2.5 Discussions and Conclusions

2.5.1 *Alibaba's Transnational Governance Facing up to Risk*

2.5.1.1 *Legal Risk: US Shareholder Class Action*

On the morning of January 28, 2015, the State Administration for Industry and Commerce disclosed the 2014 White Paper on Administrative Guidance to the Alibaba Group. At the time, the report pointed out that the Alibaba online trading platform had five major problems, such as strict control of subject access, weak review of commodity information, chaotic management of sales behavior, flaws in credit evaluation, and lax control of internal staff. There is no special market subject in front of the law. The main executives of Alibaba must have a bottom line awareness and employ bottom line thinking to overcome arrogance. After the publication of the white paper, Alibaba Group was subject to class action in the United States for allegedly "concealing investigations by the regulatory authorities," which involved a total of seven law firms.

The United States has a well-established tradition of protection and class action for small- and medium-sized investors. This makes the United States a preferred overseas destination for many Chinese companies to list and seek funding. However, many companies see only the rich sources of funds, great market liquidity, and high price-earnings ratios, but ignore the fact that the United States is one of the most mature financial capital markets in the world, and its strict market supervision protects small- and medium-sized investors. Mature concepts, laws and regulations have increased legal risks and related costs for Chinese companies listing in the United States. Class action is a US-specific litigation system recognized by the US Federal Civil Procedure Regulations.

Since publicly issued securities involve public investors, any investor can hire a lawyer to initiate a class action proceeding on behalf of other investors in the event of a securities fraud. Moreover, in the United States, in a class action lawsuit like this, the plaintiff does not need to pay the law firm in advance, but after the success of the lawsuit, settlements can be more than 50%. On the other hand, in the United States, there are a lot of arbitrage opportunities because of the wealth of financial instruments and financial derivatives. Through cooperation, funds, consulting companies, and law firms can use asymmetry of Sino-US information to make short-selling Chinese companies profitable. As a general rule, consulting companies use information sources in China to obtain information that is not conducive to listed companies. It may be real or fabricated false information. The consulting company then cooperates with the hedge fund to short the stock of a Chinese listed company through message guidance and capital operation, and use the stock price fluctuation to profit from it. After the stock price fluctuates, it cooperates with the law firm, and the shareholders file a lawsuit against the listed company, claiming compensation for the losses caused by the fluctuation of the stock price of the tradable shares, and the law firm acts as a class action lawsuit.

Legal risk is one of the most common types of risk in the process of Chinese companies going abroad. Sina, Netease, UT Starcom, Ninetowns, and McCawlin have all suffered one or more rounds of class action suits.

2.5.1.2 *Opportunities and Risks from VIE Infrastructure*

The variable interest entity (VIE) vehicle, which also known as agreement control, means that the invested company has actual or potential economic benefits, but the company itself has no complete control over the economic interests, but actual or potential. The primary beneficiary controlling this economic benefit needs to consolidate this VIE. The VIE architecture has been recognized by GAPP in the United States, and the "VIE Accounting Standards" has been created specifically for this purpose. The VIE architecture is implemented through a non-equity agreement arrangement. The protocol control model is generally composed of a three-part structure, namely, an overseas listed entity, a wholly foreign-owned subsidiary (WFOE, Wholly Foreign Owned Enterprise) or a foreign-invested company (FIE), and a licensed company (a foreign-restricted business license). Holder, the WFOE and the licensed company signed the VIE agreement to obtain the relevant rights and interests in the licensed company. Among them, overseas listed entities may adopt Cayman Company, Hong Kong Shell Company, among others, due to various considerations, such as taxation and registration convenience. Multiple or even multiple modes of coexistence.

(1) VIE risk

In 2009, Alibaba's board of directors authorized the management to legally obtain payment licenses through the adjustment of shareholding structure, and set up Alipay domestic companies under the agreement control structure. Alipay's domestic company transferred from Alipay, a wholly owned subsidiary of Alibaba Group, to Alibaba E-Commerce Co., Ltd., a wholly owned subsidiary of Jack Ma and Xie Shihuang, for a total of about RMB 330 million. After the equity transfer, in the first quarter of 2011, Jack Ma unilaterally decided to break between Alipay and Alibaba Group on the grounds that the agreement could not obtain a third-party payment license and protocol control relations endangered national economic security. Jack Ma's unilateral termination of the Alipay VIE led to a discussion of risk associated with the VIE resurfacing, and eventually to extensive discussions and concerns in the industry.

Policy risk recognized, the VIE structure has not yet been subject to specific rules by the Chinese regulatory authorities. It is in an awkward situation of "illegal prohibition is legal"; tax and foreign exchange control risks, adopting the VIE framework to sign agreements, will involve a large number of related party transactions. Price transfer and anti-tax avoidance issues sees compliance playing a decisive role. In terms of foreign exchange control risks, the transfer of domestic enterprise profits to WFOE through agreements, may face foreign exchange control risks when profits exit. Non-direct control of risks, due to the VIE model means that under some circumstances, listed companies have no equity control over domestic-funded enterprises, and there may be problems that management cannot participate in and control.

(2) The opportunity that the VIE brings to Alibaba

Alibaba partner system can be implemented in part, also benefit from the variable interest entity structure of China's internet restrictions on foreign investment caused by the factors that have a major impact on obtaining actual control over Ma and other members of Alibaba founding team, to some extent the degree of Shanghai's foreign shareholder's control over Alibaba Group is beyond its reach. Institutional factors and their changes will have a further impact on the corporate governance structure. For example, the Ministry of Commerce of China is preparing a new Foreign Investment Law to regulate the VIE model. In 2015, the Foreign Investment Law of the People's Republic of China was drafted. If the policy is introduced, it may have an impact on the actual control structure of Alibaba. Moreover, the differences in the political system of the country, the degree of marketization, the degree of perfection of laws and regulations, and the dominant corporate governance structure will affect the organizational structure design and the acquisition of the founder's control.

2.5.2 *Evaluation of the Partnership System*

2.5.2.1 *Comparison of Partnership System and Dual Equity System*

The partnership system is an attempt by the founder to maintain control under the conditions of enterprise expansion and continuous dilution of equity. There is a difference between the dual equity structure system. The dual ownership structure originated from the media industry. A family that controls many newspaper companies believes that the truth and objectivity of the news cannot be interfered with, so it is necessary to avoid the company being manipulated by capital through a dual ownership structure. After that, the dual ownership structure, as a means for management to pursue power and achieve the purpose of small groups, became popular among high-tech enterprises. Alibaba's partner system means that most of the members of Alibaba's board of directors are nominated by a group of partners consisting of Alibaba's internal seniors, rather than the number of shares allocated by the number of shares. The realization of the dual shareholding structure is to issue two types of stocks with different degrees of voting rights through the enterprise. The holders have different rights in the same stock. For example, the voting rights held by the management of the company may be 10–1, with voting rights held by ordinary investors.

The two objectives are similar. The multiple shareholding structure realizes the control of the company by a small amount of equity in the same way as the shares, while the partner system further allocates the seats on the board based on the equity, realizing the control and cash flow rights. The partnership system reflects the further expansion of the source of control, allowing partners, such as Jack Ma, to retain majority voting rights with less than 20% of equity.

2.5.2.2 Control Through Institutionalization

Salancik and Pfeffer (1977) argued that when they are in power, the dominant coalition has the power to create charters, rules, procedures, and information systems that limit the potential power of others and continue their own power, institutionalizing power. The key is to create a strategy to legitimize one's authority and reduce the legitimacy of others. The emergence of Alibaba's partner system is the product of Jack Ma and his team's institutionalization of power to guarantee absolute control. According to Edwards, the simple control system that mainly depending on individuals may be replaced by a more complicated one, which is not based on individuals, and even technical and bureaucratic structure as time goes by. The strength of such bureaucratic settings (such as acting rules, company policies and so on) lies in their impersonal appearance. The control structure created by Alibaba's partnership system also changed the control of Jack Ma and the management team of Alibaba into control of Alibaba by Jack Ma and his team of partners, from individual or group control to structured control. For Ma and his partners, the advantage is that, first, their power advantage is somewhat concealed, and it seems to be restricted to the company's normative structure, rather than individual privilege. Second, people with structured power need no other means of mobilization. Being able to pursue their interests, people will automatically assume that these people are "qualified" to have a say in situations that affect their interests.

2.5.2.3 "Coordination Control" and Establishment of Common Values and Culture

Alibaba's partnership system reflects a degree of conservatism control to some extent. The form of coercive control is based on a considerable degree of consensus among members of the organization, a high level of coordination, and a degree of self-management of members. The team consisting of a group of senior executives who are highly aware of and matching Alibaba culture and key executives of the subsidiaries. The team is based on shared values. The legitimacy of the team is derived from Jack Ma, Joseph C. Tsai, and other partners. The authority of these "company operators, business builders, cultural inheritors and shareholders," with the roles of founder, shareholders, executive directors, managers, etc., is more likely to take into account the long-term and short-term benefits. The form of the partnership team belongs to a powerful norm based on the premise of values, and becomes the rational rule of Alibaba Group's rational decision-making. At the same time, control is expressed in the values, norms, and rules of the team, through the substantive rationality and formal rationality mixes as a "public rationality" system that controls the behavior of team partners, and the powerful combination of peer pressure and rational rules in coordination control will give stronger oversight. Because partners must strongly agree with Alibaba's values and goals, its norms and rules, and the price of this kind of control is, "If they want to resist their team's control, they must be willing to risk their human dignity, being made to feel unworthy as a 'teammate'."[2]

2.5.2.4 Embodiment of Entrepreneurial Value

The Alibaba partnership system reflects changes in the balance of human capital and financial capital. For a long time, the system of equal rights has reflected the importance of financial capital. Financial capital plays an important role in the growth and development of the company, but for the human capital of the company's development, especially the founder's manpower. The role of capital is not reflected. In the information technology era, the role of people is more prominent. The reason why the partner system can be implemented and accepted by investors is largely due to the fact that the team of partners such as Jack Ma is itself Alibaba Group. The important resources, they are an important component of the value of Alibaba Group. In the future choice of corporate governance model, the value of the founder and founder team should be taken into consideration. The same shareholding system is fair, but the lack of financial capital is the beginning. For people, if they cannot take their own value into consideration, the allocation of control rights based on equity is not conducive to the long-term development of the company. The partnership system is a useful attempt in this regard.

[2] Barker J. R. (1993). Tightening the iron cage: Concertive control in self-managing work teams. *Administrative Science Quarterly*, 38(3), 408–438, p. 436.

2.5.3 *The Impact of Corporate Financing Choices on Control*

As the corporate financing dilution process progresses, the founder's power base changes with the organizational environment, and the acquisition and maintenance of its control rights also faces challenges. The main manifestation is the dilution of property resources. At this time, in order to better maintain control, the founders will take certain measures to maintain their power. The accumulation of knowledge resources of the founders on finance and governance has influenced their financing decisions. The founders of Alibaba and their team members have relevant financing experience. Jack Ma has experienced frustrated experience with investors, and Joseph C. Tsai is familiar with the operation of investors, so consideration is given to investor selection and organizational design to avoid excessive dilution and loss of control. Alibaba's first dilution ratio was 40% higher. Jack Ma and others reduced the dilution ratio in the subsequent financing dilution by 13% (21.67%). When introducing Yahoo, it reduced its holding by 15.3% (32.55%). In the process of continuous financing, the accumulation of experience and knowledge of the founder team or the founder on the investment and financing of the investor has affected the choice of the investor, the speed of the dilution of the equity, and thus the proportion of the financial resources of the founder. Changes in the company's control. Knowledge power based on knowledge resources plays a role in the influence of corporate governance structure and financing decisions, complementing the equity logic and helping founders make better use of their financial resources. In the whole financing process, investors are mainly VCs which tend to follow specialization logic. Compared with the founders, there are significant differences in resource allocation between the two, professional VC education and management background makes it more business value for the enterprise, but lacks the value of technological innovation, and the financial return is the strategic goal of its investment company. The founder is more technologically innovative, VCs and founders have a kind of interdependence, VCs rely on the founder's intellectual resources, and the founder relies on VC's financial resources. The mutual resource dependence promotes the maintenance of the cooperative relationship and guarantees cooperation for a period of time.

To sum up, established in 1999, Alibaba's executive team and shareholder composition reflect the international structural characteristics. The addition of Joseph C. Tsai and overseas VCs meant Alibaba was doomed to having to meet the needs of transnational governance and confronting its specific set of challenges. The governance problems caused by the internationalization of the group's senior management team, governance issues formed by the internationalization of the shareholder structure, the governance of the distribution of ownership and the distribution of control rights and the internationalization of the business structure, the issue of the parent–subsidiary relationship, risk management issues brought about by cultural and institutional distance between countries during overseas listings are now all firmly part of Alibaba Group's cross-border governance ecology.

References

Demsetz, Harold, Lehn, Kenneth. The Structure of Corporate Ownership: Causes and Consequences. *Journal of Political Economy*, 1985, 93(6): 1155–1177.

Salancik, Gerald R., Pfeffer, Jeffrey. Who Gets Power—And How They Hold on to It: A Strategic-Contingency Model of Power. *Organizational Dynamics*, 1977, 5(3): 3–21.

CHAPTER 3

Transnational Governance at Geely Auto During Its Acquisition of Volvo

3.1 Introduction

Zhejiang Geely Holding Group (Geely Automobile) was founded by Li Shufu in 1986 as the Arctic Flower Refrigerator Factory. In 1996, Geely Group was formally established, and in 1997, it began making cars, setting into the automotive industry by way of talent and technology, and developing rapidly. According to 2014 statistics, Geely Automobile was worth more than USD 17.85 billion (i.e., RMB 110 billion), and had been in the world's top 500 companies list for two years in a row. It has now been a China top 500 company for the past 11 years, and in the top ten Chinese automobile companies for 9 years straight. It is known as an innovator as well as core national car exporter.

Headquartered in Hangzhou, Zhejiang Geely Holding Group now owns Geely Automobile, Volvo Car, and London Taxi. Among them, Geely Automobile has built manufacturing bases in Zhejiang province's Taizhou and Ningbo, Xiangtan in Hunan, Jinan in Shandong, and Chengdun in Sichuan. Geely retails more than 10 vehicle products as well as a full range of 1–3.5 L engines with matched manual/automatic gearboxes. The company has a comprehensive sales network in China,

In this case study, Zhejiang Geely Holding Group is referred to as Geely Automobile or Geely.

© The Author(s), under exclusive license to Springer Nature Singapore Pte Ltd. 2020
R. Lin et al. *Corporate Governance of Chinese Multinational Corporations*,
https://doi.org/10.1007/978-981-15-7405-4_3

with more than 700 proprietary 4S stores and up to a thousand service outlets; nearly 200 overseas sales and service outlets; and investment of ten millions of USD in a national 24/7 call center. By the end of 2014, Geely had sold over 3.5 million units, making it well-known nationwide.

Geely established a research institute in Hangzhou, Zhejiang Province to form a complete development capability for complete vehicles, engines, transmissions, and automotive electronics. Car design is handled by centers in Shanghai, Gothenburg, Barcelona, and California. The European Research and Development Center (CEVT) was established in Gothenburg, Sweden, to create a globally competitive modular infrastructure for medium-scale car production.

Geely has implemented a "constant responsibility to the brand for longterm customer satisfaction" campaign and prioritized quality control, passing the ISO9001 quality management system, TS16949: 2009 quality management system, ISO14001: 2004 Environmental Management System, ISO/IEC27001: 2005 Information Security Management system, OHSAS18001: 2011 occupational health and safety management system among other environmental certifications. Geely also obtained international certifications, such as Gulf GCC, EU EEC & ECE, and Australian ADR. Based on a new developmental concept of "pursuing the main goal, being more than a sum of its parts, and promoting the outstanding" and core value of "living a happy life with Geely as companion," Geely Holdings Group endeavors to keep innovating, and along with its talented team, grow to become an influential, competitive, and respected global top-500 automobile group.

3.2 Transnational Governance Evolution

Specific reasons why companies take the leap to internationalize tend to be very different. Their different perspectives and external factors are all part of the decision-making process. However, whatever the reason, a company's international operations begin with a consideration of overall strategy, seeking a wider range of competitive advantages. In general, Geely was motivated to expand overseas to find new customers for existing products and services, find low-cost resources, and build core competitiveness. Geely's acquisition of Volvo was designed to secure Volvo's brand and technology. The merger became a key action in the company's internationalization process.

3.2.1 *The Background of the Acquisition*

Geely was very focused on brand strategy, as can be seen from Geely Automobile's slogan, "create a big brand, innovate at Geely." It also developed an "Eleventh Five-Year" strategic plan based on the notion of "pursuing the main goal, being more than a sum of its parts, and promoting the outstanding." By 2015, it planned to build 15 overseas production bases and achieve half the total export target it had set in the five year plan to became internationally competitive. Volvo would help Geely achieve its brand strategy. From 2002 to 2008, they were active South Korea, the Middle East, Malaysia, the United Kingdom, Russia, Nigeria, and Mexico, either by selling, investing, or producing. The acquisition of Volvo was historic.

By comparison, Volvo, a famous Swedish car brand, was rich and established. Founded in 1927 in Gothenburg, Sweden, by Gustav Larson and Arthur Gablesen, the Volvo Group is the world's leading manufacturer of commercial transportation and construction equipment, providing trucks, buses, construction equipment, marine and industrial application drive systems, and aerospace engine components, as well as financial and after-sales services. Volvo is Latin for "moving forward." In 2008, it had more than 19,000 employees worldwide, manufacturing plants and assembly lines in Sweden, Belgium, China, and Malaysia, and sales and service networks in more than 100 countries and regions around the world, including 2400 sales outlets. Its cars are divided into four series: sedan (S series), business wagon (V series), SUV (XC series), and convertible/coupe (C series). From beginning to end, safety, environmental protection, and quality are core values and commitments to every one of its 6 million car owners. Volvo is the largest car company in Northern Europe, the largest industrial group in Sweden and one of the top 20 car companies in the world. And in 1999, it was acquired by Ford for USD 4.65 billion.

In the aftermath of the 2008 financial crisis, Ford revealed it had run up losses of USD 39 billion between 2004 and 2009, and Volvo sales were not picking up. In 2008, Volvo suffered huge losses (such as those shown in Table 3.1 and Fig. 3.1). Ford tried to sell Volvo to extract funds and get out of trouble fast. Ford needed to do this to guarantee the continued operation of Ford back in the United States.

Table 3.1 List of Ford Motor Company's 2004–2008 Corporate Financial Status (unit: USD 100 million)

Year	*Income*	*Profit*	*Loss*
2004	1716	35	–
2005	1769	14	–
2006	1601	–	−126
2007	1725	–	−27
2008	1463	–	−147

Source http://auto.sina.com.cn/z/walkintovolvo/

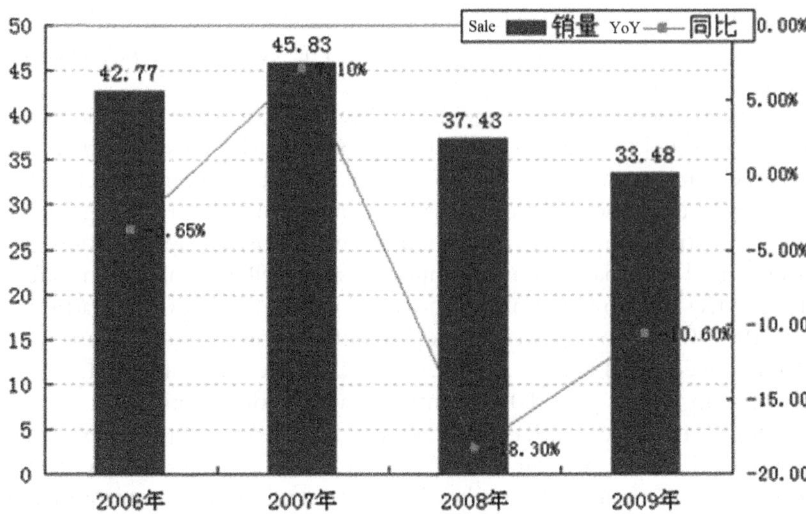

Fig. 3.1 Volvo sales from 2006 to 2009 (unit: 10,000 cars)

It is important to note why Geely bought Volvo. Their sales had been declining over recent years. The financial crisis meant Ford had to deal with huge losses, and Volvo was becoming a burden. Volvo understood Geely's corporate culture (Geely means 'lucky') and recognized its successful overseas acquisitions (British Manganese Bronze, DSI automatic transmission), and appreciated its ambitious development plans for Volvo. Not to mention, Li Shufu lent his personal charms to the takeover offensive. In addition, Geely had followed Volvo for eight years from 202 l and this laid the foundations for its successful acquisition. In addition, achieving a successful merger and acquisition, whether Geely could export its own vehicles to the world, and whether Volvo's US market could be further expanded, were all key issues of pre-acquisition preparation and negotiation, which also included post-acquisition cross-border governance.

3.2.2 Geely's Volvo Takeover

Geely had been paying attention to Volvo since 2002, and had been in official communications with Ford for more than three years when, at the tail end of 2008, it submitting a bid to Ford for the first time. This proposal, which had taken a whole year to elaborate upon, gave Ford a good first impression.

On March 28, 2010, Zhejiang Geely Holding Group and Ford Motor Company finally signed an equity acquisition agreement, with Geely taking 100% of Volvo for US$1.8 billion. Besides equity, the agreement covered intellectual property, parts supply and R&D relations between the three parties, Volvo, Geely, and Ford.

On August 2, 2010, Geely Chairman Li Shufu and Ford Chief Financial Officer Lewis Booth attended the completion ceremony in London UK, confirming that Zhejiang Geely Holding Group had full equity in the Volvo Car Corporation of Ford Motor Company including related assets (such as intellectual property). Geely's successful completion of the acquisition of Volvo took some time, as shown in Table 3.2.

3.3 Analysis of Transnational Governance Evolution

3.3.1 Multinational Parent Company (Geely) Stakeholder Governance

Geely had been paying attention to Volvo since 2002, and was officially in discussions with Ford for more than three years. This laid solid foundations for other stakeholders to offer their support to Geely's plans. Zhang Xiaoqiang, deputy director of the National Development and Reform Commission (NDRC),spoke positively about the acquisition during the 2010 "Rethinking the Asian Development Model" Boao Summit.

From a procedural perspective, to approve Geely's acquisition of Volvo, the division of functions first had to be investigated by the China's National Development and Reform Commission in conjunction with

Table 3.2 Geely's acquisition of Volvo

Date	*Milestone*
March 10, 2009	Geely hires financial family Rothschilds in bid to buy Volvo
May 11, 2009	Geely's acquisition of Volvo prioritized as support for Renault purchase fades
August 31, 2009	Geely officially bids for Volvo, becoming the only bidder to date
September 9, 2009	Geely's profit growth makes it number one in the sector, parent company to bid for Volvo
September 23, 2009	Geely officially announced investment by Goldman Sachs Capital Partners
September 29, 2009	Foreign media said Geely to buy Volvo for USD 2.5 billion
October 28, 2009	Ford Motor Company announces Geely to be Volvo's preferred bidder
October 29, 2009	Geely's official website claims the company has become Volvo's preferred purchaser
November 23, 2009	Volvo (China) publicly responds to Geely's acquisition rumors
December 3, 2009	US Crown Consortium Challenges Geely to Submit New Bidding opens for Volvo.
December 14, 2009	The Ministry of Commerce expresss support for Geely's acquisition of Volvo
December 23, 2009	Ford and Geely sign Volvo Framework Agreement
December 24, 2009	The Swedish government welcomes Geely's acquisition of Volvo
January 26, 2010	The Swedish government takes the initiative to invite an acquisition of Volvo
March 26, 2010	Volvo's union says it does not support the Geely acquisition plan
March 27, 2010	Geely signs a contract to acquire Volvo for up to USD 2 billion on March 28, 2010
March 28, 2010	Geely announces a Volvo plant will be built in China
March 30, 2010	Geely Volvo holds a press conference in Beijing

Source http://finance.sina.com.cn/focus/lsfxsjgx/index.shtml

various departments, and then reported on to the State Council. Zhang Xiaoqiang suggested that as long as Geely's team had a decent plan for the acquisition, the NDRC would back them. Because Geely was a recently established private company, it took two or three years of research preparation, before an agreement was reached to acquire Volvo cars. This shows that Chinese businesses, whether private or state-owned, are constantly striving to improve their international business capacity, via upgrading management and developing distinctive business propositions with an international vision.

In addition, the China's Ministry of Commerce expressed support for Geely's USD 1.8 billion acquisition of the 100% stake in Volvo and related intellectual property rights. Wang Chao, Deputy Minister of Commerce, said that the acquisition of Volvo by Geely was a guide to how Chinese companies could "go out into the world." The government was encouraging, but the parties still needed to abide by the rules. Geely accomplished this through careful research and preparation.

3.3.2 *Local Government and the Banks*

Based on the financial records, on August 2, 2010, adjusting for the depreciation of the euro and other factors, Geely paid pension obligations and working capital of USD 1.5 billion to complete the final acquisition settlement, of which USD 1.3 billion was paid in cash and USD 200 million went toward paying off Ford's short-term financial commitments (the remaining unpaid USD 300 million will be adjusted based on the relevant data for the second half of pensions obligations, with the total price not exceeding USD 1.8 billion).

The acquisition funds came from Geely Holding Group, Chinese-funded institutions, and international capital markets. On the basis of maintaining good relations with the government, Geely adopted an innovative strategy of using financing alliances at home and abroad. Specifically, when Geely acquired Volvo for USD 1.8 billion, Daqing, Shanghai, and Chengdu governments provided support amounting to USD 1 billion (i.e., RMB 7 billion) using local finance platforms. The Chengdu government requested cooperation between Chengdu Bank and China Development Bank's Chengdu Branch in Geely's acquisition. They provided USD 295 million (i.e., RMB 2 billion) and USD 148 million (i.e., RMB 1 billion), respectively, in low-interest loans. Geely had to pay only around one-third in the first three years, and interest would be charged only after this. Daqing and Shanghai State-owned Assets Supervision and Administration Commission provided a total of USD 591 million (i.e., RMB 4 billion) of M&A funds, and in return Geely promised to establish factories in these two places. The European Investment Bank and the Belgian Bank also provided Volvo with USD 796 million (i.e., 600 million euros) and USD 263 million (i.e., 198 million euros) of low-interest loans for post-merger operations under the guarantee of the Swedish government and the Flemish regional government. The above-mentioned banks and financial support provided by the government were extremely important for Geely's successful acquisition of Volvo. How this was managed is inseparable from good stakeholder governance at Geely.

3.3.3 *Stakeholder Governance of Multinational Subsidiaries (Volvo)*

In addition to handling its relationship with stakeholders, such as the Chinese government and the banks, the key for Geely to maintain good communication with Volvo's stakeholders, including employees and unions, as well as the Swedish government, which continued to lend its support.

3.3.3.1 The Swedish Government

According to a report in the Swedish News Agency, as early as 2004, the Swedish and Chinese governments signed a cooperation agreement in Gothenburg, Sweden's second largest city, regarding Volvo. The Swedish Investment Promotion Agency (ISA) suggested Geely should established an automotive product design center in Gothenburg and cooperate with Swedish industry. Unfortunately, Geely was not ready yet. However, this initial discussion laid foundations for the acquisition of Volvo in 2010.

At the beginning of 2010, Swedish State Secretary Haglon visited Li Shufu in Hangzhou to learn more about Geely's proposed acquisition of Volvo. Thereafter, Swedish Business Daily reported that Haglon said, "Positive signals have been exaggerated." A major obstacle in the negotiation process between the two parties was that Geely insisted on obtaining all Volvo's IP rights, while Ford resolutely opposed this. Haglon added: "Now I can only say that the two sides have not yet agreed." Geely's Volvo project spokesman Yuan Xiaolin was surprised but did not envisage more difficulties than before, because of an auspicious light on small companies to acquire Volvo, itself challenging. Geely did not flinch, persevering with Swedish government communication, until March 28, 2010, according to CCTV news reports, the Swedish Investment Agency chief representative in China Lan Chenyong said that Sweden was a veteran automobile powerhouse and the acquisition of Volvo by Geely was a big deal for Sweden. The Swedish government supported the conclusion of the transaction.

3.3.3.2 Trade Unions

As early as July 2009, the Volvo union stated that although Geely seemed to be a serious potential buyer, it could not change the position of the union, namely that Chinese investment could not be good for Volvo. The union questioned Geely on both formal and informal occasions. On March 10, 2010, shortly after the Swedish media broke the news that Geely had raised the USD 2.1 billion needed to acquire Volvo, the union said that Geely still needs about USD 1.4 billion to resurrect the Volvo brand and expressed doubts about Geely's financing ability.

At a critical moment in the negotiations, despite Geely's commitments, the Volvo union still called on the Swedish government to pay attention to this matter in order to prevent large-scale layoffs after Volvo was sold. When Ford's representative was paralyzed, Geely Chairman Li Shufu volunteered in poor English: "The three words I want to say are I love you! I love you, I also love the Volvo brand and can run Volvo. It is Geely's responsibility and obligation to protect the Volvo employees and protect the interests of Volvo employees!" Li Shufu instantly won the favor of Volvo union representatives which was partially based on his attempt to communicate.

Li Shufu made a written commitment not to lay off employees and to protect the interests of Volvo employees. He also invited Swedish media and union representatives to visit Geely headquarters in China and personally answered their questions and those of the media. At the end of January 2010, the union delegation visited China and received a satisfactory responses from Geely on many key issues. Later, the Volvo Unions issued a joint statement expressing acceptance of the Geely Group as a shareholder, and with this show of "Volvo Love," the biggest obstacle to the deal, trade union resistance vanished.

3.4 Impact of Transnational Governance Evolution

3.4.1 Volvo's Governance Structural Adjustment

3.4.1.1 Board Governance

After the acquisition, Volvo's board governance was mainly reflected in changes to the decision-making process of the board of directors. As Volvo wanted to expand its penetration into the Chinese market, its organizational structure had to undergo certain adjustments. Thus, on

September 25, 2010, during the second board meeting after the merger, Li Shufu and Stefan Jacoby admitted that "Volvo would have to undergo a procedural change." The biggest change was in the decision-making process employed by the board of directors. Management makes recommendations to the board of directors, and the board of directors agrees or rejects these recommendations. Before the merger, Volvo's board was restricted, with some issues needing to be reported to Ford management and decided by the Ford board. Post-acquisition, the Volvo board can make its own decisions.

3.4.1.2 Executive Management

After the acquisition, Volvo established a new international operations team. In mid-July 2010, Geely announced the new chairman and vice-chairman of Volvo Car Corporation, Li Shufu as chairman, and Hans-Olov Olsen, former president and CEO of Volvo Cars, as vice-chairman. According to the annual report disclosed by Volvo, in 2010, 12 members of the executive management team were recruited internally at Volvo. None of them came from Geely Group, again reflecting Volvo's independence. The board members of the new Volvo Car Company included Håkan Samuelsson, Dr. Herbert H. Demer, Lone Fønss Schrøder, Huo Jianhua, and Guan Stephen Jacob (shown in Table 3.3). From the perspective of nationality, the directors were from Sweden, Denmark, Germany, and Canada. On the Chinese side, only Li Shufu and Huo

Table 3.3 Volvo board members (in 2010)

Member	*Title*
Li Shufu (Chairman)	Founder and Chairman of Geely Holding Group
Jörgen Olsson (Vice-Chairman)	Senior Vice President, Global Marketing, Ford Motor Company
Shen Hui	Vice President of Fiat Group China
Håkan Samuelsson	Chairman and CEO of MAN Group, Germany
Herbert H. Demel	Magna Magna Executive Vice President
Lone Fønss Schrøder	Wallenius Rederier/Lines President and Managing Director
Winnie K.W. Fok	Investor AB Senior Consultant

Source Company annual reports

Jianhua participated. Moreover, apart from Li Shufu and Shen Hui, none of the other members of the board of directors had a Geely background. Geely gave basic powers including personnel management, financial management, and asset management to Volvo. The board had a diverse background and wide-ranging experience, guaranteeing its independence in decision-making. The original Volvo's global management would be basically retained, which created a "Volvo governs Volvo" scenario.

3.4.2 Relationship Between Volvo and Geely

After the acquisition, Volvo continued to maintain its core values of safety, quality, environmental protection, and modern Swedish design. After the transaction, to ensure a smooth transition, Ford continued to cooperate with Volvo Cars in various fields but not hold any ownership in the Volvo Car business. After the transaction was completed, Ford continued to provide drive systems, stamped parts, and other auto parts for Volvo Cars at different stages; during the transition period, Ford Motors has also promised to be in engineering, information technology, support for molds and other aspects of conventional parts. In addition, Ford Motor and Geely also reached an agreement on the use of intellectual property. The agreement allowed both Volvo Car and Ford to implement their own business plans and reasonably avoid misuse. These agreements also allowed Volvo Cars to transfer some of Ford's intellectual property to third parties, including Geely.

After the successful completion of the acquisition of Volvo, Geely Group and Volvo established the "Volvo-Geely Dialogue and Cooperation Committee," which was a new governance structure. The members of the organization include Geely and Volvo, and in addition to these eight members, Li Shufu personally serves as the chairman of the committee, and the committee conducts extensive exchanges on automobile manufacturing and other aspects. From the name of this committee alone, Volvo was put in front, in accordance with Chinese culture, to show respect and its higher status. Geely Group and Volvo are not in a relationship between management and management, but a relationship of dialogue. After a pleasant dialogue, a cooperative relationship has developed. The two parties are equal (each side has four participants), representing informal, voluntary, non-binding, non-legal decision-making deliberation and decision-making bodies.

In addition, the "Volvo-Geely Dialogue and Cooperation Committee" stipulates that in the future, the two parties will, under this dialogue mechanism, purchase and market-related products for automobile manufacturing and automotive products, new product development and related technologies, marketing and sales of potential products to potential customers, and talents. Extensive exchange will take place in training, idea exchange, and information sharing. If the parties agree to carry out specific project cooperation through negotiation, the specific terms of cooperation shall be signed by both parties. The relationship between Geely and Volvo represents peer-to-peer cooperation, and Volvo is being uniquely governed by way of a special "Dialogue and Cooperation Committee."

3.5 Conclusions

During the acquisition of Volvo by Geely, the latter successfully completed the acquisition through good communication with its stakeholders before the acquisition. Through the acquisition, the adjustment of Volvo's governance structure and the good relationship governance between Geely and Volvo achieved the success of post-acquisition integration. For the relationship between Geely and Volvo, Li Shufu, the chairman of Geely Automobile, called it a brotherhood, rather than a father–son relationship. He emphasized that the relationship between Geely and Volvo was not management and management, but peer-to-peer. Though Volvo governs according to its own principles, the connections between Geely Automobile and Volvo Cars can be referred to as "the dance of a snake and elephant," enabling Geely Automobile to move forward on its path to international development.

Li Shufu appeared on CCTV on June 15, 2015, pointing out that under his leadership Volvo has turned a profit for the past two years, and that Geely could now develop its long desired own brand strategy. Geely was indeed a dark horse in transition. In the five years since acquiring Swedish car brand Volvo, Geely Automobile has integrated international resources, enhanced its technological capability, and stepped out on a new road of brand building. Reviewing the entire history of Geely's acquisition of Volvo, it is not hard to see that good transnational governance has played and continues to play an important role in preparation, process, and integration, and further development in the future will continue to rely on continuous improvement of transnational governance.

CHAPTER 4

Transnational Governance of Jinjiang Group's Acquisition of Interstate Hotels and Resorts

4.1 Introduction

A professional hotel management team and an independent central reservation system are core features of any hotel management company. The former demonstrates a talent advantage and ensures smooth operations, while the latter integrates hotel resources and optimizes room sales channels via a global distribution system which forms the basis for market analysis and sales decisions. These two elements are prerequisites for becoming an international hotel group.

As of June 30, 2015, Jin Jiang Hotels owned or managed more than 3000 hotels worldwide, which gave them a total of 360,000 guest rooms in 55 countries. In 2005, it established a global distribution platform, referred to as HUBS1, to establish an international hotel management team and its own global center reservation system that Jin Jiang Hotels decided to acquire Interstate Hotels & Resorts in 2010. After the merger, Jin Jiang Hotels' board of directors exercised the function of transnational governance. The domestic hotel management team and the foreign management team realized an exchange would be valuable. Interstate

In this case study, Shanghai Jin Jiang International Hotels (Group) Co. Ltd., will be referred to as the "Jin Jiang Hotels."

© The Author(s), under exclusive license to Springer Nature Singapore Pte Ltd. 2020
R. Lin et al. *Corporate Governance of Chinese Multinational Corporations*,
https://doi.org/10.1007/978-981-15-7405-4_4

Hotels & Resorts management team could expand its business, cultivate international hotel management talent, establish a reservation system, and take over the international hotels. This is the story of China's first international hotel management company.

4.2 Transnational Governance Evolution

4.2.1 Background

Jin Jiang International Hotel Management Co. Ltd., is a listed company of Shanghai Jin Jiang International Hotels (Group) Co. Ltd. (hereinafter referred to as "Jin Jiang Hotels"), one of China's largest integrated tourism conglomerates, Jin Jiang International Hotel Management Group has six business divisions as its core business, namely investment, travel-related services, and transport services, hotels, tourism, passenger transportation, logistics, and real estate. Jin Jiang International Hotel Management Co. Ltd. was listed in Hong Kong in 1994 as Jin Jiang Hotels (H2006) and its subsidiary was listed on the Shanghai Stock Exchange (Fig 4.1).

Jin Jiang Hotels is China's largest high-end hotel management group. Its affiliated hotel brands can be divided into three categories, namely, Jin Jiang brand hotels, luxury hotels, and business hotels, all ranked between 3 and 5 stars. J. Hotel is Jin Jiang Hotels' new super five-star brand, Marvel is a new-style business travel brand, and Jin Jiang Star is the group's budget brand. At present, Jin Jiang's greatest growth comes from its line of budget hotels, Jin Jiang Inn.

The main business of Jin Jiang Hotels is investment in and management of starred hotels. Its main subsidiary, Shanghai Jin Jiang International Hotels Development Company Limited, manages and invests in Jin Jiang Star. In 2010, Jin Jiang Hotels began implementing an international strategy. Together with Delaware-based Thayer Group, they launched a joint venture acquisition of Interstate Hotels & Resorts.

4.2.2 Overview of Governance at Jin Jiang Hotels

Jin Jiang Hotels is principally engaged in the investment in starred hotels. Its subsidiary, Jin Jiang International Hotel Management Co. Ltd., is responsible for hotel management, while also engaging in passenger transport logistics, travel agencies, and overseas M&As. It holds shares in Shanghai Jin Jiang International Hotels Development Co. Ltd. and is the controlling shareholder of Jin Jiang Hotels (Fig. 4.2).

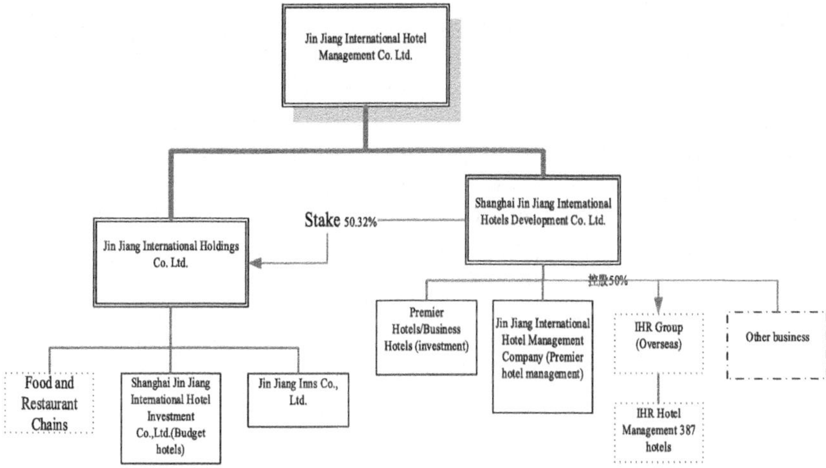

Fig. 4.1 Organizational structure of Jin Jiang International Hotel Management Co. Ltd (*Note* Shanghai Jin Jiang International Hotels Development Co. Ltd., mainly operates Jin Jiang Inn Co. Ltd. budget hotel business and catering and transportation business)

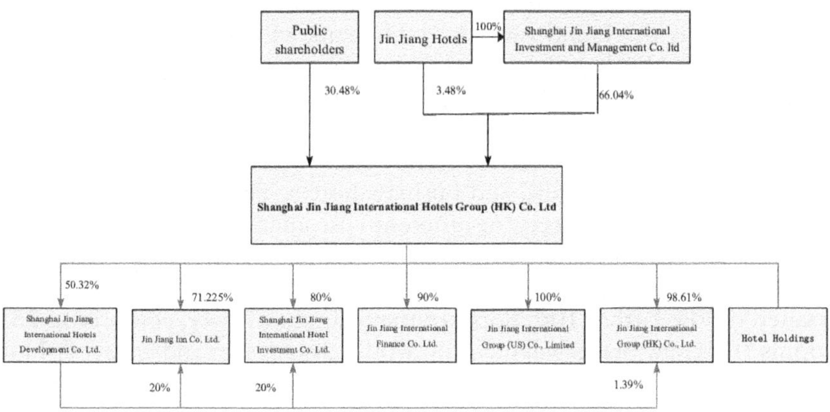

Fig. 4.2 Structure of Shanghai Jin Jiang International Hotels (Group) Co. Ltd

Jin Jiang Hotels consists of a nominated committee composed of directors, supervisors, and management personnel, an audit committee, a remuneration committee, and a strategic investment committee for group governance. As of December 2009, the organizational structure of the board of directors, board of supervisors, and company executives of Jin Jiang Hotels is shown in Fig. 4.3. Among them, Xu Zurong was the general manager of Jin Jiang California and manager of the integrated business management department and president of Jin Jiang Inn and investment director and general manager of Jin Jiang Hotels. Han Min is in charge of Jin Jiang International M&A and director of Shanghai Jin Jiang International Travel listed company. The board of directors is composed of committees, but does not reflect an international business orientation. For example, it lacks global governance capabilities.

4.2.3 Operation and Development of Jin Jiang Hotels Before the Acquisition

Jin Jiang Hotels' brands are divided into two main categories, including starred hotels and budget hotels, or more specifically, 4-star, high-end hotels and business hotels for business travelers in the mid- to high-end market. Its hotel brands include J.Hotel, Jin Jiang, and Marvel.

Jin Jiang is the brand owned by Jin Jiang Hotels. In the accommodation sector, the brand has five categories of products, namely 5-star hotels, 4-star hotels, 3-star hotels, resorts, and serviced apartments. In the face of different target markets for starred hotels, the hotels under the Jin Jiang brand can be divided into three categories, namely traditional hotels, luxury hotels, and business hotels. The hotels range from 3 to 5 stars to meet the needs of different customers.

"J" stands for Jin Jiang Group. The J.Hotel brand is a new high-end super five-star brand launched by Jin Jiang Hotels. The first hotel will be located on the 84th–110th floors of the Shanghai Tower, comprising 258 rooms. This new brand will focus on world-class design and attract fashion clients from around the world via the latest international technology.

Marvel is a new kind of business hotel brand launched by Jin Jiang Hotels. Brand positioning lies somewhere between 3 and 4 stars. The target market includes young and middle-aged business travelers. There are now two Marvel hotels, one in Shanghai and one in Chengdu.

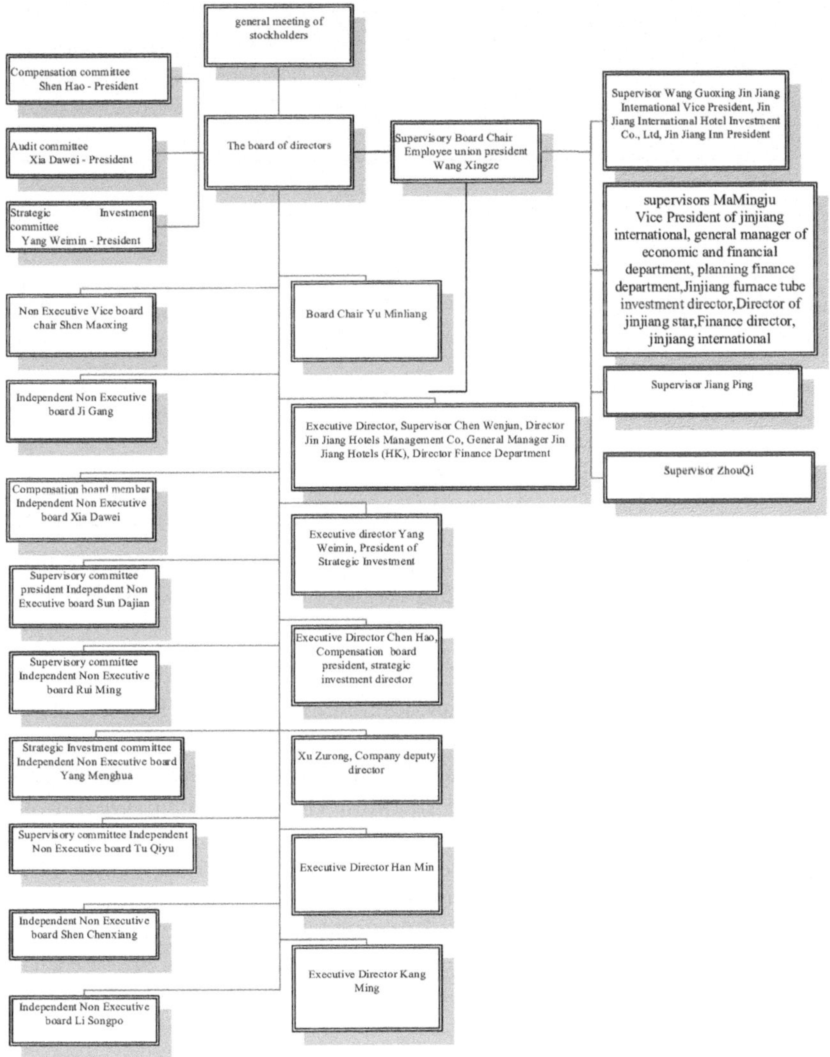

Fig. 4.3 Shanghai Jin Jiang International Hotel Group's Executive Organization Chart, Board of Directors, and Board of Supervisors

In operation (As at 31 December 2009)	Hotels in which the Group held Hotel Interests and managed by the Group		Hotels in which the Group held Hotel Interests but managed by third parties		Hotels owned by third parties but managed by the Group		Hotels owned by third parties but operated under franchises granted by the Group		Total number of hotels in operation	
	Number of hotels	Total number of Rooms	Number of hotels	Total number of Rooms	Number of hotels	Total number of Rooms	Number of hotels	Total number of Rooms	Number of hotels	Total number of Rooms
Hotel Category										
Landmark Hotels	6	1,666	–	–	–	–	–	–	6	1,666
Luxury Hotels (excluding Landmark Hotels)										
– 5-star hotels	4	2,467	2	974	16	5,458	–	–	22	8,899
– 4-star hotels	9	3,837	2	944	26	5,774	–	–	37	10,555
Sub-total	13	6,304	4	1,918	42	11,232	–	–	59	19,454
Commercial Hotels										
– 3-star hotels	6	1,112	–	–	5	1,206	–	–	11	2,318
– 2-star hotels	4	564	–	–	–	–	–	–	4	564
Sub-total	10	1,676	–	–	5	1,206	–	–	15	2,882
Jin Jiang Inn Budget Hotels	122	19,021	–	–	–	–	211	25,780	333	44,801
Total	151	28,667	4	1,918	47	12,438	211	25,780	413	68,803

Fig. 4.4 Statistics of hotels in operation (*Source* Jin Jiang Hotels [2009]. *Annual Report*. Retrieved from https://www1.hkexnews.hk/listedco/listconews/sehk/2010/0428/ltn20100428426.pdf)

Jin Jiang Inn was the first budget hotel brand in China. It offers cheap, safe, and comfortable hotels for business travelers in low- to mid-end markets. In December 2009, it had more than 546 hotels with 89,251 rooms, located in 187 large and medium cities in China. Operational details are shown in Fig. 4.4.

From 2005 to 2008, the number of hotels and operating income of Jin Jiang Hotels rose every year. In 2009, the group's operating revenue was RMB 3.321 billion, after the global financial crisis sent its reverberations around the world in 2008. The 5-year revenue statistics are shown in Fig. 4.5.

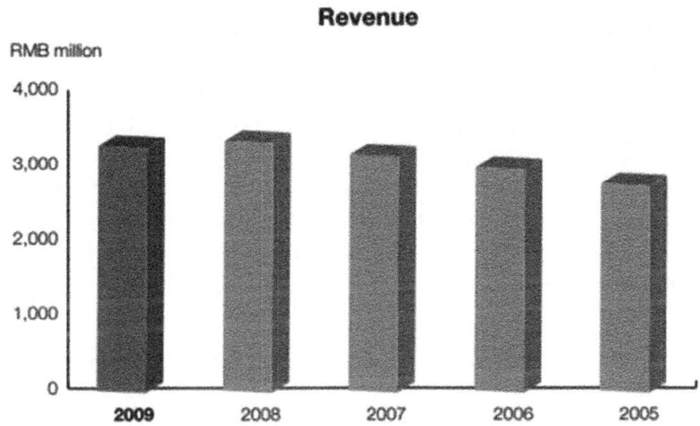

Fig. 4.5 Shanghai Jin Jiang International Hotels (Group) Co. Ltd. Revenue (million RMB, 2009–2005)

4.3 Analysis of Transnational Governance Evolution

4.3.1 Background of US Interstate Hotels & Resorts

Interstate Hotels & Resorts (commonly referred to as 'Interstate') is the largest independent (third party) hotel management company, comprising three categories of accommodations, including 100% owned, interstate, and other enterprises, with a minority stake in the hotel. The third commissioned interstate under third-party management. As of December 2009, Interstate had 315 three-star hotels in nine countries, offering 46,000 guest rooms. The company has interests in 56 properties, including six wholly owned assets. Among existing hotels, direct investment and equity participation accounts for 65%. Interstate controls considerable real estate, and in the long run, there is significant potential for appreciation.

4.3.2 Organizational Structure of US Interstate Hotels & Resorts

Interstate Hotels & Resorts is listed on the New York Stock Exchange (NYSE: IHR), and it has a very scattered shareholding structure. It provides hotel-entrusted management, development services, construction and design consulting services. Prior to M&A, direct investment to expand the hotel business has been the group's main strategy.

The successful development of Interstate Hotels & Resorts' operation and management is inseparable from its high-quality management team. This has served as an important guarantee for the operation and management of its subordinate hotels, and the company enhances the value of its assets by directly investing them and operating each hotel soundly according to best practices.

4.3.3 *Operations at Interstate Hotels & Resorts*

In 2007, Interstate Hotels & Resorts expanded significantly, acquiring six hotels and shares in 51 others. However, not long after these transactions were completed, the financial crisis took hold of the industry, and operations at multinational hotel groups were seriously affected. Interstate Hotels & Resorts was hit hard, and the banks urged repayment of their loans. The group was at risk of breaking its capital chain. Their 2008 annual report indicated that net losses were more than USD 18 million. At the lowest point in 2009, the group's share price fell below USD 3, a loss of 80% from its high. According to annual figures, in 2009, the group's assets shrank in value by 41–60%, or a total equity value of less than USD 300 million. A broken capital chain seemed inevitable.

4.3.4 *The Host Country's Local Partners*

4.3.4.1 *Operating Conditions at Thayer Lodging Group*

Founded in 1991, Thayer Lodging Group is a privately held hotel company based in Annapolis, Maryland. As a company, it is a founder and advisor to hotel investment funds, and one of the United States' premier direct investment companies, as well as the largest hotel investment group in the country. The group invests in hotels, IT, aviation, electronics, and real estate investment trusts (REITs) among other sectors. In 2006, their portfolio of investments earned more than USD 5 billion. The tourism and hospitality industries are of particular interest to Thayer.

Thayer has assets worth more than USD 12 billion, investments in 13 hotels, and includes the management of 3975 rooms. It invests in Marriott Hotels, Starwood, the Hyatt, and other premium brands, with ownership rights in more than 34 hotels, with 73,000 rooms under management.

4.3.4.2 Thayer Lodging Group's Strategy

Thayer aims to leverage its wide-ranging experience to advise entrepreneurs and their investment targets, providing strategic advice to help them grow across the travel industry. When it comes to hotel investment, Thayer selects a variety of high-value targets, including valuable individual hotels, groups, and management companies. Their strategy is largely focused on increase the commercial value of investment assets through hotel refurbishment, repositioning, management changes, channel management, as well as the use of cost controls, and innovative capital structures.

4.3.5 Jin Jiang Hotels' Acquisition of Interstate Hotels & Resorts

4.3.5.1 Motivation

The speed of development in China's hotel industry has attracted worldwide attention. In 2009, Jin Jiang Hotels ranked among the top 300 hotel brands in the world, based on scale alone. However, there is still a significant gap between the world's leading hotel chains and most Chinese hotel chains in terms of marketing innovation, employee management, and notably, cross-cultural management.

In 1982, the Hong Kong Peninsula Group officially took over management of the Beijing Jianguo Hotel, marking the first entry of a foreign-owned hotel group into the mainland hotel market. In 1984, the State Council issued the Proposal on Promoting the Management and Management Methods of Beijing Jianguo Hotel, which set off a wave of interest in better understanding hotel management practices abroad. This was also the year in which the Holiday Group landed in China. In 1985, the international hotel group Accor entered the mainland market, and since then, the number of international hotel groups entering China has continued to increase. Looking back, they came in three waves. The first steps were taken in the 1980s, official entry lasted from the late 1980s to the 1990s and the targeting of hotel brands for different markets was the primary focus in the early twenty-first century.

As multinational groups flooded into China, they not only formed networks, chains, and clusters, but also took control of more and more of China's own local hotels. About half of China's four-star hotels are now foreign-funded and managed. International hotels also brought in innovative changes in marketing, service, and management, which put local hotels under tremendous competitive pressure. By 2005, the world's top ten hotel groups had all entered the mainland Chinese market. Altogether, 47 brands from 31 international hotel management groups have settled in China, including Intercontinental Hotel Group, Marriott International Hotel Group, Accor Group, Starwood Hotel & Resort Group, Hyatt International Hotel Group, and Shangrila International Hotel Management Group. They have all brought their mature reservation systems, global distribution networks and perfect management systems and service standards with them to China's high-end hotel market. As of 2010, incomplete statistics indicated at least 2583 four-star plus hotels were operating in China, with more than 1000 of them being managed by foreign hotel management brands. China's hotel management group faced significant challenges building their brands in the high-end hotel segment, design of global distribution and management systems and the implementation of service standards. Such systems can only be developed by benchmarking mature foreign hotel management groups.

In the *Opinions of the State Council on Accelerating the Development of Tourism Industry* published in 2007, the government clearly "supports qualified tourism enterprises going global." With its macroeconomic background, Jin Jiang Hotels began its internationalization strategy and introduced the international hotel management team and system through the acquisition of mature foreign hotel management groups, and improved its own system by leveraging the management experience of overseas hotel management companies, which led to the Jin Jiang brand's push into the international hotel market.

4.3.5.2 Target Gathering Process

In 2005, Jin Jiang Hotels and private investment specialist Thayer Group jointly established a global distribution platform (i.e., HUBS1) in Shanghai. At the same time, Jin Jiang Hotels initiated its internationalization strategy with a hunt for suitable M&A targets.

In 2008, Jin Jiang Hotels and the wholly owned subsidiary of Thayer established a US joint venture. Total investment in the two-way joint venture was not to exceed USD 100 million. They already had a US-based M&A target: Interstate Hotels & Resorts. In 2009, Jin Jiang Hotels and Thayer Group each invested 50% to establish a wholly owned subsidiary company, HAC, in the United States. In 2010, all acquisitions of Interstate Hotels & Resorts were completed through HAC, with Jin Jiang and Thayer holding half the shares each. The process of this cross-border M&A of Interstate Hotels & Resorts is displayed in Fig. 4.6.

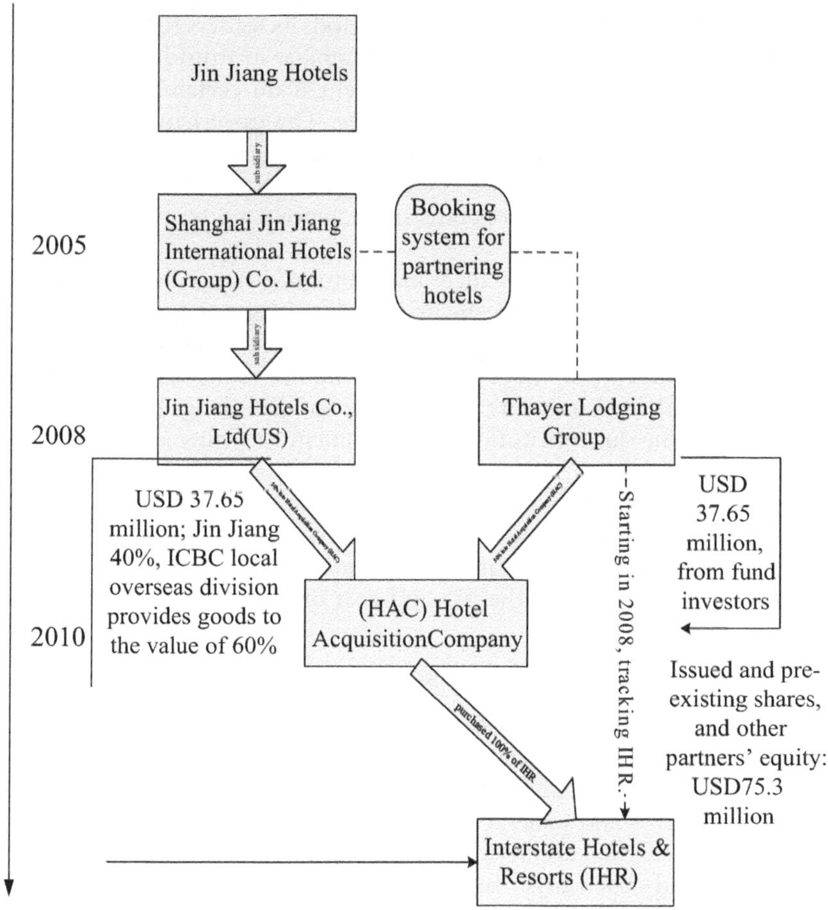

Fig. 4.6 Jin Jiang Hotels' M&A process

4.3.5.3 *Governance Issues During Jin Jiang Hotels' Cross-Border Acquisition*

At play during Jin Jiang Hotels' takeover of Interstate Hotels & Resorts were larger issues such as institutional and cultural differences between the United States and China. In 2008, Jin Jiang Hotels established a company in the United States to prepare for its acquisition, which was successfully carried out two years later. In this short period, its leaders had to acknowledge the significance of operating in an unfamiliar institutional, economic, and cultural environment. The management team certainly experienced an inferiority complex in the United States. The governance issues were how Jin Jiang Hotels should adapt to the changing social environment and economic environment of the United States to obtain "legality" and thus be able to continue to operate and achieve long-term development of enterprises.

The large institutional distance and cultural distance between China and the United States directly affected the legitimacy of Jin Jiang Hotels' acquisition of overseas subsidiaries. The question of "legality" rested on a study of institutional theory, emphasizing the role of enterprises in an institutional environment. In the case of Jin Jiang Hotels, this is embedded in the dual institutional environment of China and the United States. Recognizing the impact of its legitimacy on the acquisition, Jin Jiang Hotels chose to put its strategy in place via a joint venture with the US-based company Thayer Group, thus obtaining an external way to legitimize its overseas subsidiary in an acquisition scenario. This enabled Jin Jiang Hotels to reduce the risk and cost of institutional differences.

4.3.6 Preparation for Cross-Border Governance in M&As

4.3.6.1 Carefully Choosing Acquisition Target

In 2008, Jin Jiang Hotels established Jin Jiang Hotels (United States) and began to look for an acquisition targets. The company was headed by an executive director and general manager. It was responsible for investing, acquiring, developing, and repositioning the Jinjiang Strategic Investment Committee and other target hotels or companies approved by the Board of Directors within the United States. By the time the financial crisis broke out, Thayer Group had identified a number of targets, including well-known brands. These were sifted through until Jin Jiang Hotels was left with one, Interstate Hotels & Resorts.

This goal identification was down to long-term preparation by Jin Jiang Hotels' overseas expansion team. Since 2005, Thayer has been tracking Interstate Hotels & Resorts. The 2008 financial crisis created conditions for the acquisition. Although Interstate Hotels & Resorts fell into serious financial trouble, it had a sound management team. Its hotels were still operating normally. Interstate was still the largest independent hotel management company in the United States, and came with recognized brand and investment value.

To acquire Interstate Hotels & Resorts, Jin Jiang Hotels tasked a lawyer with studying the relevant US company, tax, and labor law. UBS and Merrill Lynch were hired as financial consultants, Baker and Hawking Law Firm as legal consultants, and Ernst & Young as auditor. This strong cooperation team conducted a six-month due diligence investigation. Financial modeling and program planning laid the foundations.

4.3.6.2 Establishment of the Special Purpose Vehicle (SPV)

Jin Jiang Hotels and Thayer decided to establish a SPV[1] hold assets at the lowest possible cost. This would bring to the overseas acquisitions benefits in terms of operational, management, tax, and time costs. Tax planning was a key advantage, facilitating future asset disposal, splitting the responsibility of upper-level shareholders, and facilitating later fund recall. Jin Jiang Hotels established this SPV as well as a financing platform for the acquisition of Interstate Hotels & Resorts.

This approach circumvented investment risks that overseas M&A have a habit of bringing to parent companies. Jin Jiang Hotels gradually promoted its Hotel Acquisition Company's bid for Interstate Hotels & Resorts with Interstate Operating Company Funds. According to US tax law, the method saved more than USD 10 million in tax, over a pure acquisition. Second, according to US labor law, the method had the potential to help the parties avoid related labor disputes right up through the integration phase. Interstate Hotels & Resorts' approval of the M&A agreement was voted on by its shareholders, and there was no objection within the company.

[1] SPV refers to an overseas enterprise directly or indirectly controlled by a domestic resident legal person or a domestic resident natural person for the purpose of equity financing (including convertible debt financing) for overseas enterprise assets or interests held by the domestic resident legal person or domestic resident. Also called special purpose vehicle (abbreviation SPV), whose function is to buy, packaging securitized assets and assets as the basis for issuance of securities, refers to accept the portfolio of sponsors and support on this issue. The special entity of the security. The original concept of SPV comes from the firewall (China Wall). The risk isolation design is designed to achieve the purpose of "bankruptcy isolation." A SPV's business scope is strictly defined, so it is a high credit rating entity that generally does not go bankrupt. SPV has a special position in asset securitization. It is the core of the entire asset securitization process, and each participant will work around it.

US law stipulates that special purpose vehicles can borrow from Chinese buyers or banks to obtain debt financing, and then merge into the target company according to the state's corporate M&A law. Chinese buyers use the equity of the special purpose vehicle in exchange for the target company's equity. In this case, the debts assumed by the SPV were merged into the target company as the companies came together. Since the special purpose vehicle disappears with the reverse integration into a US target company, it does not result in a multilayered holding level, which is beneficial for Chinese companies in applying for indirect credit on foreign tax obligations regarding US dividends.

4.3.7 *Post-acquisition Governance at Interstate Hotels & Resorts*

Interstate Hotels & Resorts is a wholly owned listed company that went through a decline due to the financial crisis and withdrew from the market in early 2010. In 2010, Jin Jiang's HAC completed 100% of the acquisition. Afterward, Jin Jiang Hotels and Thayer Group became the two shareholders of Interstate Hotels & Resorts, holding 50% each. Jin Jiang Hotels (United States) became the core manager and controller of Interstate Hotels & Resorts following the acquisition. The relationship between parent and subsidiaries is shown in Fig. 4.7.

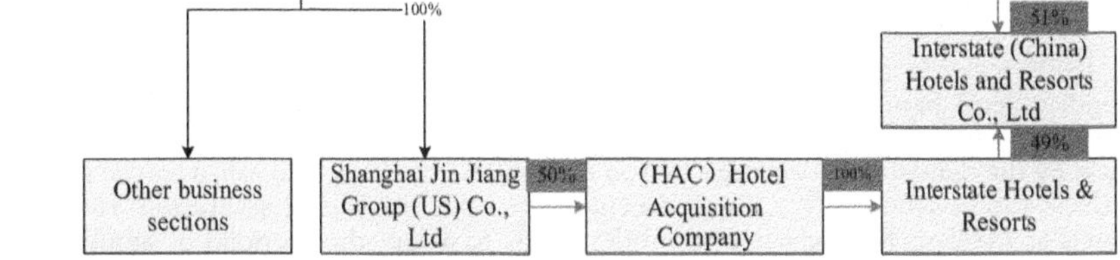

Fig. 4.7 Core company framework of Shanghai Jin Jiang International Hotels (Group) Co. Ltd. in December 2010

The resort hotel company jointly launched by Jin Jiang Hotels and Interstate Hotels & Resorts is controlled by Shanghai Jin Jiang International Hotels Group (HK) Co. Ltd., and adding resorts to the portfolio has made up for Jin Jiang Hotels' lack of resort business and lack of experience in resort operations.

Jin Jiang Hotels and Thayer Group jointly established and appointed a new board member of Interstate, US operations director of Jin Jiang Hotels Yang Weimin, to serve as Interstate Hotels & Resorts co-chairman, and co-chairman of the Interstate China. Chen Hao would serve as the Interstate Hotels & Resorts Director, Han Min as US Interstate Group Director. Thayer had one seat on the Board of Directors of Interstate Hotels & Resorts, but was not directly involved in its hotel operations management business. The organizational structure of the board of directors of Jin Jiang Hotels as of December 2010 is shown in Fig. 4.5. Interstate Hotels & Resorts holds a board meeting four times a year. For major decision-making issues, the company will actively communicate and coordinate with foreign directors before the meeting. The original senior operations team retained management equity incentives.

Jin Jiang Hotels still retains the operation management team of Interstate Hotels & Resorts. In addition to sending members of the board of directors, it has not made any personnel adjustments to the original management team, has not interfered with the management and operation of its hotel group, and has maintained the stability of the management of Interstate Hotels & Resorts. As promised, salary levels were kept, and a plan was made to establish equity incentives for net profits of 8% and to establish a long-term management incentive mechanism (Fig. 4.8).

Jin Jiang Hotels did however implement a series of internal integration and strategic restructuring exercises at Interstate Hotels & Resorts. Taking into account the exchange rate and currency spread between Chinese and US banks, Jin Jiang Hotels teamed up with ICBC's Shanghai Branch and other financial, taxation, and industrial and commercial departments to successfully complete the original acquisition in March 2011 by financing a repayment of US dollar debts via ICBC. US-funded banks with a maximum interest of 9% of USD 128 million borrowing and debt restructuring saved Interstate Hotels & Resorts USD 6 million in annual fees. Interstate Hotels & Resorts was also able to acquire 121 management contracts under Blackstone Group. According to those in the know, Interstate expects that by the end of 2011, the total number

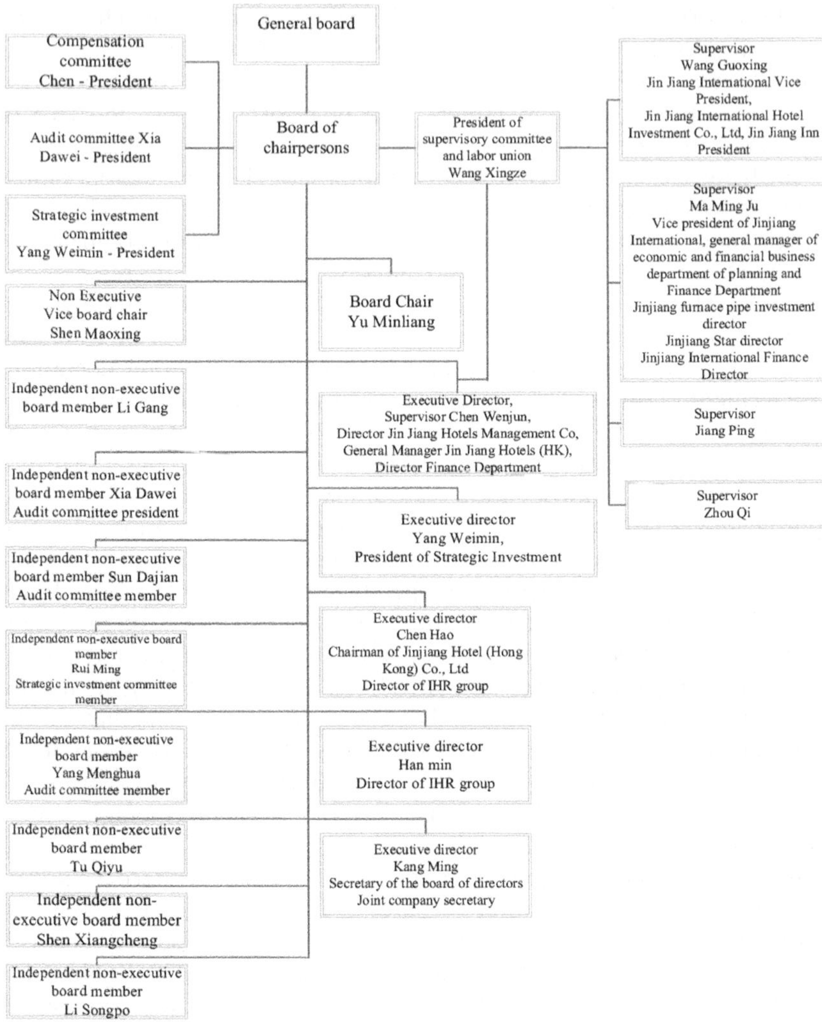

Fig. 4.8 Structure of the board of directors of Shanghai Jin Jiang International Hotels (Group) Co. Ltd. after the acquisition

Table 4.1 Shanghai Jin Jiang International Hotels (Group) Co. Ltd. income statement (as of June 30, 2011)

Business segment	*Revenue: (unit 1000 RMB)*
Star-rated hotels	1,172,078
Budget hotels	882,289
Food and restaurants	109,586
Interstate Hotels & Resorts group	1,382,101
Vehicle and logistics	1,570,559
Travel agency	797,720
Other operations	16,856
Total revenue	5,931,189

of hotels it managers will have increased to over 380. According to the Jin Jiang Hotels' 2011 Interim Report, Jin Jiang Hotels brought in a revenue of USD 214 million (i.e., RMB 1.382 billion) for the six-year period, accounting for 23% of Jin Jiang Hotels' operating income (i.e., USD 918 million, which is around RMB 5.931 billion) in the first half of the year (see Table 4.1).

After Jin Jiang Hotels acquired Interstate Hotels & Resorts, its income range and total increased significantly, as net profits also grew. According to the company's financial statements, Jin Jiang Hotels' acquisition of Interstate Hotels & Resorts led both groups to achieve financial profitability.

4.4 Impact of Transnational Governance Evolution

4.4.1 *Relationship Management Between Parent and Subsidiary Companies*

The hosting framework for running Interstate decided on by Jin Jiang Hotels was to have a board of director system meet four times a year. For major decisions, the company would actively communicate and coordinate with foreign directors before the meeting. Jin Jiang Hotels would still retain the operational management team of Interstate Hotels & Resorts. In addition to sending members of the board of directors, it has not made any personnel adjustments to the original management team, and promised that their original salary level will not drop, and established a net profit of 8%. Set up a plan for equity incentives.

The main purpose of Jin Jiang Hotels overseas acquisitions was to fill other hotel business segments and promote the international development of the parent company via human resources and the global distribution system. Under this strategic premise, the main relationship between the parent and subsidiary company is that the subsidiaries are backing up the short-term business of the parent company. From this perspective, the Interstate Board not only executed the parent company's strategy, but also monitored the performance of subsidiary managers to ensure that strategic decisions of the company were in line with the overall goal of Jin Jiang Hotels. In terms of high-level governance, with the growth of overseas subsidiaries' operating hours, host country executives can better manage local employees and obtain legitimacy. This means Jin Jiang Hotels has not interfered with its hotel group management operations and instead has tended toward the maintenance of Interstate Hotels & Resorts, keeping the group's management stable. Research on incentive mechanisms proves that the impact of executive compensation in overseas subsidiaries on international knowledge flow leads to more knowledge sharing. Jin Jiang Hotels has established a long-term management incentive mechanism for the Interstate Hotels & Resorts in order to have better access to the subsidiary's international experience, thereby making up for shortfalls at Jin Jiang Hotels.

4.4.2 *Feeding the Parent Company*

Jin Jiang Hotels will become the talent training internship base for the hotel industry in China. Sending hotel management personnel to Interstate Hotels & Resorts to learn international hotel management is the fastest way to build an international hotel management team. A large number of Chinese managers who have experience in managing overseas hotels will be at the forefront of foreign hotel and property expansion in the future, and the basis of their success.

Since 2011, around 100 Chinese managers at all levels have been transferred to hotels in the United States to serve for three years as managers at Interstate hotels. This has strengthened their ability to manage overseas hotels, while improving their individual ability to work internationally. Chinese staff have gradually entered all aspects of Interstate Hotels & Resorts management. Interstate Hotels & Resorts has fed expertise back to the parent company, nurturing future talent in the industry in China and elsewhere in the world.

4.4.3 Promoting Internationalization of the Parent Company

The establishment of an independent central reservation system and global distribution system is a must for any international hotel group. Without these two systems, hotel reservations cannot be made to overseas markets, room sales are not available, and there is no overseas market pricing system. Adding Interstate Hotels & Resorts, Jin Jiang Hotels now has more than 46,000 overseas rooms at its disposal, and 360,000 guest rooms in total. Such scale requires a central reservation system. The central reservation system and global distribution system generate additional overseas business.

After the completion of the acquisition, Jin Jiang Hotels set up a global sales office, designed a global distribution manual, and connected up room sales with international business units. This was the first step for Jin Jiang Hotels to start to engage in selling to an overseas market.

4.4.4 Group Business Development

Jin Jiang Hotels and Interstate Hotels & Resorts have joined hands to set up new Chinese hotel management platform, developing China's independent hotel management business, and incorporating unbranded independent hotels in the branding and chain management system. On this platform, the two parties have jointly established a resort business, filling in the gap in Jin Jiang Hotels' business portfolio.

Among China's domestic hotel management companies, none have a resort brand as yet. This is because resort operations and room sales are more difficult than city hotels. Building a self-owned resort brand requires a central reservation system and a global distribution system to support room sales, as well as overseas sales channels to make up for local off-season room sales. Interstate Hotels & Resorts management personnel were absorbed into the Jin Jiang Hotels management company to realize mutual flow, accelerate the establishment of the resort operations teams, and train Chinese resort management personnel.

4.5 Discussions and Conclusions

4.5.1 Improvement of Efficiency of Cross-Border M&As

When state-owned enterprises expand overseas, subjectively they face dilemmas when it comes to multinational operating game rules, as well as difficulties with the target country's investment environment. Objectively, they face the challenge of addressing security concerns and learning how to integrate culturally. Therefore, first of all, look for partners with rich market, legal and investment experience to improve the efficiency of the internationalization process and avoid the above difficulties.

4.5.2 Improvement of Legitimacy[2]

The institutional differences between the home country and the host country are the main factors that make it difficult for Chinese companies to obtain local legitimacy. The use of a special purpose vehicle with a host partner founded by the acquired company might reduce the distance between the two countries making up the system, embedded as it is in the host system environment. A company also risks trouble in design and acquisition financing when building a platform, as the entity is controlled. In addition, during the acquisition process, an SPV is to be used in various tax planning structures.

4.5.3 Building a Hosting Framework

When overseas subsidiaries rely on their own hotel operations management teams and existing dynamic capabilities and knowledge to complete strategic tasks of the parent company, they manage subsidiaries through the design of the board of directors system, while retaining the senior management team of the original hotel group and conducting equity incentives.

[2] Legitimacy is referred to as "under the norms within a social construction system, values, beliefs and define the framework for the activities of the appropriateness of the entity, the appropriateness and desirability of the general perception and ideas."

4.5.4 Using the Theory of Incentives Mechanism

The parent company implements an incentive mechanism for the senior management team of overseas subsidiaries, which can effectively promote the feeding back of the subsidiary's knowledge to the parent company. When the parent company must rely on the human resources and expertise of the overseas subsidiaries to support the parent company, it will establish a management and control framework by implementing effective incentive mechanisms for the senior management of the subsidiaries. This is done so that the strategic development of the subsidiaries is in line with the parent company's goals, and thus, overseas subsidiaries are better embedded in the strategic development of the parent company.

CHAPTER 5

The Construction and Evolution of Lenovo Group's Transnational Governance Capability

5.1 Introduction

Lenovo Group was established in 1984 with an investment of USD 86 thousand (i.e., RMB 200,000) from the Institute of Computing of the Chinese Academy of Science and just eleven science and technology personnel allocated. Now it is a major diversified IT group, and an internationally recognized technology giant. Since 1996, Lenovo's computer sales have been ranked first in China's domestic market. As a global leader in the personal computer (PC) market, Lenovo is committed to developing, manufacturing, and selling reliable, secure, and easy-to-use products and services that help its customers and partners around the world succeed. Lenovo produces desktop computers, servers, notebooks, printers, PDAs, motherboards, mobile phones, and all-in-one computers. In 2013, Lenovo became the world's largest PC manufacturer, selling more computers than any other company. On December 7, 2004, Lenovo Group signed an asset purchase agreement with IBM to acquire its PC business unit, obtaining the Thinkpad brand, core IBM technology, research and development (R&D), as well as its international management team. This move had a huge impact on Lenovo's internationalization strategy. Subsequently, Lenovo Group bought Japan's NEC, Germany's Median, IBM's X86 server, and Motorola.

Lenovo's global headquarters are in Beijing, and together with its US headquarters in Raleigh, North Carolina, form its two operations centers. As a global leader in the PC market, Lenovo is committed to developing,

© The Author(s), under exclusive license to Springer Nature Singapore Pte Ltd. 2020
R. Lin et al. *Corporate Governance of Chinese Multinational Corporations*,
https://doi.org/10.1007/978-981-15-7405-4_5

manufacturing, and selling the most reliable, secure, and easy-to-use technology products and quality professional services to help customers and partners around the world succeed. According to the 2015 Global Fortune 500 list, Lenovo ranked 231st with an annual revenue of USD 46.3 billion. It has been the world's largest personal computer manufacturer for two consecutive years, while in smartphones, tablets, and servers, it is now ranked global third (Fig. 5.1 and Table 5.1).

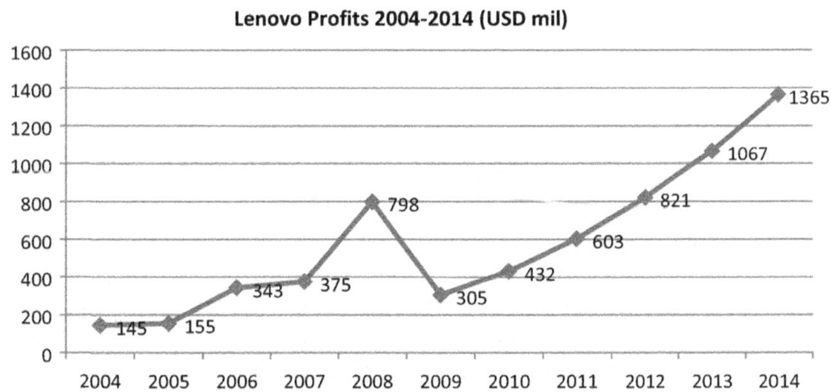

Fig. 5.1 Lenovo Group's 2004–2014 profit (unit: USD mil)

Table 5.1 Milestones in Lenovo Group's transnational endeavors (2003–2015)

Year	*Milestones*
2004	Lenovo became the first global partner of the International Olympic Committee in China
2004	Acquired the IBM PC business unit and entered the global PC market
2011	Lenovo Group acquired 36.66% of German electronics manufacturer Medion for EUR 231 million. After the transaction was completed, Lenovo doubled its market share in Germany and became the third largest manufacturer in the world
2011	Lenovo Group and Japan NEC announced a joint venture to form the largest Japanese PC group
2014	Acquired Motorola from Google for USD 2.9 billion
2014	Acquired IBM's X86 server business for USD 2.3 billion

5.2 Transnational Governance Evolution

5.2.1 *Periods of Evolution*

Lenovo Group has experienced eight periods for its transnational governance evolution.

The first period (1984–1987): This period was seen as one of great developmental potential in IT. Most computer companies were engaged in trade. Ni Guangnan served as Lenovo's chief engineer, and innovated "Lenovo Hanka" to form a fully functional Lenovo Chinese character system. Lenovo formally entered the IT industry, combining industry and trade as a "technology + trade" company. At this point, the company had a linear functional organizational structure.

The second period (1988–1993): The PC market was developing fast. Hong Kong Lenovo Computer Co., Ltd. was established, and Lenovo's first-generation Lenovo 286 Microcomputer was launched. The company established a linear functional structure, centralized command, and began cooperation by division of labor.

The third period (1994–1998): Multinationals entered the Chinese market, and the computer industry became highly competitive. Hong Kong Lenovo Computer Company was listed, Lenovo's organizational structure changed, the Microcomputer Division was established and an E series of budget computers was launched in China. Lenovo Group Holdings was established. Management functioned in a decentralized mode with coordinated control, as shown in Fig. 5.2.

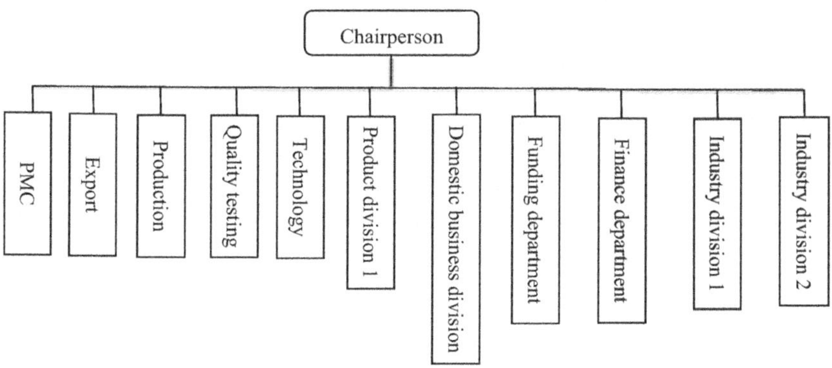

Fig. 5.2 Organizational structure of Lenovo Group in 1993

The fourth period (1999–2000): The development of computer and computing communication technology accelerated the development of the IT industry and the internet. Lenovo established an internet portal. Hardware manufacturers began turning into internet service providers. Lenovo Group introduced an enterprise resource planning (ERP) system and began running on business department lines. Its ERP system led to better integrated group resources, and enhanced the systems' collaborative capacity. The division of labor in each department became clearer.

The fifth period (2001–2003): When the internet bubble burst, the IT industry was at its peak. Lenovo Group had split into Lenovo Computer and Digital China, and had implemented a number of large-scale mergers and acquisitions. In doing so, its organizational structure gradually flattened, until it centered on commercial customers (large, small, and medium-sized enterprises) and consumer customers (families and individuals). Five business groups were established: commercial IT, consumer IT, IT services, mobile communication, and internet services, and Lenovo began to transform from a unified PC manufacturer into a company with a diversified strategy. A matrix organizational structure was developed, customers of each business group were brought together, leadership was unified, and group resources were more effectively shared.

The sixth period (2004–2008): The domestic PC market was fiercely competitive, and Lenovo now faced intense challenges. In 2004, Lenovo Group made the decision to acquire IBM Thinkpad. This has resulted in major organizational changes to the new Lenovo Group. The new organizational structure took effect on October 15, 2005. Lenovo's original business and the recently acquired IBM PC business were merged into one unified organizational structure, including operations, supply chain and sales systems. In order to build on the industry-leading innovation capabilities of both ThinkPad and Lenovo, the new group has integrated its global product and marketing divisions into a global entity. This product group will be led by Fran O'Sullivan, senior vice president and chief operating officer of Lenovo Group, who previously served as senior vice president of Lenovo Group and CEO of Lenovo International. The product group is responsible for the global business of Lenovo, Thinkpad, and IBM-Think products. It consists of two international business groups, desktop computers and notebook computers. It also comprises special services such as digital, customer service, and quality control.

The seventh period (2009–2012): With the success of Lenovo Group's acquisition of IBM Thinkpad, Lenovo Group accelerated its steps of internationalization. Since 2009, Lenovo has made numerous structural adjustments. In 2009, Lenovo divided the business into two major business groups: mature and emerging markets. With this adjustment, Lenovo set up Think and Idea product groups. In early January 2012, Lenovo Group once again made structural adjustments to divide its global business into four regions: China, North America, EMEA (Europe, Middle East, and Africa), and Asia-Pacific–Latin America. Lenovo Group announced that the company would carry out a further restructuring, which would see it divided into two major business groups: Lenovo Business Group and Think Business Group.

The eighth period (2013–present): With the rise of the mobile internet, Lenovo Group successfully acquired IBM Thinkpad, X86 small and medium-sized server, Motorola mobile phones, Germany's second largest electronics factory Median factory, and Japanese NEC Electronics. Lenovo Group's global strategy and business have undergone major changes, especially a shift to mobile internet and cloud computing services. Lenovo Group still has strong momentum, and continues to achieve high revenue and profit, as seen in a recently released performance report. At the same time, it is the world's leader in PC business, and has just announced the largest acquisition plan in the company's history. Since April 1, 2014, Lenovo Group has established four relatively independent new business groups:

- PC Business Group (including the Lenovo brand and the Think brand) is under the responsibility of Gianfranco Lanci, the current leader of Lenovo Europe, Middle East, and Africa (EMEA). PC Business Group will continue to expand our global leadership position in the core PC business, drive profitability, and breakthrough innovation.
- Mobile Business Group (smartphone, tablet, smart TV), led by Liu Jun, who currently leads the Lenovo Business Group (consumer and mobile products). The mobile business group's goal is to become a profitable global player in the fast-growing range of smartphones and tablets, and to develop smart TV services.
- Corporate Business Group (servers and storage), headed by Gerry Smith, who leads the business in the Americas. The goal of this business group is to build a new, fast-growing profit engine based on Lenovo's existing solid enterprise-level business. The recently announced acquisition of the IBM X86 server business will be incorporated into Smith's organization upon completion of regulatory approval.

- The cloud service business group (including Android and Windows software) is the responsibility of He Zhiqiang, senior vice president and chief technology officer of the current Lenovo Group. The Cloud Services Business Group aims to further establish a business ecosystem and achieve expansion and value-added services.

5.2.2 *Improvement in the Evolution of Lenovo Group's Transnational Governance Capability*

According to structural changes at the board of directors and senior management level across the identified eight evolutionary periods, the development of Lenovo's transnational governance capability can be divided into four stages: (1) Basic stage: before April 30, 2005, when the acquisition of the IBM PC Division was officially approved by the US. During this stage, Lenovo Group laid the foundation for internationalization, implemented equity reforms, and launched a new visual identity, which has already occupied the first-class measures in the market in the domestic market share. Therefore, Lenovo Group proposed to implement the internationalization strategy based on the domestic market; (2) Transitional stage: after the acquisition of IBM PC Division, the first CEO Stephen M. Ward began his tenure. The new Lenovo Group turned from a domestic to a multinational company, and entered a transitional phase of corporate governance structural change, business adjustment, and cultural integration. This lasted from April 30 to December 20, 2005. At this stage of corporate governance, the chairman of the board was Yang Yuanqing and the CEO was Stephen M. Ward; (3) Conflict stage: the new Lenovo Group secured its second CEO, William J. Amelio. After the transition period led by the first CEO, the new Group needs someone to carry out strategic adjustments, establish a new global supply chain, reduce overall operating costs, improve multinational governance capabilities, and enhance the Group's competitiveness further. However, during this process, problems in language, culture, and communication meant that fierce conflicts between Chinese executives and foreign executives inevitably broke out, caused by different governance mechanisms. From December 20, 2005 to September 2, 2009, the CEO was replaced by William J. Amelio, formerly of Dell Company. Yang Yuanqing became Chairman of the Board; (4) Formation stage: from September 2, 2009 to the present. After continuous adjustments to governance structure and mechanisms, the new coordinated structure provided an institutional guarantee for the implementation of Lenovo's global strategy. With this, the new Lenovo Group's global governance capabilities were formed. The chairman during this stage of corporate governance was Liu Chuanzhi and the CEO was Yang Yuanqing. The main task was to launch a comprehensive "double-fisted boxing" strategy. Its rollout globally has significantly improved cross-border governance capabilities.

(1) Basic stage

The premise of Lenovo Group's transnational governance capability was the decision to conduct transnational operations. Before this, Lenovo Group carried out a series of changes, including equity rights, business development, and organizational structure, and introduced a proposal for the Group's internationalization strategy.

The early reform of the equity rights system of Lenovo Group laid the institutional foundation for Lenovo's transnational operations. At this stage, Lenovo Group experienced two major equity rights reforms. The first was in 1996 when the China Academy of Science and Technology allocated 35% of dividends to Liu Chuanzhi and his team, which was a breakthrough change at the time. The second was on April 12, 2002. The Chinese Academy of Sciences funded the establishment of the State-owned Assets Management Co., Ltd. of the Chinese Academy of Sciences. On behalf of the Chinese Academy of Sciences, it was responsible for the management of the institute's state-owned assets of wholly owned and shareholding enterprises and the exercise of the rights of investors in accordance with the law. On December 3, 2002, the Chinese Academy of Sciences transferred the state-owned assets corresponding to the capital contribution and corresponding rights of Legend Holdings to the State-owned Assets Management Co., Ltd. of the Chinese Academy of Sciences. After the completion of this transfer, 65% of shares in Legend Holdings were held by the State-owned Assets Management Co., Ltd. of the Chinese Academy of Sciences, and 35% by Legend Holdings itself. This early reform of equity rights played an important role in the development of Lenovo.

The business development and organizational structure transformation of Lenovo Group was the basic organizational guarantee for Lenovo's transnational operations. At this stage, business had evolved from early PC business to client-centric (commercial and consumer customers), with a diversified strategy comprising five business groups: commercial IT, consumer IT, IT services, mobile communications, and internet services. The organizational structure of the company evolved from an early linear functional structure to a matrix organization capable of accommodating business development and corporate diversification (Table 5.2).

The proposal of Lenovo Group's internationalization strategy is an important prerequisite for Lenovo's transnational operations. Lenovo Group launched the TOP program in 2002. In 2003, the brand

Table 5.2 Lenovo Group's business and organizational structural changes

Period	*Business and organizational structural changes*
1984–1987	The IT market has great potential for development, and most computer companies are engaged in computer trading. Ni Guangnan served as the chief engineer and developed "Lenovo Hanka. Lenovo began to enter the IT industry and realized the integration of technology, industry and trade in the form of "technology + trade"
1988–1993	The PC market developed rapidly. Hong Kong Lenovo Computer Co., Ltd. was established, and the first-generation computer "Lenovo 286 Microcomputer" was launched. The company established a linear functional structure, centralized command, and began to work together
1994–1998	Multinational companies enter the domestic market and the computer industry is competitively motivated. Lenovo of Hong Kong was listed, Lenovo established the Microcomputer Division, launched the E series of China's first economical computer, Lenovo Group Holdings was established, Lenovo's organizational structure changed significantly, and the business unit + functional management was established to coordinate control. Decentralized operation mode
1999–2000	The development of computer and communication technology has accelerated the development of the information industry and the internet. Lenovo established a portal website and started to implement the ERP project. The hardware manufacturer began to change to an internet service provider, and Lenovo adopted the organizational structure of the business unit
2001–2004	The internet bubble burst and the IT industry was at its peak. Lenovo Group was divided into Lenovo Computer and Digital China. It has implemented several large-scale mergers and acquisitions and flattened its organizational structure. It has reorganized its business customers (large, small, and medium-sized) and consumer customers (family or individuals). The five business groups: commercial IT, consumer IT, IT services, mobile communication, and internet services began to transform from a unified PC company to one with a diversified strategy. At this stage, a matrix organizational structure was established, and the customers of each business group were unified and group resources shared

completed its visual identity, laid the foundation for internationalization, and proposed its vision: high-tech, services, and international. This vision remained in place as Lenovo focused on its core business—personal computers and related products and explored mobile communication equipment, to ensure that resource investment and business focus matched. Given the rapid changes in the market environment, Lenovo had to establish a more customer-oriented business model, that is, dual mode business structure: T mode (transaction, direct consumer "transaction") and R mode (establishing "relationships" with large customers) to improve the overall operational efficiency of the company. At the same time, the company decided on internationalization in preference to simple diversification.

(2) Transition l stage

Lenovo Group acquired the IBM PC business unit in 2004, which caused major changes in the organizational structure of the new Lenovo Group. After the merger, the original business and the IBM PC business were integrated globally to form a unified new organizational structure. The new organizational structure will take effect on October 15, 2005. After the completion of the acquisition of the IBM PC Division by Lenovo Group, the integration of the high-level organizational structure begins. Former Lenovo Group CEO Yang Yuanqing took over as chairman, and the CEO of the new Lenovo Group was served by Stephen M. Ward, IBM executive and vice president of the Personal Systems Group. At the 13 senior management levels of the new Lenovo Group, the proportion of the former Lenovo and IBM PC business was 7:6, similar to the equity ratio. The formation of such a combination is the result of communication and compromise between the two parties.

Financial investor GA was willing to invest in Lenovo's M&A project, but hoped to maintain stability during the transition period, by retaining managers of the acquired company as CEO, the other party being IBM.

The board of directors of Legend Holdings also had doubts about whether Lenovo management could control an international company. At this time, choosing Yang Yuanqing to sit in the position of "co-pilot" to learn how to be CEO of an international company was the right choice. Therefore, Liu Chuanzhi made the decision to become an ordinary director from the position of chairman of the board and make Yang

Yuanqing chairman of Lenovo Group. IBM CEO Peng Mingsheng chose Stephen M. Ward as CEO. His explanation was as follows:

> I think we have to keep customers first. We want to play up this brand, and Stephen M. Ward has a close relationship with our customers. In the first two years, the new Lenovo needs a person who can retain them. If you have no customers, all the supply chain in the world will not of use to us. I had to convince Liu Chuanzhi and Yang Yuanqing to choose someone who could do this. There are also people who disagree, saying that Ward is not a very strong leader. This may be true. He has been responsible for the sales of Thinkpad instead of R&D. But initially we need to be able to retain customers, not the person who designed the product.

To integrate the business and corporate culture of the new Lenovo Group as soon as possible, reduce cultural differences, and increase exchanges, the new Lenovo Group has taken a series of measures: (1) the original Lenovo's own adjustment. Although the original Lenovo Group has a cultural atmosphere that is in line with world-class enterprises, IBM, which is an internationally renowned company with a unique corporate culture, is relatively immature and lacks international experience. Therefore, after the merger and acquisition, Lenovo Group regarded respect, frankness, and compromise as the basis of cultural integration. Lenovo Group made a choice on the basis of maintaining its core culture and respecting the other culture so as to achieve the purpose of seeking common ground. (2) The new Lenovo Group set up dual headquarters. In order to reduce cultural differences, Lenovo adopted English as the company's official international language.

(3) Conflict stage

After Lenovo's organizational integration, a business process reorganization was more and more urgent. The new Lenovo Group needed to reduce the cost of the entire supply chain to ensure profitability of the new Group. Foreign directors James G. Coulter (on behalf of TPG) and William O. Grabe (on behalf of GA) were very smooth in their post-integration dealings, "business as usual" was the appropriate response. Bill Amelio, president of Dell Asia Pacific, was an expert from the TPG talent pool which led him to be appointed CEO, and Yang Yuanqing to stay on as chairman.

The main ways Lenovo went about improving cross-border governance capabilities at this stage were: (1) Adjustments to the senior management team personnel. After Bill Amelio became CEO, he quickly built a personal executive team. (2) Reorganize business processes, reduce costs, and build a global supply chain. During Bill Amelio's tenure, Lenovo laid off 30% of staff, 70% of whom were IBM employees in high-cost North American and European countries. Synergy between Lenovo and IBM PC was based on cost control and the structural transfer of production and manufacturing. Bill Amelio not only launched the project, but also implemented the global strategy. He also completed a task vital to any global company—supply chain transformation, carried out by Gerry Smith. (3) Appoint a Chief Diversification Officer. In January 2007, Yolanda Lee Conyers from Dell served as the chief diversification officer of Lenovo Group, mainly responsible for in-depth study of specific characteristics of Lenovo Group in China and the West, resolving cultural conflicts of team members and poor communication. The problem was making everyone in the company work toward a common goal, while respecting individual differences among team members, so as to help Lenovo's leadership team get the best strategy for team integration in East and West. Lenovo was the first Chinese company to set up a "Chief Diversification Officer" position (Table 5.3).

(4) Formation stage

In the 2008/2009 financial year, Lenovo Group made a loss of USD 226 million, and as a result, the board of directors asked Liu Chuanzhi to step back in as chairman and for Yang Yuanqing to become CEO, replaced Bill Amelio. This meant that Yang Yuanqing's international study phase was over and he took up the mantle of Lenovo Group to return it to global competitiveness.

With the success of Lenovo Group's acquisition of IBM Thinkpad, Lenovo Group accelerated its internationalization. Since 2009, Lenovo conducted a number of structural adjustments. In 2009, Lenovo divided its business into two major business groups: mature and emerging markets. With this adjustment, Lenovo also established a Think product group and an Idea product group. In early January 2012, Lenovo Group divided its global business into four regions: China, North America, EMEA (Europe, Middle East and Africa) and Asia Pacific-Latin America.

Table 5.3 Bill Amelio's executive team established

Name	*Position*	*Joined*	*Previous positions*
Gerry Smith	Serving as Senior Vice President of Global Supply Chain, responsible for the Group's global sourcing, logistics, supply chain planning and manufacturing operations	Joined Lenovo in August 2006	Former Vice President of Dell Display Business
David Schmoock	Serving as Senior Vice President of Center of Excellence, overseeing the operations of the Center of Excellence, including key business, customer activities, and inventory management	Joined Lenovo in August 2006	Former Vice President of Marketing, Dell Asia Pacific/Japan
David Miller	Senior Vice President and President of Asia Pacific	Joined Lenovo in August 2006	Formerly president of Dell China/Hong Kong
Christopher J. Askew	Senior Vice President, Global Services	Joined Lenovo in August 2006	He has served as Vice President of Asia Pacific and Japan for Dell Services and has extensive experience in the service business. British nationality
Rory Read	Senior Vice President of Operations, President of the Americas in 2007	Joined Lenovo in August 2006	From IBM
Kenneth DiPietro	Senior Vice President of Human Resources	Joined Lenovo in August 2006	He has worked in Dell/Microsoft and has extensive experience in human resources and organizational development

Lenovo Group announced that the company will carry out a new organizational restructuring. After this adjustment, the company will be divided into two major business groups: Lenovo Business Group and Think Business Group.

With the rise of the mobile internet, Lenovo Group successfully acquired IBM Thinkpad, X86 small and medium-sized servers, MOTO mobile phones, Germany's second largest electronics factory Median, Japan NEC Electronics, completed the Lenovo Group's global layout. Lenovo Group began to shift to mobile internet and cloud computing services. Lenovo Group continued to maintain a strong momentum of development, and once again achieved a new high in revenue and profit in the recently released performance report. At the same time, it was the world's leading PC leader and just announced the largest acquisition plan in Lenovo's history. In order to maintain a strong momentum and build an organizational structure that can help new business growth, Lenovo Group today announced changes in organizational structure and changes in the senior management team. Since April 1, 2014, Lenovo Group has established four new and relatively independent business groups: (1) PC Business Group (including Lenovo brand and Think brand), and is currently led by Lenovo Europe Middle East and Africa (EMEA) Gianfranco Lanci is responsible. (2) Mobile Business Group (smartphone, tablet, smart TV), led by Liu Jun, who currently leads Lenovo Business Group (consumer and mobile products); (3) Enterprise-level business group (including server and storage), by current leadership Gerry Smith of the Americas is responsible. The newly announced acquisition of the IBM X86 server business was to be incorporated into Smith's organization upon completion of the approval process; (4) The cloud service business group (including Android and Windows software) will be the senior vice president and chief technology officer of the current Lenovo Group He Zhiqiang's responsibility.

5.3 Analysis of Transnational Governance Evolution

Based on the definition of multinational corporate governance, it points out the composition of the internal governance structure and governance mechanism of multinational corporations, clarifies the connotation of the governance ability of transnational corporations, and proposes the theoretical framework for the formation of multinational corporations' governance capacity.

5.3.1 Theoretical Framework

5.3.1.1 The Connotation of Multinational Corporate Governance

Corporate governance is a set of institutional arrangements that focus on decision science and coordinate stakeholder-centric stakeholder relationships. Compared with corporate governance in general domestic enterprises, multinational corporate governance is not only a system for supervising the relationship between managers and shareholders. Due to the geographical dispersion of multinational corporations, a higher proportion of foreign shareholders and host country stakeholders are bound by the host country system. This increases the coordination costs and governance complexity of multinational corporate governance. Therefore, multinational corporate governance fundamentally transcends the general domestic corporate governance framework. Multinational corporate governance has the corporate governance characteristics of general enterprises, and has a new connotation of the fiduciary responsibility of various stakeholders across national borders and regions. Multinational corporate governance mainly refers to the diversified global business of transnational corporations, clarifying the distribution of power, responsibility, and interests among key players in global decision-making of multinational corporations. There are two main levels: governance at parent company level and governance at subsidiary level. Parent company governance includes equity of the parent company, and how powers and responsibilities are distributed and supervised. Governance at the subsidiary level involves how foreign affiliates deal with shareholders and other local stakeholders, feedback to the parent company and integration with the parent company.

5.3.1.2 Internal Governance Structure and Governance Mechanism of Multinational Corporations

The internal governance structure of multinational corporations mainly includes the structure of the board of directors and the structure of the senior management team. The structure of the board of directors includes the size of the board of directors and the structure of the board of directors; the executive team structure mainly refers to the staff structure of the senior management team, such as the nationality of the senior management team, the international experience of the industry, and the average age. As a form of network organization, multinational corporations have the characteristics of network governance mechanism. Powell (1990) proposed that the governance mechanisms of network organizations include trust, learning, and innovation mechanisms. Jones et al. (1997) believe that the social mechanisms of the network include Restricted Access, Collective Sanctions, Macroculture, and Reputation. From the perspective of the network, Sun Guoqiang (2003), suggested that the micro-mechanism of network governance is proposed, including learning innovation, incentive constraints, decision coordination, and benefit distribution. Therefore, the internal governance mechanism of multinational corporations is a micro-governance mechanism, including learning innovation, incentive constraints, decision coordination, and benefit distribution.

5.3.1.3 Definition of the Governance Capacity of Multinational Corporations

Scholars at home and abroad do not have a clear definition of the governance capabilities of multinational corporations. Studies of corporate governance capabilities have mainly been made by Li Wei'an's research team at the China Corporate Governance Research Institute of Nankai University. They constructed the Chinese Listed Company Corporate Governance Index. After 10 years of releases, it was found that the effectiveness of governance at Chinese listed companies has significantly improved. Therefore, they propose that the governance capabilities of Chinese listed companies will gradually improve along with the governance structure and mechanisms, to build a relatively complete governance structure with rules of compliance and accountability as core institutional elements. It can be seen that the formation of corporate governance capability follows the continuous adjustment and optimization from structure to mechanism, and finally achieves a dynamic process of improvement in effectiveness. Therefore, according to the characteristics of general domestic companies in multinational corporations, this paper defines the multinational corporate governance ability as the adjustment and optimization of multinational corporations through internal governance structure and governance mechanism to achieve dynamic interaction with the external environment to achieve the key internal and external resources. Structure and integration to enhance the ability of multinational companies to compete globally. To put it simply, the ability of multinational corporations to govern is a capability for multinational corporations to integrate their internal and external key resources and capabilities through reasonable institutional arrangements to achieve sustainable competitive advantage. The formation of multinational corporate governance capabilities is a dynamic process. This paper considers multinational corporate governance capabilities as a form of dynamic capability.

5.3.2 *Analysis of the Formation of Lenovo Group's Transnational Governance Capability*

In this part, this case study puts forward the theoretical framework of corporate environment and strategy—corporate governance structure and governance mechanism—the evolution of multinational corporate governance capabilities. According to the theoretical framework, the four key stages of the formation of the multinational governance capability of the Group are analyzed.

(1) Basic stage—Equity reform lays foundations for internationalization

In the basic stage, Lenovo Group's board of directors with Liu Chuanzhi as the chairman and the executive team with Yang Yuanqing as CEO face fierce competition in the domestic PC market and the rapid development of the technology in the PC industry. For the long-term development of Lenovo Group, the Group's equity reform clear up equity, and modernize the system. The chairman of Lenovo Group in Lenovo Group's "master-style governance mechanism," that is, through the equity incentives, the CEO of Lenovo Group and the core members of the senior management team hold the equity of Lenovo Group, becoming the "owner" of Lenovo Group, to large extent, it has inspired Lenovo's CEO and executive team to work hard for the long-term development of Lenovo's group. Therefore, in the face of the domestic PC industry environment, Lenovo Group decided to base itself in the domestic market, enter the international market, and implement an international strategy for the long-term development of Lenovo Group (Table 5.4).

Through the above analysis, Lenovo's transnational governance capability formed the basic stage, Lenovo Group's equity reform and equity incentives, making Lenovo Group's CEO and executive team become the "owner" of Lenovo, Lenovo Group Chairman and CEO, through the insight of the industry environment, for the long-term development of Lenovo Group, and thus propose an international strategy, this is the premise of the formation of Lenovo's transnational governance capabilities.

Table 5.4 Characteristics of the formation of transnational governance capabilities in the basic stage

Evolutionary stage	*Key variables*	*Evidence (typically cited)*	*Result*
Basic stage	Environment and strategy	Competition status: After China's accession to the WTO in 2001, the domestic market is highly competitive and faces the country Foreign famous brands such as IBM, Dell, and HP are competing, and they also face Tsinghua Tongfang, Founder, and Wave Chaos and other domestic brands compete; 2004 domestic notebook market is still IBM, HP, Toshiba When foreign brands dominate, sales are much higher than domestic brands Technical status: PC product technology development and market changes, product life cycle is shortening The variety of products has increased significantly Strategy: Lenovo's market share is gradually being eaten by international manufacturers, compared with cost control and technological innovation International manufacturers do not have an advantage, and the diversification strategy is not going smoothly	Based on the environment of the domestic PC industry, the board of directors of Lenovo Group put forward a foothold in the domestic market, proposed an international strategy, and turned to the global PC market

(continued)

Table 5.4 (continued)

Evolutionary stage	*Key variables*	*Evidence (typically cited)*	*Result*
	Governance structure	Board structure: Chairman of the Board is Liu Chuanzhi, CEO is Yang Yuanqing; board member is 7 The board of directors with international experience is one person, one foreign director, and one foreign member With domestic directors 1:6 TMT structure: 17 executives with 1 foreign education background executive, no foreigners Executive members, executives with no international experience	The board of directors and senior management team have fewer international members and lack international experience

Evolutionary stage	*Key variables*	*Evidence (typically cited)*	*Result*
	Governance mechanism	Equity mechanism: Lenovo experienced two important property rights reforms: in 1995, the Chinese Academy of Sciences will be 35% The right to pay dividends to Liu Chuanzhi and his team; in 2002, the Chinese Academy of Sciences invested in Lenovo Holdings and corresponding The state-owned assets corresponding to the equity are freely transferred to the State-owned Assets Management Co., Ltd. of the Chinese Academy of Sciences After the completion of the state-owned shares, the Chinese Academy of Sciences State-owned Assets Management Co., Ltd. holds Lenovo control 65% of the shares, Lenovo Holdings employees hold 35% Equity incentives: Liu Chuanzhi proposed that the CEO of Lenovo Group and the core members of the senior management team will become the masters of Lenovo through equity incentives, proposing that "the master here cannot make demands on all members. The true core strength of a company must become the master, enjoy the power and benefits of the owner, but also assume the responsibilities and risks that go alongside"	The reform of the equity mechanism has laid the foundation for Lenovo's internationalization; the governance mechanism of the "owner enterprise" has guaranteed the long-term development of the company
	Governance ability	At this stage, Lenovo's market is mainly in China. It has achieved the first market share in the domestic PC market, and has established a modern enterprise system. The perfect corporate governance structure and governance mechanism laid the foundation for Lenovo Group International	A sound corporate governance structure and governance mechanism have been established

(2) Transition stage—the formation of Lenovo's transnational governance structure

In order to achieve internationalization, Lenovo Group completed the most crucial step in the acquisition of the IBM PC business unit, with the help of IBM's brand resources, human resources, and technical resources to achieve internationalization. In the face of global market competition, the new Lenovo Group faces the tremendous changes in the internal and external environment of customers, suppliers, and partners around the world. Lenovo urgently needs to adjust its structure and strategy to adapt to the new environment. Therefore, the new Lenovo Group has carried out a series of adjustments to the governance structure. The board of directors of Lenovo Group has changed from the original 7 to the current 11 and the board of directors has grown in size; the ratio of foreign directors to domestic directors of the board has been 1:6, adjusted to 5:6 now, to become a more international board of directors. The size of the TMT team has been adjusted from the original 17 to the current 16 people, and the scale has not changed much. However, the ratio of foreign teams to domestic teams has changed from no foreign executives to 9:7. These foreign executive team members have rich international experience and play an important role in the internationalization of the new Lenovo Group (Table 5.5).

In order to enable the new Lenovo to achieve business integration and cultural integration as soon as possible, the new Lenovo has adopted a series of governance mechanisms. First of all, the new Lenovo uses English as the working language in the communication mechanism, requiring all employees of Lenovo to learn English. Secondly, the new Lenovo Group sets up dual headquarters to better carry out business development. Finally, the new Lenovo Group learns mechanism. It is from the original IBM PC business executives as a "coach," the domestic senior management team, including Yang Yuanqing, lacks international experience, and needs to learn how to manage an international business while sitting in the "co-pilot" position alongside the foreign executive team. Through the adjustment of the above governance structure and governance mechanism, the new Lenovo Group initially achieved the strategic goals of the transitional phase, and the new Lenovo Group's transnational governance capability was initially formed.

Table 5.5 Characteristics of the formation of transnational governance capabilities in the transition stage

Evolutionary stage	*Key variable*	*Evidence (typically cited)*	*Result*
Transition stage	Environment and strategy	Industry environment: After the acquisition of IBM PC business, the internal and external environment of the new Lenovo Group has become heavy Changes, external face of the global market competition of brands such as Dell, HP, while the new Lenovo still faces accreditation of IBM PC customers, suppliers, and partners in Linyuan; internal staff adjustment Major changes in business languages, working methods, business processes, etc. There are serious cultural conflicts Strategy: Integrate business processes after mergers and acquisitions to ensure that global customers do not lose, adjust Lenovo Group Structure and governance structure to adapt to Lenovo's strategy	New Lenovo Group establishes appropriate organizational structure and governance structure to adapt to changes in the external environment

(continued)

Table 5.5 (continued)

Evolutionary stage	*Key variable*	*Evidence (typically cited)*	*Result*
	Governance structure	Board structure: Chairman Yang Yuanqing, CEO is the former IBM PC business unit general manager Stephen M. Ward. The board of directors is 11 members; there are 5 foreign directors, 5 board members with international experience, and the ratio of foreign directors to domestic directors is 5:6 TMT structure: 16 senior management team, 9 executives with international experience, 9 foreign executives, 9:7 foreign executives and domestic executives	Initially formed an international board of directors team and an international executive team structure

Evolutionary stage	*Key variable*	*Evidence (typically cited)*	*Result*
	Governance mechanism	Communication: New Lenovo Group adopts English as the working language. If the law completely understands the foreign executives, it will not communicate well (Qiao Jian) Learning: 5 years after the merger, Lenovo employees collectively learn English and cultivate a mentality of returning to zero (Jia Zhaohui) "In the future if I have to face continuous work more than 48 hours, Ravi Marwaha (senior vice president of worldwide sales) set me up an international manager model, an international manager's way of life" (Chen Shaopeng) Yang Yuanqing was appointed chairman of the new Lenovo Group, and the CEO is Stephen M. Ward, in order to let Yang Yuanqing sit in the position of "co-pilot" to learn how to control an international company (Liu Chuanzhi) Coordination: New Lenovo after the merger, set up Beijing and New York dual headquarters; a few years after the merger, the new Lenovo used a "one company, two systems" model	Coexistence of "master enterprise" governance and "professional manager" governance on the basis of conflict and tolerance
	Governance ability	Within a year of Lenovo's acquisition, the new Lenovo Group operates and promotes brands in 65 countries and regions, ensuring product interaction, quality, and service. These measures effectively retain most of the customers, and retain 98% of employees, expanding the global market share, becoming the world's third largest PC manufacturer after HP and Dell	The new Lenovo Group's transnational governance structure was initially formed, the governance mechanism was weak, and the cross-country performance was initially improved

Through the above analysis, in the transitional phase, the relationship between the environment and strategy of the new Lenovo Group—governance structure and governance mechanism—i.e., transnational governance capability is shown in Figure 7. In the transition period, Lenovo Group faced the global PC industry competition after acquiring the IBM PC business unit. At the same time, the new Lenovo Group faced internal business adjustments, retaining employees and global customers. Therefore, the changes in the environment and strategy of Lenovo Group have caused the adjustment of the new Lenovo Group's transnational governance structure, especially the board of directors and the TMT team, and become an international team. This requires the establishment of a corresponding governance mechanism to solve the original Lenovo Group executives and coordination and communication issues of foreign executives. Through case studies, it was found that Lenovo's foreign executives and domestic executives, Lenovo's board of directors and senior management team realized interaction through learning mechanism, communication mechanism, and coordination mechanism, which guaranteed the realization of the strategic goals of Lenovo Group's transitional stage and initially formed the Lenovo Group's transnational Governance ability.

(3) Conflict phase—the formation of Lenovo's transnational governance mechanism

The new Lenovo Group has undergone a smooth transition period and basically maintained "one company, two systems" during the transition period. It has not fully utilized the advantages of the two companies. The new Lenovo Group faces fierce competition from the global industry and is in urgent need. Conduct global business adjustments to reduce costs and achieve synergies. Therefore, during the conflict phase, Lenovo Group's board of directors from the PC industry supply chain to do the best Dell Group Asia Pacific President William J. Amelio dug into the new Lenovo Group's second CEO to complete the Lenovo Group's strategic goals. In order to complete the strategic goal, the newly appointed CEO quickly formed a very personal senior management team to carry out the supply chain transformation. Most of the team came from Dell, which triggered the adjustment and optimization of the new Lenovo Group's executive team structure (Table 5.6).

The stronger William J. Amelio dismissed the former Lenovo Group executives during the formation of the senior management team, sparking

Table 5.6 Characteristics of the formation of transnational governance capabilities in the conflict stage

Evolutionary stage	*Key variable*	*Evidence (typically cited)*	*Result*
Conflict stage	Environment and strategy	Industry environment: The industry environment has changed since 2006, and its logo is the mobile internet Now, the IT industry is consumerized. Before the IT industry as a production tool to support enterprise production efficiency The number of PCs worldwide has grown substantially, surpassing corporate PCs in market share Facing Acer, fierce competition from global PC vendors such as Dell, Toshiba, and HP Strategy: Lenovo itself needs to build a global framework for cost transfer and supply chain transform, reduces supply chain costs, and conducts global business operations	Under the competitive pressure of PC manufacturers such as Dell, which is good at supply chain management, the new Lenovo Group will carry out a global strategic layout, reduce costs, and transform the global supply chain

(continued)

Table 5.6 (continued)

Evolutionary stage	*Key variable*	*Evidence (typically cited)*	*Result*
	Governance structure	Board structure: The chairman of the board is Yang Yuanqing, and the CEO is replaced by William J. Amelio, former president of Dell Asia Pacific. Board members 12 people; foreign directors have 6 board members who have international experience of 6 proportions, and foreign and domestic directors 6:6 TMT Structure: Executive Teams 17 people, executives with international experience 11 people, with foreign executives 11 proportion of people, foreign executives and national executives of 11:6. Executive changes is relatively large, it has five executives from Dell added new Lenovo Group in 2006	For the strategic implementation of the new Lenovo Group, the governance structure has been greatly adjusted and optimized
	Governance mechanism	Communication: Chief Diversity Officer, to create a "United Nations" new Lenovo Group, resolve issues such as cultural conflicts and poor communication between executives from China and foreign executive team members Learning: Continue with Yang Yuanqing as chairman of the new Lenovo Group, and William J. Amelio as CEO. Let Yang Yuanqing sit in the position of "co-pilot" to learn how to control an internationalization Company (Liu Chuanzhi) Coordination: The conflict between the strong "professional manager" governance mechanism and the "owner enterprise" governance mechanism, Lenovo's "brother culture" tries to retain the old Lenovo's executives, and the new CEO actively builds a private "Dell" team, strong replacement of inappropriate "old Lenovo" executives	The most intense period of conflict between the two governance mechanisms

Evolutionary stage	*Key variable*	*Evidence (typically cited)*	*Result*
	Governance ability	The second CEO of the new Lenovo still insists on corporate customers, does not pay attention to the personal consumer market, and sells Lenovo mobile terminal business, ignoring the changes in the industry environment, eventually leading to a loss of 226 million yuan in the 2008/2009 fiscal year	The new Lenovo Group's transnational governance structure and governance mechanisms have been formed

a governance mechanism characterized by "professional managers" represented by William J. Amelio and chairman Yang Yuanqing. Representation of the conflict of the "owner enterprise" governance mechanism. Not only does it stay at the conflict level between the chairman and the CEO, but also problems such as culture, ideas, and language communication have caused conflicts among the senior management of the new Lenovo Group. In order to resolve this conflict, Xinlian Lenovo Group has set up the position of Chief Diversified Officer to create a "United Nations" within the new Lenovo Group to resolve cultural conflicts and communication between executives and foreign executives from China. The problem of poorness enables them to form a joint effort to achieve the company's strategic goals. In this process, the learning mechanism is the driving force. The Chinese executives represented by Yang Yuanqing need to continue to sit in the position of "co-pilot" CEOs to learn international management experience.

In summary, in the conflict phase, Lenovo Group has developed a strategy to reduce costs, build a global supply chain, and achieve synergy based on the PC industry environment. In order to realize this strategy, Lenovo Group first carried out a series of governance structure adjustments and optimizations, realized the interaction between the chairman and CEO, and the Chinese and foreign executives team, and the governance mechanism is to resolve the conflicts generated by the interaction process and complete. The institutional guarantee of Lenovo's strategic goals has thus completed the key steps in the construction of the new Lenovo Group's multinational governance capabilities.

(4) Formation stage—synergy between Lenovo's transnational governance structure and governance mechanism

In the conflict stage, due to macroeconomic factors and the short-term behavior of CEO William J. Amelio as a professional manager, the performance of Lenovo Group declined. The board of directors, Liu Chuanzhi, decided to replace William J. Amelio and let Yang Yuanqing re-appointed as CEO. The new Lenovo Group, Liu Chuanzhi re-elected as chairman. In response to the environment of the PC industry and the industry changes brought by the mobile internet, the new Lenovo Group began to implement the "double-fisted boxing strategy" in the world, that is, "our strategic framework is to be like double fists: our left fist protecting our head and heart, consolidating two core businesses: China business and global corporate customer business. These two arms must maintain good profitability to ensure our overall success. Our right fist must be on the attack, to be able to score, seize emerging markets and global trading opportunities, including the growth of consumer business and SMEs" (Yang Yuanqing) (Table 5.7).

In order to complete the Lenovo Group strategy, leaders basically formed a stable senior management team, the ratio of foreign executives to Chinese executives is 10:8. Lenovo has grown into an international company. Since Lenovo's chairman and CEO realigned with the first phase, the difference is that Lenovo's current executives are completely an international team with rich international experience. The formation of Lenovo's diversified corporate culture makes the governance mechanism of Lenovo's "owner's enterprise" and the internationalization of Lenovo's senior management team's governance structure. It is the institutional guarantee for the realization of Lenovo's strategic goals, and it is

Table 5.7 Characteristics of the formation of transnational governance capabilities in the formation stage

Evolutionary stage	*Key variable*	*Evidence (typically cited)*	*Result*
Formation stage	Environment and strategy	Industry environment: The US financial crisis occurred in 2008, which quickly triggered the global economic crisis The environment is bad, the PC industry is completing the transition from enterprise PC to consumer PC, netbook The rapid rise is a sign of the full rise of consumer PCs, netbooks are cheap; global corporate customers The market is shrinking by 20%, while the consumer PC business is growing by 20% Strategy: Lenovo has completed the international learning phase, due to changes in the industry environment, Lenovo Group launches "double boxing strategy"	Launch "double-fisted boxing strategy" and seek global strategic advantages

(continued)

Table 5.7 (continued)

Evolutionary stage	*Key variable*	*Evidence (typically cited)*	*Result*
	Governance structure	Board structure: Liu Chuanzhi re-elected as chairman and Yang Yuanqing re-appointed as CEO. Board members 11; have 4 foreign directors, and a ratio of foreign to domestic directors of 4:7 TMT Structure: Executive teams 18 people, with 10 foreign executives, foreign executives and executives of the country in the ratio of 10:8	Formed a relatively stable transnational governance structure
	Governance mechanism	Cultural integration: "Western-style toilets and squat toilets" (Kang Youlan); "In the Lenovo China Building, a branded coffee shop was introduced; Redefining diversity, the diversity we talked about in Lenovo is about cultural differences, including: Region, gender, educational background, age, religion, experience, language, personnel relations, sexuality; Differences in orientation, physical ability, job function, race, and ethnicity, and other individual characteristics" (Qiao Jian) Coordination: The "professional manager" governance mechanism and the "owner enterprise" governance mechanism are perfectly combined to form a good coordination mechanism	The two governance mechanisms are better integrated

(continued)

Table 5.7 (continued)

Evolutionary stage	*Key variable*	*Evidence (typically cited)*	*Result*
	Governance ability	The new Lenovo Group has formed a reasonable cross-border governance structure and effective governance mechanism, so that the two can achieve synergy. Lenovo Group has achieved a series of results in the global market: in 2011, it acquired 36.66% of the German electronics manufacturer Medion for 231 million euros. After the transaction was completed, Lenovo doubled its market share in Germany and became the third largest manufacturer to complete the strategic layout of the European PC market. In the same year, it announced a joint venture with Japan NEC to form the largest Japanese personal computer group and enter the Japanese market; In 2014, it acquired Motorola's mobile smartphone business from Google for USD 2.9 billion and laid out its mobile terminal business. In the same year, it acquired IBM's X86 server business for USD 2.3 billion to lay out the server market	New Lenovo Group has grown into an international company

also the important sign that Lenovo's transnational governance capability had taken root.

In summary, the relationship between Lenovo Group's environment and strategy-governance structure and governance mechanism-transnational governance capability is shown in Fig. 5.3.

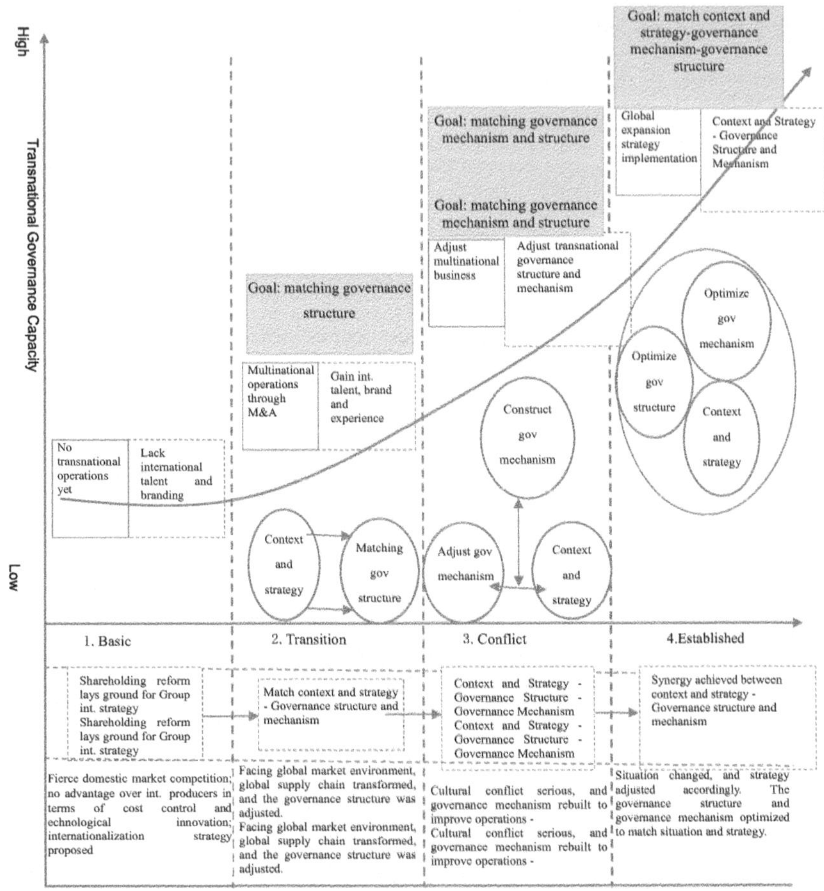

Fig. 5.3 Climate and strategy at Lenovo—governance structure and mechanisms—evolution of transnational governance capability

5.4 Summary and Conclusions

Based on a dynamic matching perspective, this case analyzes the evolution of Lenovo Group's transnational governance capabilities and identifies the key influencing factors affecting the evolution of Lenovo's multinational governance capabilities. The Chinese company improves and upgrades its business in the transnational business process. Transnational governance capabilities provide important theoretical implications. The theoretical contributions of this research are as follows: (1) Defining the connotation of transnational governance capability, and through the evolution of Lenovo Group's transnational capabilities, it is concluded that the formation of transnational governance capability is a dynamic evolution process. Previous studies on the formation of corporate transnational governance capabilities are relatively rare, and are mostly based on static perspectives. The research of this paper analyzes the enterprise environment-strategy, transnational governance structure, and transnational governance mechanism from the perspective of dynamic matching, and then builds the ability of transnational governance. (2) From the perspective of multinational corporations in emerging economies, this case study analyzes the process and mechanism of the evolution of governance capabilities of multinational corporations in emerging economies. The derived process model of this paper has important theoretical significance. It describes the formation process of transnational governance ability of multinational enterprises in developed countries, which has important reference value for transnational operations of other emerging economies. By exploring the matching levels and matching content, as well as the relationship between environment-strategy, governance structure, and governance mechanisms, this study reveals how emerging economies can build transnational governance capabilities in transnational operations and gain competitive advantage in international markets.

References

Jones, C, Hesterly, WS, Borgatti, SP. A General Theory of Network Governance: Exchange Conditions and Social Mechanisms. *The Academy of Management Review*, 1997, 22(4): 911–945.

Powell, WW. Neither Market Nor Hierarchy: Network Forms of Organization. In BM Staw & LL Cummings (Eds.), *Research in Organizational Behavior*, 1990, (12): 295–336. Greenwich, CT: JAI Press.

Sun Guoqiang. Relationship, Interaction and Collaboration: Governance Logic of Network Organization. *China Industrial Economy*, 2003, (11): 14–20.

CHAPTER 6

The Equity Governance Model of the Wuhan Iron and Steel Corporation (WISCO)'s Overseas Investment

6.1 Introduction

Wuhan Iron and Steel Corporation (WISCO) was the first large-scale iron and steel venture created after the founding of the People's Republic of China. Construction began in 1955 and was completed on September 13, 1958. It is a core state-owned enterprise directly managed by the Central Committee and State-owned Assets Supervision and Administration Commission of the State Council. WISCO owns advanced steel production process equipment in mining, coking, iron making, steel making, steel rolling, and supporting public and auxiliary facilities. It is an important high-quality plate production base in China and has made important contributions to China's national economy and modernization. WISCO was listed in the global Fortune 500 rankings for six consecutive years, at 500th in 2015. WISCO headquarters now has a production capacity of 18 million tons of steel, and through the restructuring of Egang Iron Mine and Kunming Iron and Steel, it has turned into a modern global steel powerhouse, and is one of the most competitive steel companies in the world.

*In order to facilitate reading, the former "Wuhan Iron and Steel Group" is referred to as WISCO or Wugang.

© The Author(s), under exclusive license to Springer Nature Singapore Pte Ltd. 2020
R. Lin et al. *Corporate Governance of Chinese Multinational Corporations*,
https://doi.org/10.1007/978-981-15-7405-4_6

WISCO currently has three main businesses, namely steel manufacturing, high-tech industries. and international trade. Steel products include hot rolled coil, hot rolled steel, hot rolled heavy rail, medium and heavy plate, cold rolled coil, galvanized sheet, tin plate, cold rolled-oriented and non-oriented silicon steel sheet, color coated steel sheet, high-speed wire. WISCO's three strategic product bases are mature. WISCO has become the world's largest silicon steel production base. Its self-initiated automobile panels supply medium and high-end cars. WISCO also makes high-performance engineering structure steel and fine products. With a leading position in the country WISCO's cold rolled silicon steel sheet and ship plate steel have been awarded Famous Brand Products in China. The company is known for its high-quality steel automobile boards, bridges, pipelines, pressure vessels, containers, cords, fire resistant weathering materials, and electrician material. The WISCO brand has been awarded national well-known trademark. According to a report released by the World Brand Lab, the WISCO brand ranked 56th, and is worth RMB 17.052 billion.

WISCO works in several sectors, including coking, refractory materials, chemicals, metallurgic powders, water slag, oxygen, rare gases, coal tar, crude benzene, ammonium sulfate, and undertakes engineering design and construction, machinery manufacturing, and processing projects at home and abroad. It also engages in transportation, logistics, warehousing, automation, overseas development, and investment financing.

6.2 Transnational Governance Evolution

The best way to understand the evolution of WISCO's corporate governance is to consider their approach to overseas project investment. WISCO overseas investment projects are concentrated in Liberia, Canada, Australia, Brazil, and Madagascar. There are mainly seven major projects, some of which are in production, some under construction, and some still subject to the outcome of feasibility studies.

6.2.1 Liberian State Mine Project

The Liberian State Mine Project, located in central Liberia is about 80 kilometers from Monrovia, the capital of the country. WISCO has a charter to operate iron mines in an area of 619 km^2. They expect to be able to secure 1.48 billion tons of mineral resources, graded on average 35.48%. Potential resources amount to 2.785 billion tons and total resources amount to 4.095 billion tons. The mining area has a railway link to a port 80 km away.

The state mine was operated by a German company before the civil war. In 2007, the Liberian government conducted an international tender for the state mining project. Zhonglilian (Hong Kong) Mining Co., Ltd. (a private company composed of four mainland companies) made a bid. With the strong support of the Chinese Ambassador to Liberia, it won 100% of equity in the state mining project on July 16, 2009. Zhonglilian was too weak to make the purchase alone, so the China-Africa Development Fund also participated. In October 2009, Zhonglilian transferred 85% of the shares to the China-Africa Development Fund, and on June 11, 2010, WISCO International Resources Investment Limited (established in Hong Kong) signed an equity transfer agreement with the China-Africa Development Fund and invested USD 68.47 million in the acquisition of a 60% stake in Zhonglilian held by the China-Africa Development Fund. The Liberian state mining project is shown in Fig. 6.1.

At the time, Deng Qilin, chairman of WISCO, said that the WISCO state mine project would act as a model and milestone achievement in economic cooperation between China and Liberia. It was the first major project undertaken by Chinese company in Africa, and a symbol of strategic engineering undertaking a "going out of China" campaign.

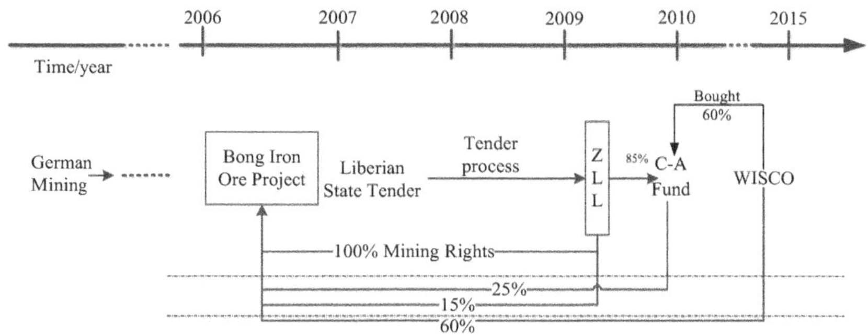

Fig. 6.1 Liberia State Mine project

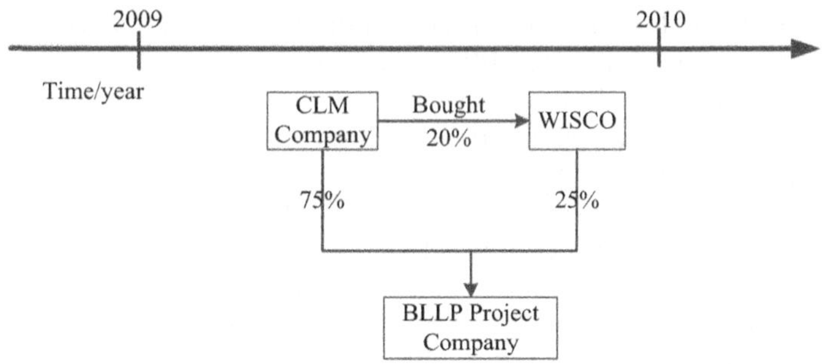

Fig. 6.2 Canadian Bloom Lake (BL) project

6.2.2 Canadian Bloom Lake (BL) Project

The transportation conditions in this project were relatively mature, and minerals on the scale of 228 million tons complied with international standards. On June 8, 2009, WISCO moved into Canada's Consolidated Thompson Iron Mines Ltd (CLM), a listed company, with an initial purchase of 19.99% of shares, purchased for about USD 143 million. With this deal, WISCO became CLM's largest shareholder, establishing a joint venture company called BLLP. This company specializes in iron ore development. The Bloom Lake (BL) project in Canada is shown in Fig. 6.2.

6.2.3 Canadian ADI Project

This project is a partnership with ADI, a publicly traded company based in Toronto, Canada. The listed company's mines are located in the north and south and consist of 1267 blocks totaling 611 km^2. Forecasted mineral resources comprise 23.7 billion tons in the south, and 300 million tons of iron ore in the northern mining area. The total mineral resources exceed total mineral resources nationally available in China.

In December 2011, WISCO invested 180 million Canadian dollars in the project, of which CAD 120 million went to buy 19.9% of the shares in listed company ADI. The latter controlled iron ore deposits in Brazil and Canada, and aimed to become a comprehensive iron ore producer. The Canadian ADI project is shown in Fig. 6.3.

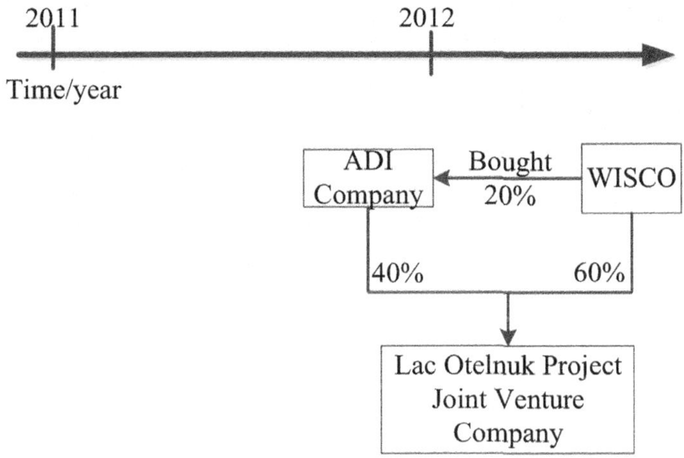

Fig. 6.3 Canadian ADI project

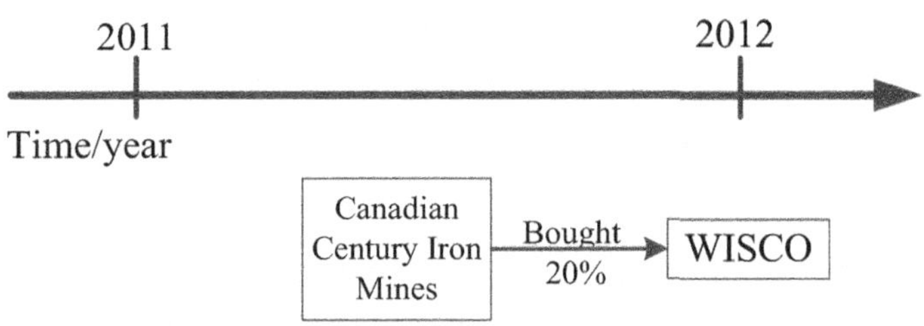

Fig. 6.4 Canadian Century Iron Mines

6.2.4 *Century Iron Mines Corporation*

Canadian Century Corporation is a listed company located in Toronto, Canada. This city has the largest concentration of mining companies in the world, followed by Australia. WISCO purchased a 24.99% stake, and cooperates with them in the form of equity participation. Century Corporation established a joint venture company on project level with several projects. The Canadian Century Iron Mines Project is shown in Fig. 6.4.

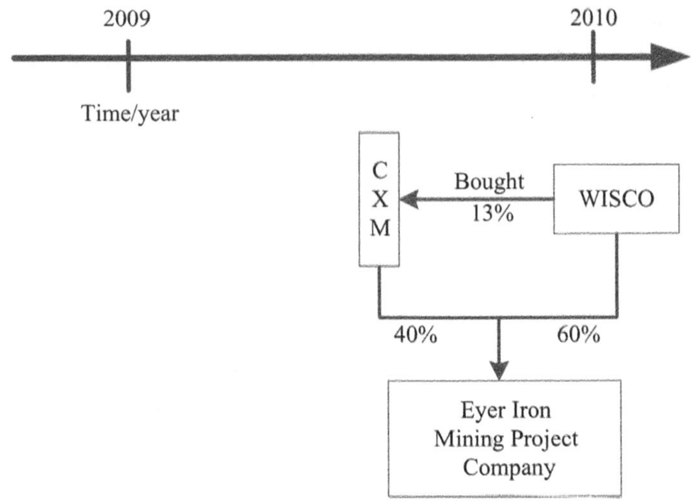

Fig. 6.5 Australian Eyer Iron Ore project

6.2.5 *Australian Iron Ore Project*

Centrex Metals (CXM) is an Australian listed company headquartered in Adelaide, Australia's southernmost city. Established in March 2001, it is mainly engaged in the development of iron ore resources on the Eyre Peninsula. It comprises of more than 2000 km^2. Exploration permits name hematite and magnetite ore. On July 20, 2009, WISCO purchased a 15% stake in CXM for AUD 10.1 million and a USD 108 million acquisition of a 60% stake in Eyre Iron Ore Mine. The Australian Iron Ore Project is shown in Fig. 6.5.

6.2.6 *Brazil's MMX Cooperation Project*

On November 30, 2009, WISCO and Brazil's EBX Group signed a cooperation agreement to carry out mining and steel production together, and on February 26, 2012, both parties completed an equity transfer in the mine project. WISCO subscribed to its subsidiary MMX (a listed company in Brazil, which directly controls two major mining areas, with a reserve of more than 3 billion tons and a grade of 33.75%). In February 2010, WISCO invested USD 400 million to acquire 21.52% of MMX Corporation and became its second largest shareholder. In October 2010, MMX

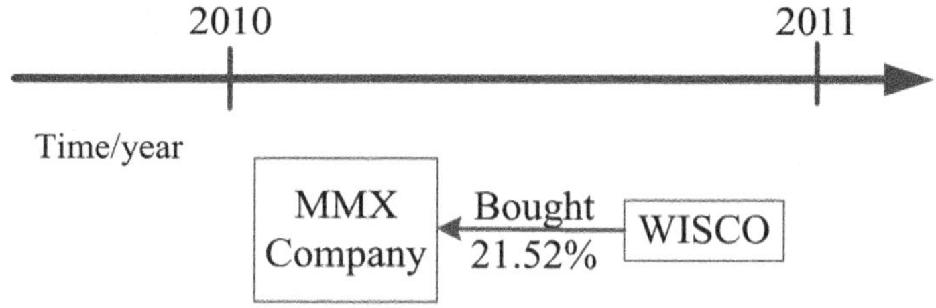

Fig. 6.6 Brazil's MMX cooperation project

issued additional shares and introduced South Korea's SAK Corporation as its strategic partner, diluting the shareholding of WISCO to 16.3%. The Brazilian MMX cooperation project is shown in Fig. 6.6.

6.2.7 Madagascar Soalala Project

The mining area covers an area of 431 km^2. It is currently known to meet the international standard resources of 888 million tons, with a potential of 1 billion tons, and average grade of 31.5%. The project is invested in by three companies, with Wuhan Iron and Steel Co., Ltd. holding 42% of the shares. The State-owned Assets Supervision and Administration Commission holds 38%, and Jinxing International Holdings Co., Ltd. (private) accounts for 20%. The Soalala project is shown in Fig. 6.7.

6.3 Analysis of Transnational Governance Evolution

As can be seen in the brief description of WISCO's seven overseas investment projects, when WISCO entered Canada, Australia, and Brazil, local mineral resources were owned by local listed companies, so WISCO could directly participate by becoming a major shareholder, and jointly develop projects on this basis. In Liberia and Madagascar, WISCO first established joint ventures or jointly purchased companies that already owned mine projects. Why do the seven overseas projects of WISCO have different entry modes, and is there a scientific basis for this?

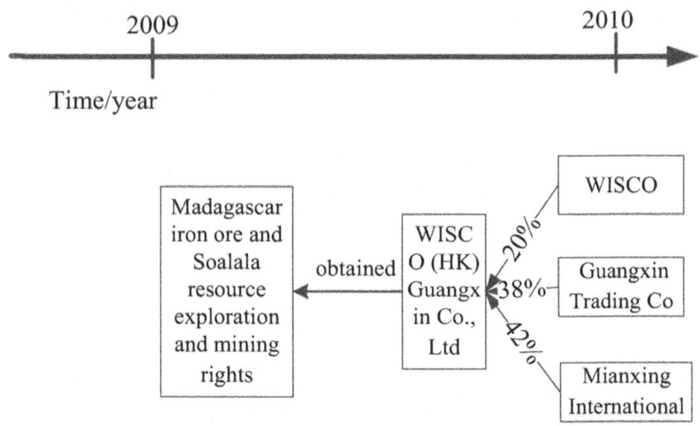

Fig. 6.7 Madagascar Soalala project

6.3.1 Analysis of the Level of the Host Country System of WISCO's Overseas Investment Projects

Existing research shows that differences in the institutional environment in different countries will have an impact on companies' transnational investment behavior. We compare the institutional environment of five countries, and score the country's institutional environment using a widely recognized global governance index. The Global Governance Index is a collaborative effort of 31 organizations that selects hundreds of independent variables and uses 37 independent data sources containing a number of institution-related factors. In 2005, Kaufmann and other founders of the Global Governance Index identified six dimensions for measuring a country's institutions: democratic institutions of government (political rights, civil rights, and human rights); political stability (the possibility of governmental threats and violence, including terrorism); government efficiency (ability and quality of public services); quality of supervision (government that promote the development of industry, the emergence of policy rates that do not conform to market rules); legal environment (quality of contract enforcement, law and order, court and the possibility of crime and violence); corruption control (referring to the use of public power for personal profit, including small and large amounts of corruption and national capture capabilities). These six dimensions fully reflect the quality of a host country's regulatory system, including

Table 6.1 The systemic environment in six countries

Country	*Year*	*Democratic deliberation*	*Political stability*	*Government efficiency*	*Government monitoring*	*Legal environment*	*Corruption control*
Australia	2009	1.40	0.83	1.70	1.82	1.73	2.08
Brazil	2009	−0.20	0.16	−0.10	0.11	−0.22	−0.12
China	2009	−1.66	−0.43	0.11	−0.20	−0.32	−0.54
Liberia	2010	−0.26	−0.46	−1.27	−1.05	−1.01	−0.53
Madagascar	2010	−0.83	−1.05	−0.95	−0.56	−0.85	−0.27
Canada	2010	1.38	0.90	1.79	1.69	1.81	2.10
China	2010	−1.63	−0.66	0.10	−0.22	0.33	−0.60
Canada	2011	1.41	1.06	1.78	1.68	1.74	2.11
China	2011	−1.58	−0.61	0.10	−0.21	−0.39	−0.56

Source Global governance indicators

administration and justice. The scores for each dimension range from −2.5 to 2.5, with higher scores suggesting a more comprehensive system (Table 6.1).

By way of the above comparison at institutional level, we find that Chinese scores are lower than the scores in Canada and Australia in each sub-indicator. Combining the investment of four projects in China in these two countries, we can see that since iron ore in these two countries are owned by local listed companies, this is where WISCO carried out iron ore mining. In cooperating with listed companies in the two countries, WISCO first purchased CLM, ADI, Century and Australia's Centrex Metals (CXM), and became the main shareholder to jointly cooperate in mining projects. The scores in China are higher than in Brazil in terms of government efficiency alone. Considering that Brazil's institutional quality is higher than China in overall terms, we find that China's investment in Brazil is similar to China's investment in Canada and Australia. Mine resources in Brazil are owned by listed company MMX, so WISCO subscribed to the listed company's shares before becoming its second largest shareholder, and only then carried out mining cooperation.

By comparing China's institutional indicators with Liberia and Madagascar, several indicators find China's institutional quality significantly higher. Combined with China's investment in these two countries, the strategy involved first finding a partner, whether it is Lizhonglian or the China-Africa Development Fund, which has already carried out commercial activities in Liberia, or Guangxin Group and Jinxing International

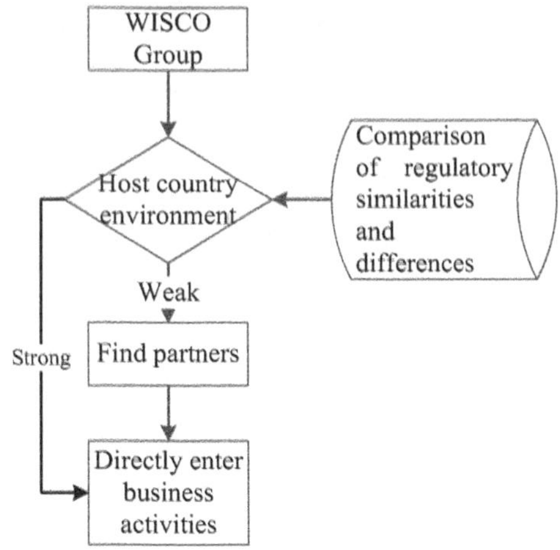

Fig. 6.8 WISCO's overseas investment decision-making logic

Holdings in Madagascar. After that, WISCO cooperated with its partners to carry out related commercial mining activities.

Through the above analysis of specific cases of WISCO, we show the logic behind the seven projects in five different countries in Fig. 6.8, calling it the "Wugang Model." But is the WISCO model scientific?

6.3.2 *Analysis of the Equity Governance Model of WISCO's Overseas Investment Projects*

As the first important decision a company needs to enter a new market (Agarwal and Ramaswami 1992; Davis et al. 2000), it will not only affect the business performance of the company (Shaver 2013), but also affect the entry of the company. The success or failure of overseas markets (Mitchell et al. 1992; Shaver et al. 1997) and the international competitiveness of companies (Cuervo-Cazurra and Genc 2012). The entry mode problem is one of the most concerned research topics in the international business field. There are many articles (Shaver 2013). When a company enters an unfamiliar environment for business activities, how to choose an appropriate entry mode requires consideration of a large number of influencing factors, such as internal capabilities, external environmental changes, and external environmental adaptation. As the economy continues to globalize, more and more companies are stepping out of the country and entering foreign markets to participate in the international competition. Academic and practical circles are increasingly concerned with entry model (Brouthers and Hennart 2007). One of the first problems facing decision-makers on entering any country is differences in institutional quality between countries.

With the academic community's attention on institutional distance, some academic researchers began to analyze this problem from two theoretical perspectives, namely transaction cost theory and institutional theory (Kim and Gray 2009). We will hold up the "Wugang Model" to transaction cost theory and institutional theory.

Differences in the international institutional environment will bring legal pressure to enterprises, and at the same time reduce the efficiency of business operations.

6.3.2.1 Transaction Cost Theory Perspective

Enterprises engaging in overseas investment processes face uncertainty in their environment, arising primarily from opportunistic behavior of partners, including strategic business partners, joint ventures, and subsidiaries of the parent company and inconsistencies with multinational corporations. In the case of information asymmetry, cooperative enterprises, or joint venture subsidiaries may engage in opportunistic behaviors for the sake of their own strategies and interests, adversely affecting parent company operations. If a host country has a good institutional environment and strong legal supervision, then the external system will support supervision of certain opportunistic behaviors, and provide protection when there is some conflict and friction. Uncertainty stems from challenges such as complexity in the external environment. If systemic quality in a host country is high, the legal and regulatory system is sound, and the host country has less political risk and less possibility of turmoil, the company will wish to cooperate. When partners cooperate, contracts will be relatively complete and business risk relatively low. When the quality of the host country system is low, the ability of the two sides to predict the environment will decline during the cooperation process, leading to higher external uncertainty and higher operational risks. Therefore, when systemic quality of the host country is relatively high, risk is relatively low, and a company can directly launch specific investment projects. When the host country's systemic quality level is low, risk is relatively high, and the company may choose partners so as to share business risks as much as possible.

6.3.2.2 Institutional Theory Perspective

When multinational corporations invest abroad, there will be pressure for legitimacy internally and externally. Internal legitimacy mainly refers to consistency between the parent company and the subsidiary company or the parent company and the specific investment project in terms of strategy or business model. External legitimacy refers to the ability of the multinational company to comply with local systems, and whether multinational companies can be recognized by partners and other stakeholders.

When a host country's system is more complete, with a fully functioning legal system, rules, and regulations are more transparent, the knowledge required for enterprises to obtain legitimacy and the laws and regulations are clear, it is easier for enterprises to obtain external legitimacy. When a host country's system is relatively imperfect, it is relatively difficult for enterprises to obtain local legitimacy. If they can find partners to share risks, it can reduce the difficulty of obtaining external legitimacy. Therefore, when a host country's infrastructure is at a relatively high level, external legitimacy is relatively easy to obtain, and specific investment projects can be directly launched. When the host country's systemic level is low, the legitimacy of a enterprise is relatively difficult to obtain, and partners are needed more than ever. Operating risks help companies reduce the difficulty of obtaining external legitimacy.

In summary, from the perspective of transaction cost theory and institutional theory, the "Wugang" model can be considered scientific.

6.4 Discussions and Conclusions

Given ongoing globalization, domestic markets are become increasingly unable to meet companies' development requirements, which means more have begun to seek international markets, opening-up broader developmental spaces. However, as companies' cross-borders, risks, and costs brought on by differences in business environment inevitably follow, so how to choose the appropriate entry mode to reduce the risk of operating in foreign markets? The case of Wuhan Iron and Steel Group, provides material for a detailed analysis of seven projects in five different countries, showing that entry mode choice is made in consideration of external environmental factors and differences between national systems.

Through research, it has been found that there are certain regularities in the investment of WISCO in these seven projects. When WISCO enters a country with a formal institutional environment superior to China, it will directly conduct business activities with companies that own mines. When WISCO enters a country with a formal institutional environment inferior to China, WISCO tends to choose partners with which to jointly invest in mining projects. We also found that companies must first recognize the difference in the institutional environment between the other country and China at the beginning of the internationalization process, in order to formulate a corresponding entry mode. When the system of the other country is relatively better than that of China, Chinese companies can quickly and easily grasp the knowledge required for the operation of the enterprise and the business model to be followed, keeping risk down and benefits high. The company can make commitments to conduct certain business activities, such as setting up wholly owned subsidiaries or directly investing in related projects. When the level of the other country's system is relatively low compared with that of China, it indicates that the laws and regulations and the political system of the other country are far from perfect. The knowledge that companies need to understand and the business operations should be observed when conducting business activities in any country. It is difficult to obtain legal and regulatory documents. At this time, it is recommended that companies choose low-resource commitments to conduct local business activities, such as finding suitable partners when investing locally, or finding Chinese companies that have already invested in the area or directly looking for local businesses. Co-investing in a company or investing in a corresponding project as a partner can help reduce investment risks.

References

Agarwal, S., Ramaswami, N.S. (1992). Choice of Foreign Market Entry Mode: Impact of Ownership, Location and Internalization Factors. *Journal of International Business Studies*, *23*(1), 1–27.

Brouthers, K.D., Hennart, J.F. (2007). Boundaries of the Firm: Insights from International Entry Mode Research. *Journal of Management*, *33*(3), 395–425.

Cuervo-Cazurra, A., Genc, M.E. (2012). Categories of Distance and International Business Research. In Wood, G., and Demirbag, M. (Eds.), *Handbook of Institutional Approaches to International Business* (pp. 219–235). Northampton, MA: Edward Elgar.

Davis, P.S., Desai, A.B., Francis, J.D. (2000). Mode of International Entry: An Isomorphism Perspective. *Journal of International Business Studies*, *31*(2), 239–258.

Kim, Y., Gray, S.J. (2009). An Assessment of Alternative Empirical Measures of Cultural Distance: Evidence from the Republic of Korea. *Asia Pacific Journal of Management*, *26*(1), 55–74.

Mitchell, W., Shaver, J.M., Yeung, B. (1992). Getting There in a Global Industry: Impacts on Performance of Changing International Presence. *Strategic Management Journal*, *13*(6), 419–432.

Shaver, J.M. (2013). Do We Really Need More Entry Mode Studies? *Journal of International Business Studies*, *44*(1), 23–27.

Shaver, J.M., Mitchell, W., Yeung, B. (1997). The Effect of Own-Firm and Other-Firm Experience on Foreign Direct Investment Survival in the United States, 1987–92. *Strategic Management Journal*, *18*(10), 811–824.

CHAPTER 7

Transnational Governance of Ping An Group's Cross-Border Acquisition of Belgium's Fortis

7.1 Introduction

In 2007, the US subprime mortgage crisis swept the world, and across the board, companies suffered. Market turbulence intensified the crisis yet further. However, for Asian countries, especially for China, as the year of "going global," 2007 was remembered. It was in this very year that China Ping An chose to make a huge acquisition, purchasing the Belgian insurance broker Fortis Group. Its massive investment and the eventual failure of the deal had a huge impact on Chinese companies considering going global ever since. Although risks existed in the market at the time, the EUR 48.6 billion market value of Fortis Group and its top ranking by the financial institutions of 15 European countries filled Ping An with longing for it to be the "testing site" of its dreams. This is what they learned.

On November 29, 2007, China Ping An formally acquired Fortis Group. Via a secondary market Dutch and Belgian joint venture, Ping An Life invested RMB 19.6 billion in 9501 million Fortis shares, accounting for 4.18%, becoming Fortis Group's single largest shareholder. Ping An continued to increase its shareholding in Fortis Group, and in as little

In this case study, China Ping An Insurance Group Co., Ltd. is referred to as China Ping An or Ping An.

© The Author(s), under exclusive license to Springer Nature Singapore Pte Ltd. 2020
R. Lin et al. *Corporate Governance of Chinese Multinational Corporations*,
https://doi.org/10.1007/978-981-15-7405-4_7

as two to three months, increased its shareholding ratio from 4.18 to 4.99%. On March 20, 2008 Ping An announced it would spend EUR 2.15 billion on a 50% stake in Fortis Investment Management Company. Ping An felt at the time that Fortis was a "good quality and cheap" target, in short, a great bargain, and it did indeed seem to be, as a world leader in both market position and influence. Ping An's decision was governed by multifold logic.

But things were not as smooth under the surface. The Fortis Group was in a bad state, with its financial situation deteriorating sharply. The share price plummeted. As of 7 p.m. on October 6, 2008 (Beijing time), Fortis shares fell to EUR 5.42 per share (about RMB 54.2), a loss of around 90%. Coupled with the impact of the financial crisis, Fortis suffered its Waterloo and was ultimately unable to regain its position of influence. Ping An could only accept it had lost. After a statistical calculation to counting the damage, the initial investment amounted to RMB 23.838 billion. Of nearly RMB 24 billion, final losses came to RMB 23 billion and in October 2, Ping An issued a notice to stop a share purchase agreement with a subsidiary of Fortis asset management, in an attempt to avoid even greater losses. Ping An's painful acquisition process was by far the largest financial transaction in China's attempt to "scrape the bottom of Wall Street." Last but not least, Ping An's Chairman, Ma Mingzhe, had been called China's "the most unqualified investor" online.

Ping An has always been a model of mixed operations in China's finance industry. This cross-border acquisition alerted potential emulators to the fact that transnational operations are not as easy as they might seem. The company is going to face a new law, system, and there are many cultural uncertainties and risks to consider. Whether taking products global or capital, these issues should not be underestimated. Transnational governance is an important system for enterprises to achieve transnational business activities. We can be sure that designing a reasonable governance mechanism according to different external environmental changes is related to success. More and more real problems reflect the importance of transnational governance. In this case of Ping An's acquisition of Fortis, why did China's Ping An, in its eagerness to go global and succeed in building transnational operations, suffer such huge losses? What is the truth behind a huge loss of more than RMB 20 billion? How to look at governance problems in transnational operations? From the perspective of transnational governance, what is the key reason to Ping An's failure? (Fig. 7.1).

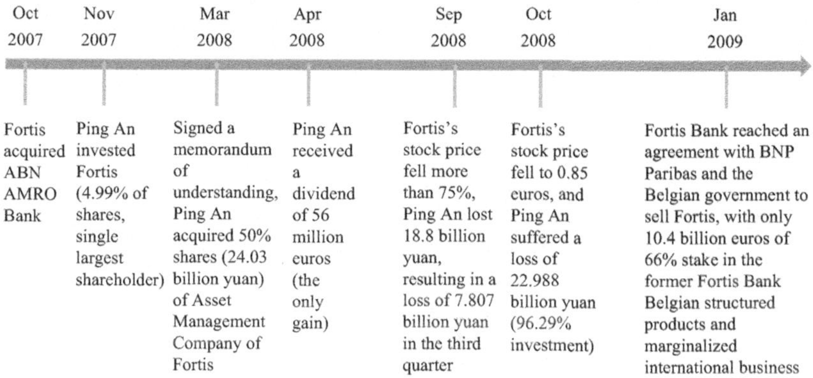

Fig. 7.1 A timeline of Ping An's investment in Fortis

7.2 Transnational Governance Evolution

7.2.1 China Ping An Background

China Ping An Insurance (Group) Co., Ltd., is one of three financial services groups that integrates insurance, banking, and investment. It has also expanded from traditional finance into non-traditional finance. Established in Shekou, Shenzhen in March 1988, it was the first joint-stock insurance company to set up in China. In June 2004, Ping An listed on the Hong Kong Stock Exchange, valued at RMB 13.826 billion. In March 2007, Ping An listed in Shanghai for RMB 38.87 billion. Ping An Group operates via subsidiaries in each of its specialized business segments: insurance (founded in 2002), life insurance (founded in 2002), trust companies (established on July 2, 1996), pension insurance, health insurance, and asset management. As for trust companies, these include Ping An Bank (formerly known as Shenzhen City Commercial Bank) and Ping An Securities (established in August 1991). The company has established China Ping An Life Insurance Limited Company, China Ping An Property Insurance Limited Company, Ping An Pension Insurance, Ping An Asset Management Limited Company, Ping An Health Insurance Limited Company. It also holds China Ping An Insurance Overseas (Holdings) Limited Company, Ping An Trust and Investment Limited Company. Ping An trusts include Ping An Bank Limited Company, and Ping An Securities Limited Company.

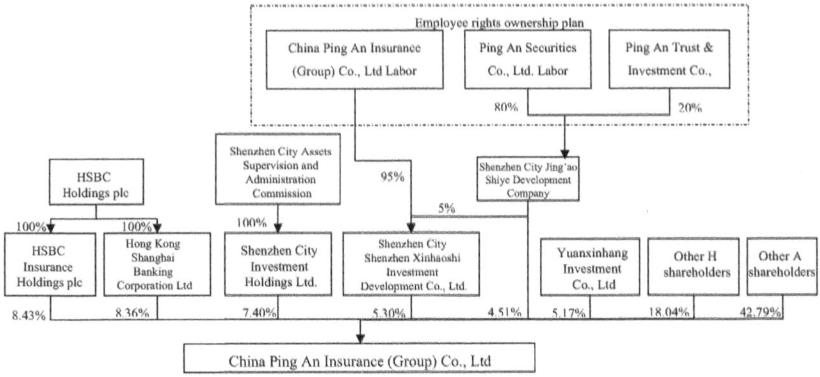

Fig. 7.2 China Ping An organizational chart (2007)

Through its subsidiaries, the company provides insurance services, as well as investment and financial services for more than 35 million individual customers and one million corporate customers. Ping An has more than 635,000 life insurance salespeople and approximately 236,000 full-time employees. As of December 31, 2014, the Group's total assets amounted to RMB 4 trillion, attributable to shareholders' equity of RMB 2895.64 billion. From the perspective of premium earnings, Ping An Life Insurance is the second largest life insurance company in China, and Ping An Property Insurance is the second largest property insurance company in China (Fig. 7.2).

7.2.2 *Organization Structure at China Ping An*

From the above chart, we see that Ping An Group's ownership structure is dispersed, there is no controlling shareholder, and an actual controller does not exist. As a private financial enterprise, Ping An Group is the first major shareholder of HSBC Holdings Co., Ltd., which is a wholly owned subsidiary of HSBC Holdings Co., Ltd., which is located in an integrated financial services company in China and has no shareholding in overseas investors. That is to say, there is almost no overseas ratio in its own organizational structure, and the degree of internationalization is very low (Table 7.1).

Secondly, the Board of Directors and senior management team of peace in 2007, 18 members of the board of directors for the organization

Table 7.1 Ping An board of directors and executive team (2007)

	International dimension
Board of directors	All Chinese
Executive team	10 people of whom two were foreigners

of peace in all the domestic staff, three executive directors, nine non-executive directors, and seven independent directors. As for the executive team members, of ten, two were foreign: Richard Jackson, with a wealth of experience in insurance, working in Commercial Union Assurance Company from 1974 to 1985, Citibank from 1985 to 2005, and served as head of international operations in insurance. His tenure was with effect from November 2005, which acted as Ping An's chief executive in financial services by the year 2012 when he resigned. The other was John Pearce, who served as deputy general manager of Ping An Group from January 15, 2007, until his dismissal at the end of 2008.

7.2.3 *China Ping An's Operation and Development Before the Acquisition*

As an integrated financial group, Ping An developed rapidly since its establishment in 1988. By 2007, Ping An's total assets reached RMB 651.10 billion, operating income was RMB 165.024 billion, and operating profit was RMB 17.167 billion. However, after experiencing the loss of the acquisition of Fortis, Ping An operating profit in 2008 plunged to RMB −2.307 billion, total assets of RMB 707.64 billion. The business development status of Ping An was as follows (Fig. 7.3).

From this it can be seen that Ping An's asset grew at a rapid rate, with a particularly strong momentum after the year 2000. The growth rate in 2004 and 2007 is even more obvious because Ping An was in the Hong Kong Stock Exchange in 2004 and 2007. It listed on the market with the Shanghai Stock Exchange and raised a large amount of funds for the development of the group (Fig. 7.4).

Successively listed in Hong Kong and Shanghai raised a lot of money, safe operating condition have a more rapid development, annual revenue increased from 2001 to RMB 41.834 billion in 2007 to RMB 165.204 billion, net profit also rose in 2001 from RMB 2.954 billion in 2007 to RMB 17.167 billion, net profit increased by 4.8 times. This rapid growth

Unit: million RMB

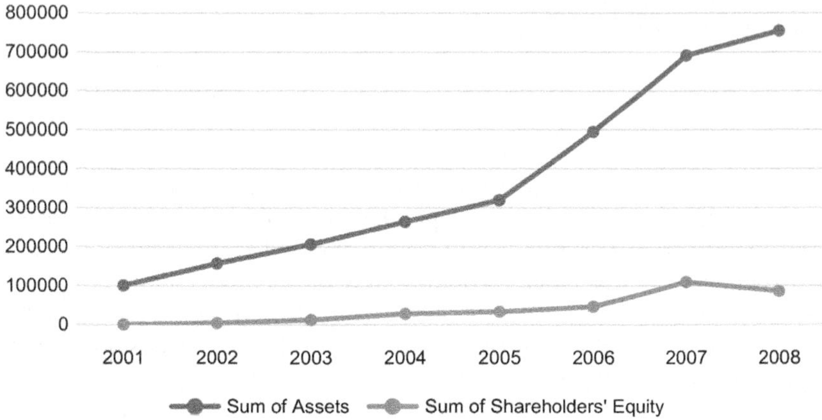

Fig. 7.3 Ping An group asset development overview (*Resource* The annual report of Ping An from 2001 to 2008)

Unit: million RMB

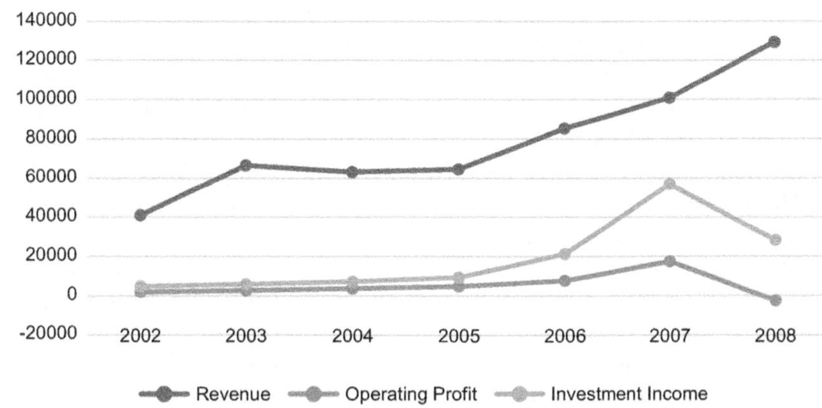

Fig. 7.4 Ping An group operating development status (*Resource* The annual report of Ping An from 2001 to 2008)

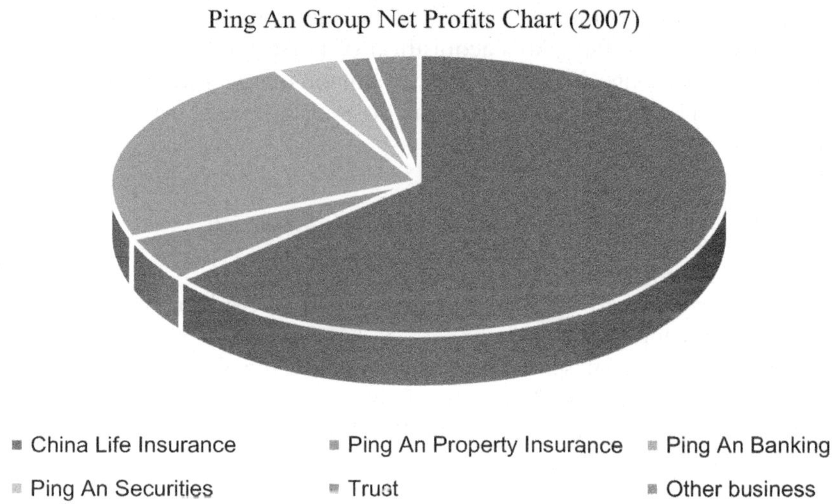

Fig. 7.5 The asset structure at Ping An group (*Resource* 2007 Annual Report of Ping An)

has given Ping An greater confidence to insist on investing heavily in Fortis.

Comprising Ping An's business operations, most of its asset structure and profit structure were composed of insurance business. The development speed of different businesses under Ping An were unusual, and the scale of insurance business had indeed grown tremendously, but business performance has gradually entered the bottleneck. As shown in the chart below, Ping An Group's insurance assets accounted for 69%, but the profit contribution was only 59% (Fig. 7.5).

7.2.4 *Transnational Experience*

Ping An has always focused on domestic business development and has little involvement in transnational operations. In 1994, Ping An introduced Morgan and Goldman Sachs as strategic investors. In 1996, China Ping An Insurance Overseas (Holdings) Co., Ltd. was established. In 2007, overseas reinsurance companies cooperating with Ping An Company were only a Munich reinsurance company and a Hong

Kong reinsurance company. There was no substantial transnational business activity before Ping An's acquisition of Fortis, and there was no real experience in going abroad for investment or mergers and acquisitions. Apart from Hong Kong, Ping An has no transnational business activities elsewhere.

7.2.5 Analysis of Fortis Situation

7.2.5.1 Background and Introduction of Fortis

Fortis was established in 1990 when a number of banks merged to form the Fortis Group. After a few years, it has become a world-renowned international financial services group active in the world of insurance, banking and investment. It is one of the largest financial institutions in Europe. Fortis Group (Euronext: FORA, Euronext: FORB, Luxembourg Exchange: FOR) is a large financial services and investment management company, including Fortis International Inc. and Fortis Bank. Fortis Group listed on Euronext Brussels, Euronext Amsterdam and the Luxembourg Stock Exchange has issued US Depositary Receipts (ADR).

The Fortis Group originally had its main base in the Netherlands, and was insurance business oriented. In 1990, the Dutch insurance giant AMEV merged with Dutch bank VSB to form a financial group that spanned two business areas, which is also the first merger of multinational financial institutions. In the same year, the group merged with AG Group, one of Belgium's largest insurance companies, at a 50% ratio, forming the predecessor of Fortis Group.

In 1992, Fortis realized that the survival of insurance required a huge network, and proposed the concept of bank assurance. Since then, it has been the Belgian ASLK-CGER, the Belgian SNCINMKN bank, the Dutch Wanbei Bank (Meespierson) and John Aiden. The income of domestic financial institutions has rapidly expanded their scale and market share. Through these mergers and acquisitions activities, Fortis, as a young financial group, has a number of established financial companies with hundreds of years of history and deep roots in the local people. For example, the Netherlands Wan Pui Bank was established in 1720; although the size of the bank can only be considered medium-sized bank, its core business—private banking business was well advanced, even the largest Dutch banking group ABN · AMRO, ING Bank Group. They are located on the bottom of the rankings. Others such as V SB was founded in 1817, ASLK-CGER was founded in 1865. These brands were retained in the early integration. These in-depth brands made Fortis look old in the highly competitive international financial community, because these companies have accumulated sufficient financial services experience in various economic cycles, and they have formed cooperative relationships with customers in their regions, making them rich. Fortis had to gain a deeper understanding of the needs of customers in different regions.

The physical form of the Fortis Group consisted of 200 banks, insurance companies, and other companies throughout the Netherlands, Belgium, and Luxembourg. Fortis's own merger and acquisition process continued until 1997 when it acquired Belgium's largest commercial bank, General Bank, which was established in 1822. After the successful acquisition of General Bank, Fortis became one of the biggest financial institutions in the Benelux countries. Almost half of the population of Belgium used Fortis Bank. Benelux was the source of 80% of profits and its business base and focus. Through the acquisition and the re-acquisition of its subsidiaries, Fortis has rapidly grown into a large multinational financial group. In the 1990s, Fortis was named the world's most successful investment banks in the United States, citing its mergers, and acquisitions and growth rates. Its return on capital rose from 12 to 17%, peaking at 21%.

In the next 10 years, Fortis focused on building its own banking and insurance alliance, cross-selling strategic positioning, and Fortis's business has gradually expanded to the world, including insurance, banking, and investment. Operating in 65 countries and regions around the world, it has about 200 companies with legal personality, providing a wide range of financial insurance services to individuals, businesses, and public institutions. In the Fortune 500 rankings in 2006, the total assets of Fortis was 112,351.4 million US dollars and ranked 18th, second only to Citigroup in the banking and financial category. After acquiring some of ABNAM-RO's business in 2007, it became one of the largest financial institutions in Europe. In the Fortune Global 500 in 2004, Fortis Group ranked 24th in terms of assets. In the 2004 Forbes World Top 500, Fortis Group ranked 38th among global financial services providers in terms of overall rankings of sales, profits, assets, and market capitalization. In the 2008 Global Fortune 500, it rose to 14th place and ranked second in the world in the business and savings banking category (Fig. 7.6).

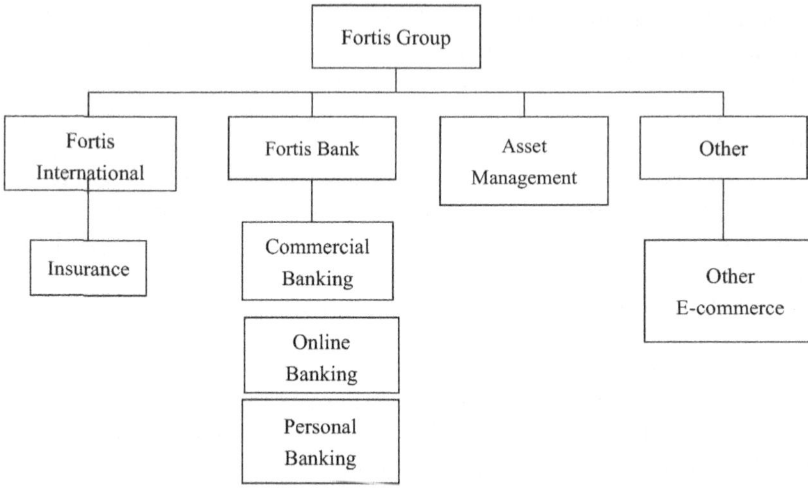

Fig. 7.6 Fortis's basic business structure

7.2.5.2 Fortis's Organizational Structure

Fortis's core business comprised the four parts of retail banking, commercial banking, investment companies, and insurance companies. It was the world's largest jointly operated finance group. Its business scope spanned Europe and Asia, including Belgium, the United Kingdom, Luxembourg, Turkey, China, Malaysia, India, and Thailand.

Fortis's shareholding structure was very fragmented, 75% of stakeholders were pension funds and institutional investors. This part of the shareholding had been striven by the Belgian government, so it was vulnerable to the influence and control of the government.

7.2.5.3 Fortis's Business Status

From the beginning of its establishment, Fortis developed very rapidly. From 1990 to 2004, Fortis' net profit increased eightfold, the market value increased tenfold, and the total investment return in the past 16 years totaled 1232%. In 2007, Fortis Group was only a medium-sized European bank and insurance group with stable income, but not in a leading position. It ranked the 20th largest bank in the world in terms of turnover in 2007.

According to the Financial report of Fortis Group, we can find that its assets are basically flat after being acquired by Ping An. During the decade from 1998 to 2007, Fortis continued to expand its market share through frequent mergers and acquisitions. Its assets also expanded from EUR 340.262 billion to EUR 871.179 billion, 2.56 times the scale of assets, net assets also expanded in 1998 from EUR 11.263 billion in 2007 to EUR 33.047 billion, net assets expanded 2.93 times. However, in terms of operating conditions, Fortis's operating profit and operating income did not increase by the same amount during the decade. During this decade, Fortis' net profit increased from EUR 1.862 billion to EUR 3.994 billion euros, 2.13 times more.[1]

Before 2006, the business development of Fortis was balanced relatively, especially the development of its bank energy. At that time, Fortis was hailed as the "double-headed eagle" of the banking insurance alliance, and the most mature and successful company in the "joint development banking insurance" financial model. But after 2006, the proportion of Fortis Bank's business began to decline, more rely on the insurance business, and its profits also decline rapidly.

In April 2007, when the Royal Bank of Scotland and Fortis announced that Standard Bank of Spain would jointly acquire ABN Amro, Fortis's stock price began to fall. On September 15, when Lehman Brothers declared bankruptcy, Fortis held EUR 137 million in Lehman Brothers bonds, EUR 270 million in reverse repo transactions, and EUR 7 million in CDS transactions. Fortis's shares continued to plummet for several days. Daily crashes exceeded 20% for a time. From January to September 2007, Fortis shares plunged more than 60%. Even so, in October 2007, Fortis paid the EUR 24 billion in cash to acquire jointly ABN Amro with the Royal Bank of Scotland and the Standard Bank of Spain.

7.2.6 How Ping An's Bought Fortis Group

7.2.6.1 Motivation

Ping An's starting point was its own needs, in order to seek overseas development, effectively broaden investment channels, spread risks across a wider scale, and achieve long-term stable returns. Moreover, the acquisition of Fortis meant getting its asset management technology for free,

[1] Hongzhen Zhao, *The Research of Ping An Investment for Fortis* [D]. Shanghai Jiaotong University, 2009.

and Ping An wants to become leader in all three core businesses: insurance, banking, and asset management. Its main source of income would remain insurance. Although the banking industry has profit contribution, its proportion is limited. Therefore, investing in Fortis Group and Fortis Investment Management Company can not only obtain investment income, but also acquire technology to accelerate the dream of a safe financial group. Ping An's vision is to become China's leading provider of integrated personal financial services, building a traditional business system based on insurance, banking, and investment, and adhering to the common development of traditional and non-traditional financial services. Fortis is related to Ping An's main business, so Ping An expects to generate a synergy effect through the acquisition of Fortis, which can achieve good business growth and returns. Fortis' continued growth in the future is the main reason for Ping An's investment in it.

Fortis is regarded as the embodiment of history and stability. In the 17 years since the establishment of Fortis Group, the average dividend rate has exceeded 6.5%. Ping An believes that this dividend rate can be sustained, then Ping An will get an ideal asset allocation in terms of revenue and time, which will also largely solve the difficult problem of matching the old policy's income. The purchase of Fortis is also based on Fortis' "bank + insurance" business model. For the mixed advantage of Fortis Banking Cross-selling, Ping An intends to quickly establish a global asset management and QDII business platform through this acquisition. Tong will also accelerate its development in China and the Asia Pacific market. A senior person from Ping An Group told the Times Weekly: "Ma's heart is very big. Buying Fujian Asian Bank and Shenzhen Commercial Bank is only the first step. Participating in international banking competition is his ultimate idea". Fortis Group' the Bank of China's model has always been regarded by Ping An as its future goal. The acquisition of Fortis is also aimed at rapidly establishing a global asset management and QDII business platform and building a global asset management platform. The domestic investment channel is simple and relatively limited. Domestic insurance funds are mainly used for bank deposits and long-term bonds, and the rate of return is much lower than that of foreign counterparts (average investment yields from 2000 to 2005 are slightly higher than 3% vs. 10% in Europe and America). The domestic insurance business model is also facing new The challenge is that Ping An hopes to carry out "institutional innovation" and seek transformation.

In addition, Ping Pui's Deputy Manager and Chief Investment Officer (CIO) John Pearce was previously a fund manager. As a professional manager, if he acquired Fu Neng, he would add a thick touch to his professional resume. This will have a very significant impact on his future career. Ma Mingzhe, chairman of Ping An, wants to make Ping An's development stronger and not to fall under the international competition. Therefore, he is eager to get out of peace and quickly gain a foothold in the international arena. Fortis has this at the time. The well-known enterprises naturally entered his field of vision and became an important acquisition target for the rapid internationalization of Ping An.

7.2.6.2 Results

With the subprime mortgage crisis in the United States sweeping across the globe, under the influence of the financial environment, due to the outbreak of the financial crisis, the stock price of Fortis began to fall. At this time, the pressure and burden caused by Fortis's rush to acquire the Dutch bank gradually emerged. The profit of the Fortis Group began to decline, the capital chain was in short supply, and its credit rating was switched to "negative."

In order to alleviate the liquidity shortage caused by the acquisition and the financial crisis, Fortis began to sell its assets. But the future looks bleak, with its shares price plummeting, even a sale of the assets can not make up the liquidity gap. On the verge of bankruptcy, the Netherlands, Belgium, and Luxembourg, these three countries forced a acquisition of Fortis's banking operations in the country, the Fortis institutions nationalized in October 2008, the three governments announced a joint Netherlands spent EUR 16.8 billion acquisition of the former Dutch Fortis Bank, the former in charge of all business. In this way, through a series of transactions and asset swaps, the interests of shareholders such as Ping An were "emptied." At this time, Ping An and the majority of small and medium-sized shareholders were aware of it, although they raised objections at the Fortis Shareholders' Meeting and also stopped selling.

But January 31, 2009, Fortis said, with BNP Paribas, the Belgian government on the sale of Fortis Insurance Belgium to arrange a series of transactions has reached a new agreement, a new protocol was adopted. Under the agreement, BNP Paribas continues to acquire a 75% stake in Fortis Belgian Bank held by the Belgian government, and the proportion of Fortis's insurance business in Belgium will be reduced from the original

100 to 10%, and the funds required will also be paid. From the original EUR 5.5 billion to EUR 550 million, in addition, BNP Paribas agreed to increase its shareholding in special purpose companies with assets of EUR 10.4 billion. After the entry into force of the agreement, BNP Paribas will receive a 75% stake in Fortis Bank Belgium and all insurance business in Belgium and 66% stake in Fortis Bank Fortis Bank Luxembourg. After some "shifting the trees," Fortis left only a EUR 10.4 billion worth of 66% of the original Fortis Bank Belgian structured products, as well as marginalized international business. For Fortis, which is on the brink of collapse, comprehensive nationalization and integration with BNP Paribas are clearly more conducive to maintaining the stability of the credit market. But for peace, this is a nightmare. After this series of operations, the Benelux three-country bank and insurance business, which is the core of the original Fortis business, has no connection with the listed company. Fortis Group was dismantled from "Yinbao Double-headed Eagle" as an insurance company whose assets only include international insurance business, part of the structured credit asset portfolio and cash. Since the core business of listed companies no longer exists, the stock price of Fortis has been hovering around one Euro since the resumption of trading. At this point, the stock price of Fortis has fallen by more than 96%, and Ping An Group has invested up to RMB 23.447 billion in investment. The remaining RMB one billion, according to its 2008 annual report, Ping An's annual provision for impairment of Fortis Investment totaled RMB 22.79 billion.

After the Fortis incident, Ping An began to realize that its internationalization level is insufficient, especially the improvement of the international governance structure, gradually stepping out of failure, steadily achieving internationalization, and gradually improving its international governance level. After gradually developed, July 8, 2013, China Ping An Insurance (Group) Co., Ltd. invested GBP 260 million to buy located landmark London financial center of the city—Lloyds Insurance company building. By the end of 2014, Ping An has set up inspection agency outlets in nearly 400 cities in 150 countries and regions, with China Reinsurance Group Co., Hannover Reinsurance Company, Allianz Reinsurance Company, Munich Reinsurance Company, and Swiss Reinsurance Company. More than 160 insurance companies and reinsurance companies at home and abroad have established business contacts.

7.3 Analysis of Transnational Governance Evolution

7.3.1 *The Issue of Control Over Transnational Governance*

Since April 2007 when the financial crisis broke out, Fortis's share price began to fall. Along with the worsening financial environment, Fortis shares continue to drop. After four times, Ping An decided to buy Fortis's shares in the secondary market for the first time at 19 euros on November 27 in 2007, and directly purchased the 4.18% stake. Then in 2008, Ping An further increased its shareholding in Fortis, reaching 4.99%. It became the first single major shareholder of Ping An, and spent a total of more than RMB 23.8 billion before and after Ping An. In June 2008, the Fortis Group in order to ensure stable cash flow announced a EUR 8.3 billion of additional time, once again safe to spend EUR 75 million to buy one of the 5%. So far, Fortis Ping An investment in this event come to an end, the cumulative Fortis investment cost of up to RMB 23.874 billion, holding 121 million shares have Fortis.

However, Ping An's investment in Fortis's investment reached as much as 23.8 billion, in order to guarantee its status as the first single major shareholder in Fortis. However, despite its shareholding ratio, it only accounts for about 5%, but Ping An is acquiring Fu. After the pass, although the proportion of shares occupied the first, there is no control over Fortis, it does not guarantee the control of Fortis, there is a risk to the management of Fortis. According to the agreement, Ping An intends to acquire 50% of the shares, but the number of shares is less than that of Fortis. It has not obtained the management rights of Fortis Investment. It is difficult to say that Ping An has truly acquired the huge asset management business of Fortis. In this way, Ping An does not directly participate in the management of Fortis, which greatly weakens the control of Fortis' investment. From another point of view, it can be said that Ping An's acquisition of Fortis has no guarantee of its own control. Ping An, as the first single major shareholder of Fortis, did not participate in the management. On the board of Fortis, there is peace. The power sent people to enter, but Zhang Zixin, the executive director of China Ping An Group and the general manager of the group, was not an executive director after joining the board of Fortis. This means that Ping An does not have any management rights to Fortis. So after Fortis suffered a crisis, it sold its core business without authorization.

In addition, in the ownership structure of Fortis, 75% of the holders of the shares are pension funds and institutional investors. The trend of this part of the equity has been actively pursued by the Belgian government, so in the business development decision of Fortis, it is easy to set aside the first single major shareholder, but China's Ping An's production is not aware of this. It does not have a clear understanding of the political interference (or government regulation, financial security) in Western countries, but thinks it is the largest single major shareholder. You can have enough right to speak. As a result, after the problem of Fortis, it took over the safety of the Belgian government to sell its core business, which undoubtedly caused a second loss to the security. So in summary, multinational companies must ensure their own control when making mergers and acquisitions, so that they are always in a favorable position.

7.3.2 Structure Defects in Transnational Governance

Ping An's own transnational governance capabilities were insufficient before investing in Belgian Fortis, and the lack of experience in overseas mergers and acquisitions can be used for reference. In addition, Fortis was considered to be a large international company at that time. Ping An rushed to invest in Fortis on a large scale in the absence of its multinational governance capabilities. The risks can be imagined. Whether it is experience or governance level, there is still a big gap in the degree of internationalization of Ping An, and its internationalization level is still in its infancy. Moreover, the experience of Ping An's existing internationalization is mostly the introduction of foreign investors into China. There is almost no experience in going out for investment and mergers and acquisitions from China. These numerous realities show that Ping An did not have the conditions for large-scale overseas mergers and acquisitions.

First of all, in terms of its own governance capabilities. On the board of Ping An, there are only two overseas directors. The degree of internationalization of its own is far from adequate. In order to acquire Fortis, in January 2007, Ma Mingzhe announced temporarily the appointment of John Pierce as vice general manager and chief investment executive (CIO) of Ping An Group. John Pierce became the leader of the Ping An International Investment Team. All of these show that the level of internationalization of Ping An's own governance structure is still insufficient. Not only that, because of its lack of governance capacity, it lacks in the decision-making of business management, which leads to management when investing. Although Ping An has done a good job in the insurance business, it is very lacking in managing the banking business. Although it can be borrowed from its major shareholder HSBC, it does not have its own experience and management team. This is very demanding. In terms of banking, it is very deadly. On the other hand China Ping An is also a capital market investment institutions, two factors show that China's Ping An investment in the Fortis Group, the route taken by and investment strategy are the continuation of the agency also are not enough, not only that, due to their own governance.

Secondly, regarding China's internationalization process, China Ping An is eager to expand abroad, but it lacks sufficient overseas M&A experience, and it has invested nearly RMB 24 billion to carry out overseas investment mergers and acquisitions. This action is obviously trade-oriented and not sufficient. Time to conduct research and evaluation, so failure is easy to cause. Ping An Group's huge investment in the acquisition of Fortis is premature for its own degree of internationalization, because in the development of Ping An, its internationalization level is relatively low, and its experience in overseas mergers and acquisitions is insufficient. In order to go out and go international, Ping An did make some preparations. For example, in 2005, Ping An Group was granted a self-owned foreign exchange fund of USD 1.75 billion and started overseas investment through Ping An Asset Management Corporation. In May 2006, China set up China Ping An Asset Management (Hong Kong) Limited in Hong Kong as China's Ping An Overseas investment management business of the main platform. But these are not enough. Ping An is one of the earliest financial institutions to introduce foreign capital, but this is not the same as going abroad to invest in M&A. Moreover, most of these so-called international operations are in Hong Kong. There is no real sense of going abroad to go to the Western capitalist countries to test the water. The lack of experience restricts the pace of internationalization of peace, and when peace goes out the first goal chosen was Fortis, which invested nearly 24 billion. This huge investment is unprecedented, so that it is easy to lose its initiative when choosing such a huge monster without any substantial experience. Losing control of it has incalculable consequences, and in fact, peace does, and the results are very painful.

7.3.3 Benefits of Host Countries of Transnational Governance Stakeholders Governance (Government-Enterprise Relations)

The failure of Ping An invest Fortis is largely due to the failure of the governance of stakeholders in the host country, which is reflected in the reality as political risk, which is also an important reason why Ping An did not get away from Fortis in time after it was hit by the financial crisis. After Fortis group was involved in the financial crisis, the financial situation of Fortis continued to deteriorate and the overall performance declined. In September 2008, the governments of Benelux countries announced to jointly contribute 11.2 billion euros to Fortis and hold 49% of the equity of Fortis bank, a subsidiary of Fortis group. Ping An was too optimistic about the government's capital injection, believing that it was a good news. However, the governments of the three countries did not carry out the capital injection as scheduled. On the contrary, they separated the business three times without the consent of the shareholders of Fortis and arbitrarily transferred the core business of Fortis group.

In this way, the intervention of the three governments increased the loss of Ping An's investment in Fortis. The Belgian government will nationalize Fortis and for this EU investors have been compensated, but Ping An did not get any compensation, and its requests to the Chinese Ministry of Commerce and Ministry of Foreign Affairs to coordinate with the Government of Belgium came to nothing. Finally Ping An filed a lawsuit against the Belgian government. Paying for a lawsuit a drop in the water compared with nearly RMB 24 billion, so it was worth pursuing.

Ping An had insufficient understanding and analysis of the management of the stakeholders of Fortis Group, and its relationship with the host government has been handled well. There was clearly a great risk. In the host country's investment operations, in addition to the large and small shareholders of Fortis Group, the host government is also an important stakeholder, and Ping An's understanding of the relationship between Fortis and government companies was asymmetric. In this way, the relationship between the target company and the host government was different from that of the host government. This made other parties assume that after the problems of Fortis, the Belgian government will definitely come out in support. Considering the interests of a foreign investor in the interests of maximizing one's own interests, there will be the result of nationalization of the Fortis Group, but Ping An has not taken effective measures to remedy it. Instead, it hopes that the three governments will not fully consider it. The impact of different stakeholders on the group's operations and the lack of awareness of political risks led to a fiasco of investment.

"Not only for insurance funds, but also for the overall overseas investment of Chinese companies, it is indeed a warning. Chinese companies must take various measures to prevent and resolve non-commercial risks when investing overseas. Risk assessment, to deal with all parties, non-governmental organizations, the media, the community, can be insured for non-commercial risks such as expropriation, government default, war, etc.; through appropriate investor nationality planning and investment path planning, to obtain higher levels of protection of investment agreements," Zhong Lun lawyer Ren Qing pointed out in an interview.

7.3.4 Transnational Governance with Asymmetric Information (Inadequate Investigation Leading to Wrong Decisions)

Ping An's investment in Fortis Group failed. From the perspective of risk, due to information asymmetry between Ping An and Fortis, and regarding the real financial and operating conditions of Fortis, Ping An did not conduct sufficient research and investigation, and thus did not realize the risk in time. Ping An did not make enough preparations at this point, ignoring the risks brought about by information asymmetry.

Fortis was a well-known international finance company, ranking top twenty in banking. Why would such a prestigious company agree to be bought by Ping An? What were some specific financial operations at Fortis that gave rise to poor results? Due to information asymmetry between Ping An and Fortis, Ping An has not conducted in-depth investigation and analysis, resulting in a series of risks. Fortis had invested in US bonds before Ping An's investment, leaving it with a huge financial deficit. Its crisis was partly due to the US subprime mortgage crisis in 2007. At the time, reputable media had made profound accusations regarding suspected financial fraudulence at Fortis Group. According to the Daily Economic News, the Belgian Evening News published "Fortis: The Great Lie" believing that Fortis's financial situation has caused the problems, not Ping An itself.

In April 2007, when the Royal Bank of Scotland and Fortis announced with the Standard Bank of Spain that they would jointly acquire ABN Amro, stocks began to fall. On September 15, when Lehman Brothers declared bankruptcy, Fortis held EUR 137 million in Lehman Brothers bonds, EUR 270 million for reverse repo transactions, and EUR seven million for CDS transactions. Fortis shares continued fall for several days thereafter. The decline, the biggest daily decline once exceeded 20%. For nine months from January 2007, Fortis shares plummeted more than 60%. Even so, in October 2007, Fortis paid EUR 240 million euros in cash and the Royal Bank of Scotland, Standard Bank of Spain jointly acquired ABN Amro. All these indicate that the financial position of Fortis is not as good as it looked on the surface. In addition, when Ping An intended to invest in Fortis, Fortis would have begun to show itself to have been affected by the subprime crisis by September 2007 when it went about buying ABN AMRO, which meant it deliberately concealed the financial impact of the subprime crisis. The report shows that as of August 2008, the group holds a total of EUR 57.15 billion in collateralized debt obligations (CDO), of which EUR 51.28 billion came from the United States. Among debt-backed bonds, about EUR 1.254 billion was at a higher risk of debt-backed bonds, but these effects were concealed by Fortis, and the real financial situation of Fortis was kept under lock and key. Other investors also concealed the truth, coupled with the existence of information asymmetry between Fortis and Ping An. The real understanding of Ping An on the actual situation about Fortis was insufficient. Ping An selected Fortis just for the bancassurance business model, but before the acquisition of Fortis group, the proportion of its business Banks gradually declined, relying more on insurance business, which Ping An did not conduct careful analysis and made no preparation in advance.

7.4 Discussions and Conclusions

Corporate transnational investment management, as an important strategic decision of a company, has a very important impact on enterprises. As the process of internationalization of Chinese enterprises continues to deepen the problem of transnational governance, it becomes more and more important. From the case of Ping An's failure to invest in Fortis, we can realize that when companies invest in transnational operations, the first thing that needs to be adjusted is their own governance structure. Governance is the most important decisive factor. Only the governance structure is well adjusted to make the right management decisions.

First of all, enterprises will enhance their transnational governance capabilities when implementing cross-border investment operations.

Governance as an important capability of the enterprise is increasingly valued by the theoretical and practical circles. In the process of going global, due to a different national environment than before, the environment of governance has undergone major changes, and the importance of transnational governance capability has also emerged. Only by improving its transnational governance capabilities can it be improved. In the face of changes in the business environment and differences in legal systems, we should respond and adjust in time to ensure that they can better achieve business and legality in the host country.

Secondly, the issue of control rights has always been a key link in corporate investment mergers and acquisitions. Therefore, enterprises must first consider this aspect when implementing investment mergers and acquisitions, and clearly understand their motivations and purposes. Is it to achieve control or to have a major impact on them? Or is it just for capital gains? Therefore, for the target company to do a good analysis of the shareholding structure, the only way is to take the initiative in the investment mergers and acquisitions.

Furthermore, the key considerations of corporate transnational operations are institutional legal and cultural differences. This difference leads to the lack of experience of the host country and the important influence of enterprises in cross-border M&A, so multinational companies are entering. The investment in the host country should be a gradual process. The theoretical community has done research on this. As early as 1977, Johanson and Vahlne proposed the theory of internationalization process. The research shows that multinational companies need to go step by step to internationalization. Most successful multinational companies go out. Following a gradual rhythm, because a company enters another country to operate, it faces many differences, and its operating environment will be very different from its original operating environment. The most important thing is the relevant knowledge and culture and system for entering the country. If you don't understand, this requires that you must carry out slow internationalization. First, you should seek an agency to export products. When you have enough understanding of the operating environment and relevant culture and legal knowledge of the country you enter, you will not make mergers and acquisitions. This will ultimately lead to local operations.

In the process of transnational investment and management, the enterprises need to face a new country, new objects, because of the natural systems, laws, and even cultural differences, inevitably there must be some information asymmetry, the companies have to make a fully detailed research and investigation and analysis on the target. Only enough information can ensure that they are in a favorable position and further guarantee their own interests. China's large-scale financial enterprises have an impulse to become bigger and stronger. They are expressed in thinking. They hope to rank hundreds or dozens of internationally and want to be the boss of the industry. However, when it comes to decision-making and action, it lacks sufficient in-depth investigations. It is easy to make a wrong estimate of the situation, leading to blind optimism. In the end, it will be a big deal. When it is not fully grasped, it will be rashly shot, which will easily cause losses and failures. In addition, in the transnational operation of enterprises, it is necessary to do a good governance relationship between stakeholders. Stakeholders can have an important impact on the local operation of enterprises, and in different countries, due to differences in their laws, systems, and cultures, they are considered. Stakeholders also have different focuses, which requires great attention when companies implement cross-border M&A investments.

CHAPTER 8

Transnational Governance of Zoomlion's Acquisition of Italian CIFA

8.1 Introduction

A state-owned enterprise founded in 1992, Zoomlion Heavy Industry Science & Technology Co., Ltd. ("Zoomlion") is mainly engaged in the development and manufacturing of high-tech equipment in the areas of engineering machinery, environmental industry and agricultural machinery. After more than 20 years of growth, the company's main products now span 11 categories, 51 product lines, and over 1200 product types. Its engineering machinery and environmental sanitation machinery both rank first in the domestic market, while its agriculturing machinery ranks among top three. Globally, the company has the most complete product chain among all engineering machinery enterprises. Zoomlion is also a multinational enterprise that continually innovates. Its two main areas of business, concrete machinery and hoisting machinery, are both among top two in the world. Zoomlion was listed on the Shenzhen Stock Exchange (2000) and the Hong Kong Stock Exchange (2010). It is the first company in the industry to be listed on A+H stocks. Zoomlion has a registered capital of RMB 7.706 billion and employs over 30,000 staff worldwide.

In this case study, Zoomlion Heavy Industry Science & Technology Co., Ltd. is called Zoomlion for short.

© The Author(s), under exclusive license to Springer Nature Singapore Pte Ltd. 2020
R. Lin et al. *Corporate Governance of Chinese Multinational Corporations*,
https://doi.org/10.1007/978-981-15-7405-4_8

Confucious ideology is deeply imbedded in Zoomlion's corporate culture. Under the slogan "sincere and modest, profound and long-standing," Zoomlion puts integrity at the core of its corporate culture. Treating staff with integrity, treating customers with integrity—integrity is the cornerstone of the company's core values, moral standards, performance standards, and corporate character. "Not competing within China, but competing for China," says Zoomlion's Chairman Zhan Chunxin, "for a multinational company that originated from an R&D institution, this is the mission of the 'national team'." Zoomlion always takes on the country's mission as its own corporate development mission. It believes firmly in building a future together with the builders (construction industry). It believes in the vision that innovation in science and technology helps build a beautiful China. It takes on the responsibility as a leader in the healthy and sustainable development of the industry. Zoomlion has always taken as its core goal and mission the global marketing of a national brand. It believes in innovation empowering China and aims to build a world-class machinery manufacturing enterprise.

According to Zoomlion's 2007 financial report (prior to acquiring CIFA), Changsha Construction Machinery Research Institute LLC ("CMI") was the biggest shareholder of Zoomlion. Zoomlion originated from CMI, who was its controlling shareholder holding state-owned (SOE) legal person share (41.8614%). The next biggest shareholder, Good Excel Group Limited Company, holds 11.1479% of shares. The remaining top ten shareholders of Zoomlion are investment funds controlled by banks, each holding a relatively small and similar percentage of shares. Details are shown in Table 8.1. In 2007, Zoomlion's shareholding structure was highly concentrated, with the two biggest shareholders holding over 50% of total shares. And with CMI holding 30% more than Good Excel Group Limited Company, Zoomlion's shareholding structure was one with absolute dominance by state ownership (Fig. 8.1).

Zoomlion spearheaded the integration of overseas resources initiated by a Chinese engineering machinery enterprise. It leverages capital to integrate quality assets globally, thereby achieving fast expansion and building a global manufacturing, sales, and services network. In 2001, Zoomlion acquired 80% of shares of the British company Powermole International. This was the very first successful acquisition of a world-renowned enterprise by a Chinese company since China's entry into WTO. In the few years that followed, Zoomlion grew steadily through

Table 8.1 Zoomlion's top ten shareholders at the end of 2007

Name of shareholder	*Nature of shareholder*	*Shareholding percentage (%)*
Changsha Construction Machinery Research Institute LLC ("CMI")	State-owned legal person	41.8614
Good Excel Group Limited Company	Overseas legal person	11.1479
Industrial and Commercial Bank of China—Hua'an Medium and Small Market Growth Stock Security Investment Fund	Other	1.7817
Morgan Stanley and Co. International PLC	Other	1.6254
Industrial and Commercial Bank of China—Yifangda Value Growth Mixed Security Investment Fund	Other	1.3612
Bank of Communications—Hua'an Strategic Selection Stock Security Investment Fund	Other	1.3083
China Construction Bank—Huaxia Advantage Growth Stock Security Investment Fund	Other	1.0595
China Construction Bank—Yinhua—Dow Jones 88 Selection Security Investment Fund	Other	1.0519
Agricultural Bank of China—Bank of Communications Shroders Selection Stock Security Investment Fund	Other	1.0519
China Construction Bank—Great Wall Brand Selection Stock Security Investment Fund	Other	0.9973

Source 2007 Zoomlion annual report

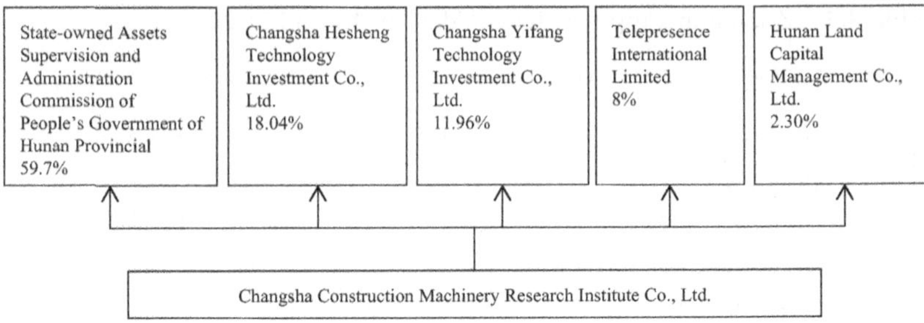

Fig. 8.1 CMI's equity structure in 2007 (*Note* Hunan Land Capital Management Co., Ltd. was renamed to Hunan Development Group, in 2009)

a series of acquisitions: in 2007, Zoomlion acquired CMI with RMB 215 million; in March 2008, Zoomlion acquired 100% of shares of Shaanxi Xinhuanggong Machinery with RMB 34 million; in April 2008, Zoomlion acquired the project assets of Dahan Automobile Company Limited; in June 2008, Zoomlion spent RMB 154 million to acquire the major state-owned operational assets of Hunan Automobile Axle Factory, equivalent to 82.73% of the latter's shares, held at the time by Hunan Province State-owned Assets Supervision and Administration Commission; in July 2008, Zoomlion purchased 82% of Huatai Heavy Industry's shares with RMB 119 million; on September 28 of the same year, Zoomlion, partnering with Hony Capital, Goldman Sachs and Mandarin Capital, completed the 100% acquisition of Italy's CIFA, with Zoomlion controlling 60% of total shares.

8.2 Transnational Governance Evolution

8.2.1 Zoomlion's Acquisition of CIFA

On September 28, 2008, Zoomlion, together with Hony Capital, Goldman Sachs and Mandarin Capital, signed the acquisition agreement with CIFA in Changsha, thereby officially completing the full acquisition of CIFA with EUR 271 million in cash. Of the shareholders, Zoomlion holds a controlling share of 60%. After the acquisition, Zoomlion became the biggest company globally in terms of market share in the concrete machinery market.

8.2.1.1 Background

In order to lessen the competitive pressure it was facing in the domestic market, and in light of its strategic target to become bigger and stronger and to enter global top ten, Zoomlion was looking to broaden its global reach.

- From 2001 to 2007, Zoomlion's share of the domestic concrete machinery market was only 25%, ranking it at number three in the engineering machinery industry in China, far below the nearly 70% enjoyed by Sany Heavy Industry, the then number one in the market. ZHAN Chunxin, Zoomlion's Chairman, expressed Zoomlion's ambition to become, within five to 10 years' time, number one in engineering machinery industry in China and top ten globally. Zoomlion's business scale at the time was far from sufficient to support this strategic target of becoming global top ten. The company needed to enter a market with great growth capacity and large enough scale. It needed to enter the international market.
- Zoomlion's main products are closely related to its fixed assets investment. Whether or not its domestic fixed assets investment can continually create market demand determined Zoomlion's sales volume and the company's continuous growth. Between 2003 and 2007, Zoomlion's domestic fixed assets investment was still increasing, albeit at an increasingly slower pace. Affected by this, the growth rate of domestic demand for engineering machinery was slowing down as well. In the meantime, however, China's major engineering machinery manufacturers were investing substantially in technological improvements. Production capacity in engineering machinery was expanding swiftly. With the typically one- to two-year-delay in the utilization of production capacity, competition in the domestic market for engineering machinery would become rather fierce. ZHAN Chunxin thought that, as the domestic engineering machinery market gradually neared saturation, diversification would become a crucial channel to relieve the pressure of the potential overload in productivity. Huge amounts of production capacity needed to be utilized by going international. Therefore, only by stepping out onto the international scene, by actively participating in overseas markets and pursuing acquisition overseas, can Zoomlion relieve the competitive pressure faced domestically and sustain

fast growth, thereby truly building a bigger and stronger Zoomlion. To this end, Zoomlion's leadership decided to broaden its horizon overseas through a series of cross-border mergers and acquisitions, integrating resources, gaining technology and market, and expanding sales network globally.

Zoomlion had other strong incentives to acquire CIFA: to enhance its technological stance, improve operational and management capabilities as well as expand sales network.

- Better technology: Zoomlion was the domestic market leader in the manufacturing of concrete machinery. Compared with a leading company in Europe however, it still had a long way to go in terms of product stability, technological advantage, and manufacturing process. Especially in brand recognition and customer recognition, Zoomlion was far behind its European peers. CIFA's product line boasts a wide range of product types, its overall technology more advanced than that in the domestic market. CIFA also had more advanced product design philosophy, production technology, and manufacturing process. Therefore, Zoomlion would gain through successfully acquiring CIFA the latter's technology, which brings significant advances in improving Zoomlion's own product performance and manufacturing process for its concrete machinery production.
- Better operations and management: Chinese manufacturing firms had been studying the technology and management models in advanced countries, for a long time. Nevertheless, just visiting and touring alone were no longer sufficient to learn. Successfully acquiring CIFA would enable Zoomlion to move CIFA's manufacturing center to China, thereby allowing Zoomlion to learn CIFA's production and operations, and creating opportunities for the managers of Zoomlion and CIFA to communicate with each other, thus helping to improve the operational and management capabilities of Zoomlion.
- Bigger sales network: in 2007 Zoomlion's export accounted for 12% of its total sales. Going forward, overseas sales would become a major player in delivering future business growth. That said, many problems surfaced as Zoomlion expanded its overseas operations,

for example, its highly underdeveloped overseas sales network and services system. CIFA had very strong market presence in Eastern Europe and Russia with high market shares as well as complete sales network and services system. Successfully acquiring CIFA would enable Zoomlion to enter Eastern European and Russian markets in a relatively short period of time. These are markets with strong potential for development. The acquisition would save a huge amount of money otherwise spent in developing these markets. The resources saved could be put into efforts to enter other markets.

8.2.1.2 Compagnia Italiana Forme Acciaio (CIFA)

Back in 2006, CIFA's majority of stocks was already purchased by Magenta, a private equity investment fund in Italy. In October 2007, both Magenta, CIFA's then biggest shareholder who needed cash to pay up some debts, and two other shareholding families publicly expressed interests to sell CIFA. CIFA's shareholding structure prior to the 2008 acquisition by Zoomlion is shown in Table 8.2.

CIFA's products and brand had a solid reputation in the concrete industry. Before the Zoomlion acquisition, it already boasted strong profitability among peer concrete machinery manufacturers in the European and US market. In Italy it ranked first in the manufacturing of concrete transportation pumps, concrete pumping trucks, and concrete mixer trucks. Among European and US manufacturers it ranked second in

Table 8.2 CIFA's equity structure prior to the 2008 acquisition

Name of shareholder	*Shareholding percentage (%)*	*Nature of shareholder*
Magenta SGR S.p.A.	50.72	Italian investment fund
Fadore S.ar.l.	10.0	Luxembourg company
Intesa Sanpanlo S.p.A.	10.0	Italian bank
Plurifid S.p.A.	27.5	The five shareholders before the 2006 acquisition, included Immobiliare BA.STE.Do.S.r.l. (7.18%), Immobiliare Novanta S.r.l. (7.18%), Pasquale Di Iorio (2.98%) and Simone Rafael Emdin (2.98%)
Maurizio Ferrari	1.78	Natural person, Chairman of CIFA

the production of concrete pumping machinery and third in the production of concrete mixer trucks. Headquartered in Senago, near Milan, CIFA has a long history in the manufacturing of engineering machinery. Globally it was the number three manufacturer in concrete machinery, closely following Putzmeister and Schwing, both German companies.

In the early years since its founding, CIFA engaged primarily in the production and sales of steel molding for reinforced concrete. In the late 1950s, CIFA expanded its product line to include concrete pumping trucks, concrete mixer trucks, and concrete transportation equipment. In the mid-1980s, CIFA developed and produced the world's first concrete spraying mechanical hand, which quickly became CIFA's star product. In July 2006 Magenta, an Italian private equity investment fund, joined hands with other investors and acquired 72.5% of CIFA's shares, becoming CIFA's principal shareholder.

In 2007, CIFA's two main products, concrete mixer trucks and concrete pumping trucks, respectively commanded 80 and 70% of market share in Italy, 23 and 20% in Western Europe, 15 and 20% in Eastern Europe, and 10 and 8% in the Middle East. CIFA had seven production bases in Italy. Its products were sold through 58 independent distributors in over 70 countries as well as 24 agencies in Italy. Its sales network covered almost all of Western Europe, Eastern Europe, the Middle East and Northern African countries. CIFA also had its distribution networks in Australia, United States, Mexico, and other South American countries.

CIFA's main products included concrete pumping trucks, concrete transportation pumps, stationary concrete pumps, concrete mixer trucks, concrete placing machinery, stabilizing mixers and equipment, concrete spraying trucks and concrete construction molding. Of these products, concrete transportation pumps, concrete pumping trucks and concrete mixer trucks were CIFA's biggest selling products, shipped mainly to Europe, Africa, and the Middle East. CIFA was one of the earliest engineering machinery manufacturers to enter the China market. While commanding over 80% of the concrete machinery market in Europe, CIFA did not deliver as outstanding performance in China. This was mainly because in China, concrete machinery industry started quite early. The concrete machinery produced by the two industry leaders Zoomlion and Sany were comparable in product performance with those from foreign peers, while their prices were 15–20% lower. Zoomlion and Sany together accounted for about 80% of the concrete machinery market in China. Foreign peers had no apparent competitive advantage here.

8.2.1.3 Process

Zoomlion's acquisition of CIFA began in the second half of 2007 and was concluded on September 28, 2008 with the signing of Acquisition and Handover Agreement. See Table 8.3 for detailed schedule.

The acquisition was carried out through setting up of a series of special purpose corporations, a common practice in the international market. Figure 8.2 shows the detailed process. First, a fully owned subsidiary was set up in Hong Kong, Zoomlion Heavy Industry (Hong Kong) Holdings Company, which in turn set up a Hong Kong based special purpose corporation, a fully owned subsidiary called Zoomlion Heavy Industry Overseas Investment Management (Hong Kong) Company Limited ("Hong Kong Special Purpose Company A"). This Hong Kong Special Purpose Company A, together with Zoomlion's co-investors in the acquisition, then jointly set up another Hong Kong based special purpose corporation ("Hong Kong Special Purpose Company B"), of which Hong Kong Special Purpose Company A owns 60%, while co-investors Hony Capital, Goldman Sachs, and Mandarin Fund own 18.04, 12.92, and 9.04%, respectively.

Table 8.3 Zoomlion's acquisition of CIFA—milestones

Time	*Milestone*
Second half of 2007	CIFA's principal shareholder Magenta Equity Investment Fund decided to dissolve CIFA and sell its CIFA shares
November 2007	CIFA officially kickstarted the public tendering process for its sale
End of January 2008	Zoomlion submitted the first round of proposal (non-binding)
February 2008	Zoomlion began due diligence investigation on CIFA
March 2008	Zoomlion submitted the second round of proposal (bining). Negotiations began
June 2008	Zoomlion and CIFA signed the final Purchasing and Selling Agreement and submitted it to Shareholder's Meeting for approval; Agreement subsequently submitted to regulatory bodies for approval and record: China Securities Regulatory Commission, National Development and Reform Commission, Ministry of Commerce, State Administration of Foreign Exchange and the provincial State-owned Assets Supervision and Administration Commission
September 28, 2008	Zoomlion signed the official Acquisition and Handover Agreement with CIFA, concluding the transaction

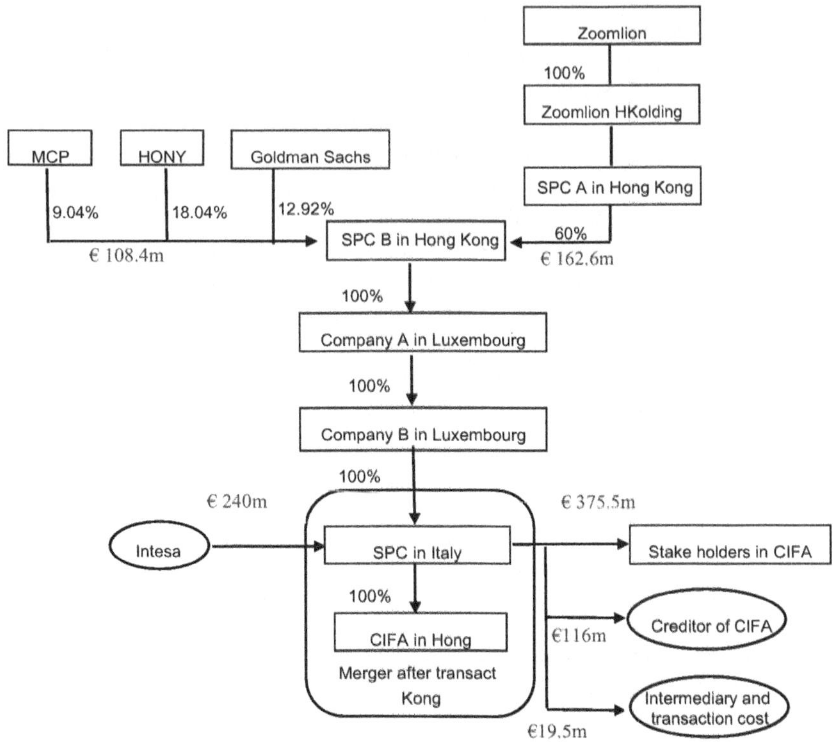

Fig. 8.2 Zoomlion's acquisition of CIFA—transaction process and structure (*Notes* MCP: Mandarin Capital Partners; HONY: Hony Capital; SPC: Special Purpose Company)

Hong Kong Special Purpose Company B went on to set up in Luxembourg a fully owned subsidiary, Luxembourg Company A, which subsequently set up another fully owned subsidiary, Luxembourg Company B. This Luxembourg Company B established in Italy a fully owned special purpose corporation, CIFA Worldwide S.P.A, to acquire 100% of CIFA's shares. After the acquisition was completed, the Italy based special purpose corporation and CIFA would combine and merge.

In this transaction, in order to acquire 100% of CIFA's shares, Zoomlion and co-investors offered a total of EUR 271 million (approximately RMB 1.727 billion), of which Zoomlion paid a consideration of EUR

162.6 million. Of the total payment of EUR 271 million, EUR 251.5 million went to the target company for the purchase of shares, while EUR 19.5 million were associated expenses. According to the Purchasing and Selling Agreement, at the time of the transaction the target company was valued at EUR 375.5 million. This consisted of the EUR 251.5 million paid by Zoomlion and co-investors, as well as EUR 124 million, which was CIFA's own long-term debt.

A Luxembourg holding company is not just one form of corporation. Usually there is public limited liability company (SA), private limited liability company (SARL) and coorporative company (SC). A Luxembourg holding company can be categorized into either a 1929 tax-free holding company or a 1990 SOPARFI trading and holding company.

A 1990 SOPARFI trading and holding company enjoys the benefits of the participation tax exemption policy of Luxembourg, with extensive tax exemption on dividends, capital gains, and liquidation distribution. However, for its profits from trading, normal income tax rates apply. Further, a 1990 SOPARFI trading and holding company can enjoy the treaty preventing double taxing which Luxembourg signed with many other European countries.

Luxembourg had fully executed EU's parent–subsidiary company guidelines, guidelines on interests and royalty fees as well as guidelines on merger. According to the above guidelines, when a 1990 SOPARFI trading and holding company's participating rights is no less than 10% of the subsidiary's shares, the company may enjoy tax-free interests, dividends, and royalty fees. Therefore, the Italian special purpose company did not need to pay tax on the interests, dividends, and royalty fees paid to its shareholders.

According to the Prevention of Double Taxing on Income and Capital and the Prevention of Tax Evasion Agreement signed on November 2, 2007 between Hong Kong and Luxembourg, when a Luxembourg company pays dividends, profits, or royalty to a Hong Kong company, the Luxembourg company is exempt from withholding income tax or can enjoy relatively low rate of withholding income tax. In the meantime, Hong Kong tax law is based on the source location principle, i.e., tax is levied only on business operated locally, not otherwise.

On top of that, both Luxembourg and Hong Kong have zero limit on foreign currency flow, allowing money to freely flow in and out. This also prompted Zoomlion to adopt the holding corporation model (Table 8.4).

Table 8.4 Tax rate comparison as per laws in Luxembourg, Hong Kong, and HK–Luxembourg prevention of double taxation agreement

	Dividend	*Interest*	*Royalty*
Italy–China agreed rate	10%	10%	10%
Italy–Luxembourg agreed rate	0/15%	0/10%	0/10%
Luxembourg–China agreed rate	5/10%	0	0
HK–Luxembourg agreed rate	0/10%	0	3%
Hong Kong rate if no agreement	0	0	4.95%

The idea behind setting up special purpose companies in Hong Kong, Luxembourg, and Italy was that, Chinese enterprises, especially enterprises with state-ownership background, when acquiring European companies, typically need to face review from and supervision by the acquiree's home country as well as the EU. The need then arises to design an acquiring entity with an eye for reducing supervision to a certain extent. Meanwhile, an appropriate structure needs to be set up to minimize the withholding income tax due to withholding income tax regulations in various countries. As per tax agreement between China and Italy, the withholding income tax rate may be as high as 30% when capital or earnings leave Italy. Through entities setup in appropriate third-party countries, such withholding income tax can be reduced or eliminated.

The setup of the above SPVs (Special Purpose Vehicles, or special purpose institutions/companies) capitalized on Italy and Luxembourg both being EU countries and therefore mutually withholding income tax free, as well as Luxembourg and Hong Kong having bilateral tax agreement which exempts capital flowing from Luxembourg to Hong Kong from paying withholding income tax. As long as the money does not flow back to China, there won't be income tax levied domestically either. This setup effectively resolved the problems of acquiree's home country supervision, withholding income tax reduction as well as supervision of overseas money flow.

After the acquisition in 2008, Zoomlion and its partnering investment fund companies together controlled all of CIFA's shares: Zoomlion 60%, Mandarin Fund 9.04%, Hony Capital 18.04%, and Goldman Sachs 12.92%.

Zoomlion and the three co-investors, Hony Capital, Mandarin Fund, and Goldman Sachs agreed that, three years after the completion of acquisition, Zoomlion could exercise at any time its right to buy co-investors' options in the holding company using cash or Zoomlion shares, unless the exit value of the co-investor in question is lower than its initial investment. Each co-investor may also sell to Zoomlion all of its shares in the holding company, provided that a four-month notice is given in writing. When exercising such rights to buy or to sell, the recipient of the options may choose to accept payment in cash or in Zoomlion's shares, but not a combination of both.

End of 2012, through its fully owned subsidiary Zoomlion Overseas Investment Management Company, Zoomlion acquired the other 40.68% of Zoomlion CIFA (H.K) Holdings Co. Ltd. (Hong Kong CIFA)'s shares heretofore held by the co-investors (Hony Capital, Mandarin Fund and Goldman Sachs) with USD 235.7 million (approx. RMB 1467 billion), thus achieving full ownership of CIFA. Hony Capital, Mandarin Fund, and Goldman Sachs fully withdrew from CIFA with a total return of RMB 300 million. Zoomlion thereof became 100% shareholder of CIFA.

Looking at Zoomlion's annual reports, Zoomlion's operational income grew 49% year-on-year in the first half of 2009; by the first half of 2010, this growth rate had reached 74%. For its concrete machinery products, the growth rates during the same periods were 62 and 99%, respectively. In other words, after acquisition, the concrete machinery business enjoyed much higher growth rates than the company as a whole, indicating that this acquisition greatly boosted Zoomlion's sales domestically, enabling Zoomlion to become the market leader in the domestic concrete machinery industry. Through this acquisition, Zoomlion integrated global resources from both sides effectively, combining strengths in product development, production process innovation, strategic purchasing, and market distribution. As a result, Zoomlion further strengthened its competitive advantage. CIFA enjoyed further improvement in its brand recognition and customer loyalty in Europe, the Gulf, North Africa, and South America. Zoomlion also saw its brand recognition and reputation climbing in Europe and Asia. Zoomlion's share of the global concrete machinery market improved markedly.

8.3 Analysis of Transnational Governance Evolution

8.3.1 *Stakeholder Governance During Zoomlion's Acquisition of CIFA*

8.3.1.1 *Zoomlion's Co-investors*

This acquisition entailed huge differences between the target country and the home country in terms of corporate culture, laws and regulations, accounting and tax rules as well as union dynamics. In light of these vast differences and associated risks, Zoomlion teamed up with three co-investors, Hony Capital, Mandarin Fund, and Goldman Sachs. To Zoomlion, there are further considerations in introducing these three investors. These partners are more familiar with the rules of the western business world. Together, the partners can form a cultural buffer zone for the acquisition and integration as well as afford a certain credibility for the acquisition.

The primary co-investor, Hony Capital, was a member of the Lenovo Holdings group of companies. Founded in 2003, it specializes in equity investment and business management. It was initiated by Lenovo Holdings, Hony's principal investor. Other investors of Hony Capital include world-renowned investment institutions from United States, Europe, Asia, and Japan. Currently Hony manages a total of around RMB 20 billion of assets. Hony Capital was one of the earliest professional investment corporations in China, with a focus on domestic investment. It is also the actual controlling shareholder of Good Excel Group Limited Company, Zoomlion's second biggest shareholder. Hony Capital is a shareholder of Zoomlion. A Chinese fund management company with a global vision, Hony has a most thorough understanding of Zoomlion's corporate development strategy, the value of the CIFA acquisition as well as the synergy that can be harnessed as a result of the acquisition. Hony Capital was the principal investor in this acquisition. Hony knew Zoomlion well through years of working together and could lend full support to the future integration of Zoomlion and CIFA.

Goldman Sachs and Mandarin Fund also played significant roles in the acquisition. Founded in 2007, Mandarin Fund is the biggest and the most important of private equity investment funds focusing on business between China and Italy. Its three major investors are China Development Bank, the Export-Import Bank of China, and Intesa Sanpaolo S.p.A,

Italy's second largest bank. Mandarin Fund has an abundance of experience in cross-border acquisitions. Specializing in investment management, it bridges the cultural exchange between Chinese and Italian enterprises. Mandarin Fund's mission is to assist Chinese companies in their globalization effort, expanding their distribution channels, building global brands and technical expertise in Europe. Mandarin Fund also helps European companies with their investment and development in China. The founding partners of Mandarin Fund have over 25 years of experience in private equity and finance. They are a local Italian team who understand the Chinese market environment. Goldman Sachs is a pure international fund experienced in investment globally.

The options agreement between Zoomlion and co-investors on stock ownership essentially allowed Zoomlion three years to integrate in exchange for 40% of the shares. The two culturally very different enterprises could take their time to merge and integrate in an orderly fashion. This agreement meant that the risks of this transaction were limited to a maximum of EUR 160 million while the benefits could be enjoyed by all of Zoomlion. The arrangement fully mobilized and utilized various resources, with unlimited prospects for actual gains. Zoomlion did not guarantee a minimum return to co-investors' investment, meaning that co-investors were under pressure, and therefore motivated, to work together with Zoomlion toward a successful CIFA post acquisition. In the meantime, in order to maximize the gain when reselling the CIFA shares back to Zoomlion, Goldman Sachs and Hony Capital would also be motivated to help Zoomlion management with post acquisition integration. The principle of shared risks and shared benefits ensured that Zoomlion and the co-investors' interests were well aligned.

8.3.1.2 Government Bodies

Zoomlion's top-notch Mergers and Acquisitions lawyers knew the overseas acquisition regulations well. To them the "road pass" from the National Development and Reform Commission was key to getting the acquisition approved at home. Zoomlion had obtained the "road pass" by the third time it met with CIFA in Changsha. The so-called road pass is an approval letter from the National Development and Reform Commission. It is the document that qualifies a company for acquisition. In fact, Sany was also eyeing CIFA. Sany went to Italy for a presentation and their offer in the first round was much higher than Zoomlion's offer.

Sany attributed their failure to eventually land the deal to the fact that "Zoomlion is a state-owned enterprise, the government is on their side."

8.4 Impact of the Evolution of Transnational Governance

8.4.1 *Changes to CIFA's Corporate Structure*

8.4.1.1 Board of Directors

As specified in Zoomlion's Letter of Intent for the acquisition, CIFA's Board of Directors post acquisition consisted of seven members, four appointed by Zoomlion and three by the co-investors.

Mr. Maurizio Ferrari, CIFA's then Chairman and CEO, continued his role as CIFA's Chairman until 2009, when he became Vice President of Zoomlion in charge of global acquisition. Mr. Stefano Marcon took over as Chairman of CIFA and was also appointed the Deputy General Manager of Zoomlion Concrete Machinery Global Management Corporation.

In Italy there is a system called internal audit system. The internal auditor looks after finance as well as corporate compliance and participates in each and every important event in the company, acting as the most crucial internal controller. There are two Internal Auditors in CIFA, both appointed by Mandarin Fund. Both had many years of experience working with Mandarin Fund.

8.4.1.2 Senior Management

For this acquisition, Zoomlion wanted to make sure it's working together with CIFA. After the acquisition, Zoomlion approached the two companies' integration accordingly: the original CIFA management team was all retained with complete trust; not one manager was sent from the Chinese side; apart from the CFO who was appointed by Zoomlion, every senior director continued to be locally employed; CIFA kept its existing operations team; the acquired business was managed locally.

"An acquired company should be trusted yet not indulged. People who do not align with the company's future directions, people who are detrimental to resources integration, people who do not follow rules, these people must be replaced," said Zhan Chunxin.

Pre-acquisition, the majority of people on the CIFA management team had "parachuted" straight from Magenta Fund. This type of fund management company typically has a group of so-called golden muscles managers, whose very task is to go into the acquired enterprise, cut costs, make numbers look good, and then resell high at the right time. Heading the team of parachuted managers at CIFA was Maurizio Ferrari, formerly a banker by profession.

"Maurizio Ferrari is very rich. His mind was not in managing the company," said HE Wenjin. Maurizio Ferrari was VIP at all the world's famous opera houses. He usually booked his tickets one to two years in advance. Nothing would make him miss his opera; everything gave way. Obviously he was not the person who could lead CIFA out of the financial crisis. After Zoomlion acquired CIFA, Maurizio Ferrari himself also had no intention of staying on. He recommended Stefano Marcon to take over as Chairman, which Zoomlion accepted. Business did not improve, however, after the new Chairman took over.

After the acquisition, Zoomlion would send an audit team at the end of each year to conduct a full audit of CIFA's operational decisions and financial status that year. Based on the audit results, Zoomlion would then suggest changes and a schedule for the changes. This was to ensure CIFA and Zoomlion could communicate under the same management context. End of 2010, Liu Jie from Zoomlion's Internal Audit who did the job that year found that CIFA staff were quite unhappy with Stefano Marcon. Mr. Marcon's background was in finance; he did not have any experience steering a manufacturing enterprise. Further, when communicating with Zoomlion, he liked to departmentalize, holding on tightly to his territory and hindering integration progress.

In July 2011, Zhan Chunxin, Qiu Zhongwei, Zhang Jianguo, and Chen Peiliang went to Milan to have the CEO replaced. Zhen told Stefano that the co-investors were not satisfied with CIFA's performance and hoped that he would leave his position. In the end the Board of Directors voted in favor of this proposal. Davide Cipolla, the then head of Technology at CIFA, was recommended by CIFA's management team to take over as new CEO.

Davide Cipolla joined CIFA after graduating in 1992. He started in the R&D department and had been with CIFA for 20 years. Before the Zoomlion acquisition, he was in charge of CIFA's supply chain, including purchasing, technical design, and production. After the acquisition, as well as overseeing CIFA's R&D, he was also responsible for the technical support for Zoomlion products and the technical integration of Zoomlion and CIFA. Just like Davide Cipolla, most people at Zoomlion also came from technical background. Communication was more smooth between technical people. GAO Zhen, a director at Mandarin Fund, also noted that during the integration process, the module overseen by Davide Cipolla was the fastest and most effective.

8.4.2 Stakeholder Governance—CIFA Staff

In August 2008 after the acquisition, Zhan Chunxin made a promise on the Italian Newspaper Il Sole 24 Ore: no laying off staff, no closing down factories. In the second half of 2008, much to ZHAN's surprise, CEO Maurizio Ferrari started laying off staff. Zhan asked him why. To which he replied, "it was acquisition time when you promised not to cut people. Now the financial crisis is here, of course I will cut people!" Zhan was very happy, "see, he was justifying it for me. From their standpoint, they also had to protect their interest, protect the company, because if the company is over, they would lose their jobs."

According to local media, CIFA had employee strikes before; there was also times of tension between union and management. Davide Cipolla mentioned that Zoomlion had never demanded that CIFA lower its human capital cost. As a business leader however, he needed to make decisions according to economic situation. CIFA had a total of around six hundred/seven hundred employees. In 2010, when market was low and there wasn't that much work to do, CIFA applied for coverage under the social security fund for one and a half years. (In Europe, when a company runs into trouble, the social security fund can provide subsidy. For example, workers work for only fourr hours in an eight-hour working day and social security would cover the remaining four hours.) CIFA's policy at the time was that employees take turns to apply for this social security and everyone shares the economic consequences.

When attacked by media about this policy, Davide Cipolla wrote the whole staff a public letter, in which he argued that the union was not looking at the problem from the whole company's standpoint. He revisited all the major milestones CIFA had achieved over the years and pleased for everyone to stick together during difficult times. "Staff also knew that this kind of strike could only lead to crisis, not real change and further development for the company," said Davide Cipolla. The letter was received with understanding from most staff. The union in the end also remarked that the protest was not directed specifically toward the company, but the Italian government who was "doing nothing" under the economic crisis.

He Wenjin shared that, at that time, China was right in the middle of the four trillion RMB Stimulus; Zoomlion was doing exceptionally well in the domestic market and was therefore able to support CIFA in its time of need. Under the joint effort by the Zoomlion and CIFA management, CIFA made it through this crisis.

8.4.3 Governance of the Zoomlion–CIFA Relationship

> "We had never thought of appropriating CIFA's technology to Zoomlion, shutting down CIFA's factories and then using that technology plus China's low production cost to produce more competitive products." "We continue to develop the CIFA brand as a high-end brand, while our products are middle market products infused with advanced technology."—Chen Peiliang

8.4.3.1 The 1/2/3 Promise

Of all the phases of an acquisition, the integration period after an acquisition stands the highest risk of failure. Starting the day the acquisition was finalized (September 28, 2008), Zoomlion promosed CIFA thus: Zoomlion and CIFA were "1" family, "2" brands with "3" basic principles, that CIFA's management team and staff were to be retained, that CIFA was to continue its independent operation, and that resources sharing was to be achieved across the global market.

8.4.3.2 Personnel Integration

Zoomlion would abide by local laws and regulations; would treat CIFA's staff as its own staff; would acquire, not cut. All CIFA staff's salary and benefits package would stay unchanged.

8.4.3.3 The Three-Person Group

To strengthen communication with the staff, Zhan Chunxin, CIFA's Chairman Maurizio Ferrari and Hony Capital's President Zhao Linghuan formed a three-person group after the acquisition to discuss periodically CIFA's development strategies. Messages were communicated by Maurizio Ferrari to CIFA's staff, ensuring smooth communication between staff and management. Observing the principle of openness and transparency, the three-person group also communicated with management as well as with staff through meetings and other means to inform people of CIFA's current status and future business adjustments.

8.4.3.4 Synergy

Zoomlion set up a "synergy office" consisting of several workstreams: marketing, technology, purchasing, and overall coordination. For every aspect of the integration, there was conversation going on between the Chinese side and the Italian side.

A "factory within a factory" was set up in Changsha. An exact replica of the Italian "working island" way of production, this would model CIFA's operations and management in Italy. The "factory within a factory" facilitated Zoomlion employees' observation and study, while making it possible to produce CIFA's unique product parts locally. Employees of different colored skins now worked on the same working platform, reflecting Zoomlion's progress in going international.

To speed up integration, Zhan Chunxin started with himself. He also asked all on Zoomlion's senior management team to join him in an intensive English course in order to help them communicate with foreign peers. He reminded himself and his staff to "do as the Romans do when in Rome," jumping out of the box of the Chinese mindset and thinking from their standpoint, which would in turn help them respect CIFA's culture, philosophy, and values.

8.4.3.5 Reverse Feeding the Parent Company

Benefiting from the high-speed growth in the China market, Zoomlion was able to support CIFA with fighting the financial crisis. CIFA in turn could repay or back-feed Zoomlion with its technology, helping Zoomlion achieve greater success in the China and world market. This is sharing of benefits and resources. After CIFA shared its technology with Zoomlion, Zoomlion shared its market with CIFA. Not only was income from overseas sales shared between Zoomlion and CIFA, profits from sales in China of the new products born out of the Zoomlion–CIFA technical integration, such as F3 generation products, were also shared by Zoomlion and CIFA.

In light of the increasing need for long-boom pumping trucks in the China market, CIFA had already relocated production capabilities for some high-end products to China to roll out products suitable for the

China market. This satisfied the need in China market while also solving CIFA's excess productivity problem. "'CIFA supply chain - China base' is managed by a team sent from CIFA. Production is carried out in China, utilizing the low production cost. The parts needed are then sent back to Italy. Zoomlion benefits from acquiring the advanced technology and opening up global markets and channels with the CIFA brand. This is resources sharing."

As technology and market sharing unfolded, synergy from the acquisition gradually came to be felt. In sales, the market was made up of two main geographical zones: CIFA sales team was in charge of the Middle East, North Africa, and Europe where CIFA had strong presence, while Zoomlion sales team was in charge of Southeast Asia, South Asia, South America as well as Southern and Middle Africa. In purchasing, Zoomlion was now able to secure supply of key parts by sourcing from international suppliers who worked regularly with CIFA, thereby lowering purchasing cost.

After acquiring CIFA, Zoomlion further perfected its global network, building a solid global supply chain. Zoomlion rolled out a series of new products incorporating CIFA's Carbotech boom technology, pumping trucks with carbon fiber booms. At 80 metres/101 metres, pumping trucks with the world's longest carbon fiber booms were successfully launched and employed in construction. After integration with Zoomlion, CIFA was able to minimize the impact of the global financial crisis through the synergy of resources sharing, complementary strengths, and accurate targeting. CIFA was among the first in US/European peers to come out of the trough. In the past three years, CIFA's operational profit grew at a compound rate of 200%, with its operational performance achieving historical new high, presenting to the world a healthy new image with sustainable growth capabilities.

The CICC report at the end of 2012 showed that CIFA crossed the line from loss to profit making as of 2012. Its scale and profitability had both recovered to the level before the financial crisis. Meanwhile, in terms of technology transfer, OEM (Original Equipment Manufacturer) for high-end products and product chain integration, the CIFA-Zoomlion synergy was starting to pay off. As next steps, further resources integration is anticipated.

8.4.4 Changes in Zoomlion's Governance Structure

As a typical state-owned enterprise, Zoomlion's acquisition of CIFA was an important milestone in SOE reform as well as in the internationalization of Chinese enterprises. On December 15, 2008, Changsha Construction Machinery Research Institute LLC ("CMI"), Zoomlion's then biggest shareholder, held a board meeting, during which these proposals and reports were submitted and approved: Liquidation Audit Report, Liquidation Report, Employment Proposal for CMI Staff following Liquidation. The shareholders of CMI also agreed to the decisions of this board meeting. Liquidation Registration Notice was subsequently issued by Hunan Province Industry and Business Administration Bureau on December 31, 2008 green-lighting CMI's liquidation.

CMI's liquidation marked the completion of Zoomlion's reform starting in 2006. After CMI's liquidation, Changsha Hesheng and Changsha Yifang as companies founded by people from CMI management and staff would now become Zoomlion's direct shareholders. This marked the finale of management incentive initiative. Among Zoomlion's top ten shareholders as per Zoomlion's 2009 financial report, State-owned Assets Supervision and Administration Commission, Hunan Province People's Government was the state-owned legal person shareholder with the highest shares (24.99%), while Changsha Hesheng and Changsha Yifang became, respectively, the third largest and the fourth largest shareholders.

In fact, as early as 2007, Zoomlion had already purchased the majority of CMI's assets, rendering CMI a shell company with little reason to continue its existence. CMI's liquidation was therefore only natural as the next development. With Zoomlion's listing on the Hong Kong Stock Exchange in 2010, Zoomlion had embarked full speed toward the international market. Looking at the 2012 financial report, Zoomlion's shareholding landscape at that point looked very different from that just before the CIFA acquisition. The top ten shareholders now had relatively even weight, with no one dominant party controlling the shareholding scene. Detailed structure is shown in Table 8.5.

Zoomlion, who originated from an R&D institute, was now diverse in ownership. State-owned shares now accounted for less than 17% of total shares. "Zoomlion's personnel appointment is now entirely up to shareholders. When the state-owned shareholder raises his hand, it's only 17%.

Table 8.5 Zoomlion's top ten shareholders as at the end of 2012

Name of shareholder	*Nature of shareholder*	*Shareholding percentage (%)*
HKSCC NOMINEES LIMITED	Overseas legal person	18.53
State-owned Assets Supervision and Administration Commission, People's Government of Hunan Province	State-owned legal person	16.19
Changsha Hesheng Science and Technology Investment Company Limited	Domestic non-state-owned legal person	5.02
GOOD EXCEL GROUP LIMITED	Overseas legal person	4.72
Zhizhen International Company Limited	Overseas legal person	2.19
Changsha Yifang Science and Technology Investment Company Limited	Domestic non-state-owned legal person	2.12
Hony Investment Industry Phase 1 Fund (Tianjin) (limited partner)	Domestic non-state-owned legal person	2.07
CCB Investment LLC	State-owned legal person	1.96
Bank of China-Yifangda Shenzhen Stock Exchange 100 Trading Open Index Security Investment Fund	Domestic non-state-owned legal person	0.86
Anhui Province Investment Group Holdings Company Limited	State-owned legal person	0.73

Source Zoomlion 2012 annual report

We have really instituted a modern enterprise mechanism," said Zhan Chunxin.

8.5 Discussion

As a typical state-owned enterprise, Zoomlion's acquisition of CIFA was an important milestone in SOE enterprise reform as well as in the internationalization of Chinese enterprises. From the acquisition of CIFA in 2008, to liquidation CM, Zoomlion's then biggest shareholder at the end pf 2008, to IPO on the Hong Kong Stock Exchange in 2010. By 2012, there was no longer one dominant shareholder among Zoomlion's top ten shareholders, while shareholding by SOE legal person was reduced from 41.8614% in 2007 to 18.88% in 2012.

In the fourth quarter of 2011, there were drastic changes in the competitive landscape in China's engineering machinery industry. Zoomlion's market share in the domestic concrete machinery sector reached 48%, while Sany Heavy Industry's share went down to 42%. Currently, Zoomlion's production and manufacturing bases are spread all over the world, with subsidiaries in over 40 countries plus marketing and sales as well as R&D branches, serving and creating values for customers in over 80 countries across 6 continents. Zoomlion is now a company with a fully fledged sales network and strong services network across the globe. In 2013, Zoomlion made major adjustment to its development strategy, shifting from focusing only on engineering machinery to developing five main modules at the same time: engineering machinery, agricultural machinery, environmental protection, heavy lifting trucks as well as finance. It was listed number 779 on the 2013 Forbes Global Top 800 Enterprises. In the field of engineering machinery, Zoomlion is now the world's number thirteen enterprise and China's number three company.[1]

As its overseas sales steadily grew over the years, Zoomlion's overseas development strategy was implemented step by step, its overseas market network unfolding in full speed. Zoomlion continued to swiftly plan its product chain building, including overseas M&A and base construction. Global resources were continuously gathering at Zoomlion. ZHAN Chunxin said that apart from building a comprehensive network, financial leasing became another important pathway in Zoomlion's overseas expansion. In February 2009, Zoomlion Heavy Industry Financial Leasing (China) Company Limited was founded, with qualifications as both a foreign-owned financial leasing company and a domestic financial leasing pilot enterprise. These independent companies together form Zoomlion's financial leasing global services network, providing high-value-add financial services globally for sales of its concrete machinery, engineering heavy lifting machinery, architectural heavy lifting machinery, and other Zoomlion products. Going forward, Zoomlion's overseas business would work

[1] https://news.d1cm.com/20190506104302.shtml.

closely with its financial leasing services, establishing financial leasing platforms wherever there is Zoomlion products to provide product-related services. Within the next few years, sales of financial leasing products are to become 50% of all Zoomlion's income from sales.

As Zoomlion moves forward in its overseas expansion, as well as looking at overseas M&A projects, Zoomlion also started to try building its production facilities and R&D center overseas. This unveiled Zoomlion's unique internationalization strategy, "Integrate and Innovate - Global Market." At the core of this strategy is the building of a globalized purchasing system suited to Zoomlion's product evolution and market evolution through integration of resources globally. Zoomlion aims to possess its own core technology and intellectual property, to train operations and management talents with a global vision, and to form its very own competitive advantage. By acquiring enterprises both domestically and abroad, it integrates businesses of various divisions, developing overseas agencies, setting up financial leasing, and implementing mergers and acquisitions. It will build a globalized manufacturing, sales and after-sales service system. It will commit to localized after-sales service and parts supply. It has drawn a sales and services market strategy suited to local markets. It will blend into local culture. It will gradually form the design-produce-sell three-in-one complete operational cycle. It will boost its corporate team spirit to build a truly global brand, ultimately becoming a company with genuinely global operations.

Entering the Zoomlion official website and opening up Market Services, you will see a map of global network. On this map is Zoomlion's global reach across five continents. Along with Zoomlion's internationalization, its overseas business has now covered over 60 countries and regions, with its products in the Middle East, South America, Africa, Southeast Asia, Russia as well as in higher end market such as Europe, United States, and Australia. Zoomlion actively participates in major international conventions and exhibitions including Bauma in Germany, Conexpo in United States, Intermat in France, CTT in Russia, and BIGS in the Middle East. Right now, the company is proactively pushing through its strategic transformation into a high-end equipment manufacturing enterprise spanning the fields of engineering machinery, environmental industry, agricultural machinery, and financial services.

8.6 Summary and Conclusions

There are three interesting aspects in the Zoomlion's acquisition of CIFA that are worth noting for Chinese enterprises planning to conduct transnational acquisitions:

- Selection of co-investors during cross-border transaction: Zoomlion teamed up with Hony Capital, Mandarin Fund, and Goldman Sachs for its acquisition of CIFA, fully utilizing these three investment companies' familiarity with the rules of the western business world to form a "cultural bufferzone" for the integration, while also affording a kind of vouch for credibility on behalf of Zoomlion.
- Setting up of special purpose corporations during cross-border acquisition: Zoomlion set up several special purpose companies in Hong Kong, Luxembourg, and Italy specifically for this acquisition, making full use of bilateral trade agreements between different locations to minimize withholding income tax.
- Trusting but not indulging the acquired company after the acquisition: immediately after the acquisition, with the exception of CFO, all on the original CIFA senior management were retained, giving CIFA complete autonomy in its operations. The three changes of CEO after, from the banker Maurizio Ferrari to the financier Stefano Marcon, and then to the technical expert Davide Cipolla, was to improve CIFA's management efficiency, which helps move forward the integration with Zoomlion.

CHAPTER 9

Transnational Governance of SANY Heavy Industry's Acquisition of Putzmeister

9.1 Introduction

Sany Group has as its corporate vision, "creating a first-class enterprise, creating first-class talents, and making a first-class contributions" and has built the well-known Sany brand. Sany Heavy Industry Co., Ltd. was founded by Sany Group in 1994 as a private enterprise. Since its inception, the company has grown at an average annual rate of over 50%. It has developed into the largest construction machinery manufacturer in China and the fifth largest in the world, as well as the largest concrete machinery manufacturer in China. Among the company's main products, pump trucks, trailer pumps, excavators, crawler cranes, rotary drilling rigs, have all become number one products in their categories in China. The market share for concrete pump trucks, concrete pump, and full hydraulic roller is not only first in China, but also first globally.

With the mission statement, "Quality Changes the World," Sany gives over 5–7% of its sales revenue every year to research and development, and is committed to upgrading products to world-class standards. Director Liang Wengen, chairman of Sany Heavy Industry, has maintained the entrepreneurial spirit of "Industry to Serve the Country" since his company was founded, and has dreamed of revitalizing national industry

In this case study, Sany Heavy Industry Co., Ltd. is called Sany for short.

© The Author(s), under exclusive license to Springer Nature Singapore Pte Ltd. 2020
R. Lin et al. *Corporate Governance of Chinese Multinational Corporations*,
https://doi.org/10.1007/978-981-15-7405-4_9

and offering a world-class brand to the Chinese nation. After entering the twenty-first century, with the leap of the country's overall strength, the Sany entrepreneurial team realized that in order to make "made in China" become "created in China" and Sany become a world brand, the companies needed to go global market, compete with other world-class companies and go overseas to "breaking new ground." From then on, the move toward internationalization began. In 2012, Sany Heavy Industry acquired concrete machinery maker Putzmeister, a Germany company with a prestigious history in the sector. This changed the competitive landscape of the entire industry and forced Sany to make real its internationalization goal.

According to the company's financial report data in 2011, the company's largest shareholder is Sany Group Co., Ltd. (56.38%), which is the controlling shareholder of Sany Heavy Industry. Liang Wengen is the largest shareholder of natural persons, and the specific shareholding ratio of other shareholders is shown in Table 9.1.

Although Sany Group Co., Ltd. holds 56.38% of the shares of Sany Heavy Industry and is the controlling shareholder of the company, Liang Wengen personally holds 58.24% of the shares of Sany Group Co., Ltd., which is equivalent to indirectly holding 32.83% of the shares of Sany Heavy Industry. In addition, Mr. Liang Wengen directly holds 3.77% of the shares of Sany Heavy Industry, so he holds a total of 36.60% of the shares of Sany Heavy Industry, which is the actual controller of Sany Heavy Industry. The property rights and control relationship between the company and the actual controller are shown in Fig. 9.1 (December 31, 2012).

9.2 Transnational Governance Evolution

9.2.1 *Sany Heavy Industry's Acquisition of Putzmeister*

9.2.1.1 *Background*

Sany Heavy Industry and Zoomlion are major competitors in the domestic machinery sector. Sany Heavy Industry had nearly 60% of the pump business in 2007 and Zoomlion had about 40%. Pumps are the core business of both companies, and they engaged in something of a "pump battle" for CIFA. In 2008, Zoomlion joined handed with Hony Capital, Goldman Sachs, and Mandolin Fund to implement a wholly owned acquisition of Italian CIFA, the third largest global concrete machinery

Table 9.1 Shareholdings of the top ten shareholders of Sany Heavy Industry Co., Ltd. (end of 2011)

Shareholder name	*Shareholder nature*	*Shareholding ratio (%)*
Sany Group Co., Ltd.	Domestic non-state legal person	56.38
Liang Wengen	Natural person	3.77
Bosera Value Growth Securities Investment Fund	Other	1.40
Tang Xiuguo	Natural person	0.62
Xiang Wenbo	Natural person	0.57
Mao Zhongwu	Natural person	0.57
Zhai Chun	Natural person	0.49
China Construction Bank—Bosera Value Growth No. 2 Securities Investment Fund	Other	0.49
China Construction Bank—Fuguo Tianbo Innovation Theme Stock Securities Investment Fund	Other	0.42
Industrial and Commercial Bank of China—SSE 50 Trading Open Index Securities Investment Fund	Other	0.42

Source Sany Heavy Industry annual report 2011

Fig. 9.1 Property right and control relationship between Sany Heavy Industry Co., Ltd. and the actual controller

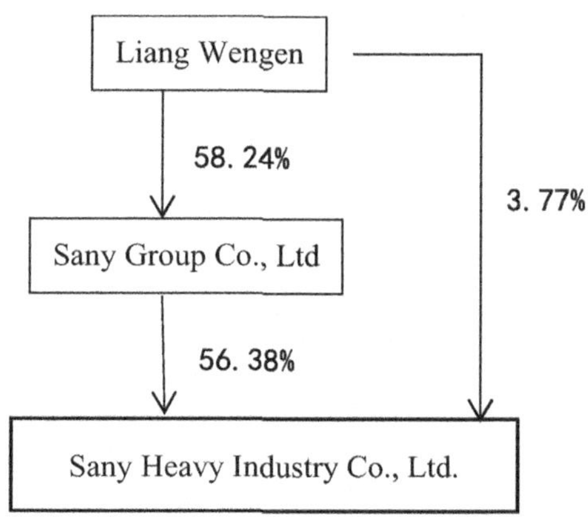

industry, for a total of EUR 511 million, acquiring a top brand and crucial technologies. This since opened the door to the European market (this merger has been elaborated and analyzed in the Zoomlion acquisition of CIFA cross-border governance case). Sany Heavy Industry, which had always been the second in the industry, was overtaken by Zoomlion in size, which further spurred on its determination to grow at any cost.

9.2.1.2 *Motivation for Overseas Expansion*

The external environment has provided very favorable support for the merger of Sany Heavy Industry, but the most fundamental reason for Sany Heavy Industry's internationalization is the company's own development appeal. Internationalization differs from localization and transnational operations. The business in each country is relatively independent, and different strategies are developed for each country's business. Quite the contrary, the internationalization strategy represents a global mindset that creates synergies and economies of scale between countries through internationalization strategies, increases strategic flexibility, and leverages market information, business activities and productivity.

The management of Sany Heavy Industry starts from a strategic height and spares no expense to acquire at an absolute advantage. The purpose is to shorten the internationalization process of Sany Heavy Industry and to possess all the technologies and patents of Putzmeister and its global base and sales system. Sany Heavy Industry will use Putzmeister's marketing system to reduce production costs from the global procurement chain. Sany's expanding global distribution network will provide Putzmeister with a significant competitive advantage and guarantee its growth prospects. At the same time, Sany will also acquire technology-leading "Made in Germany" products and innovations to enrich its products. The combination will also gain a strong overseas distribution and service network.

9.2.1.3 *Enhancing Brand Awareness*

One of the goals of Sany Heavy Industry's acquisition of Putzmeister is to achieve its brand strategy: to obtain Putzmeister's global marketing, maintenance, and service network platform through mergers and acquisitions, which can help Sany Heavy Industry greatly accelerate the internationalization process; Putzmeister's patented technology and core technology strengthen Sany Heavy Industry's R&D strength and talent technology advantages, and comprehensively improve product technology; to open up the upstream and downstream industry chain and further expand the share of construction machinery in the international market. The integrated resources of these three aspects will help Sany Heavy Industry to build the first brand of global concrete machinery manufacturers.

Founded in 1958, Putzmeister is one of the world's most well-known construction machinery manufacturers. It is the world's first brand of concrete machinery, the technical leader of concrete machinery in the international market, and the group company of global sales network. In the field of concrete pump truck manufacturing, it has long been a world leader. Putzmeister is headquartered near Stuttgart, Germany, and has subsidiaries in more than a dozen countries around the world. The company was originally owned by two companies under the name of its founder, Karl Schlecht, with Karl Schlecht Gemeinnützige Stiftung holding 99% and Karl Schlecht Familienstiftung holding 1%. Putzmeister's global market share is as high as 40% for a long time, and more than 90% of its sales revenue comes from overseas, and overseas markets are spread over more than 110 countries around the world. As of 2011, the company had more than 3000 employees and achieved sales of 570 million euros.

In some of China's national key projects (such as the Yellow River Xiaolangdi Project, Ertan Hydropower Project) and Asia's first Shanghai Oriental Pearl TV Tower, Putzmeister has played an irreplaceable role. Putzmeister has been creating and maintaining many world records in the field of hydraulic piston pumps: displacement, delivery distance, lift, product range, diversity of materials that can be transported, and more. In the world's tallest building, the Burj Khalifa in the UAE, Putzmeister has set the latest world record for concrete transport at height—603 meters.

Because it has been focused on market segments, Putzmeister has maintained a steady but not fast pace of development for more than half a century. With the growth of the global economy, the company entered the high growth period in 2003 and reached peak annual sales of EUR one billion in 2007. Then came the financial crisis and the double attack from Chinese competitors. Sales revenue and profits began to decline. In 2010, the annual sales revenue decreased to EUR 550 million and net profits to EUR 1.5 million.

In 2003, Putzmeister entered the high growth period with global economic growth. In 2007, sales revenue reached an all-time high of one billion euros. In 2008, affected by the global financial crisis and Chinese competitors, the sales and profits of Putzmeister began to decline. In 2008, the revenue was 450 million Euros, and the first loss in the 50 years since the company was founded. After 2008, under the influence of the global debt crisis, the performance of Putzmeister rebounded slowly. According to public data, as of December 31, 2010, the net worth of Putzmeister was EUR 177 million. In 2010, annual sales brought in EUR 550 million and net profit of EUR 1.5 million. In 2011, the annual sales income was 560 million euros and net profit of six million euros. In 2011, revenue was only 57% of the highest point in history, and net profit was about one-tenth of the highest point in history. Putzmeister CEO, 80-year-old Karl Schlecht, explained why he wants to sell up: First, because his children had little interest in inheriting the company, and second, in recent years, the innovative ability in Chinese construction machinery companies such as Sany Heavy Industry, has been improved, which squeezed the profit margins of international brands such as Putzmeister. The more deadly cause was the European debt crisis. In collective operations, such companies are weak and their market prospects are bleak.

(1) *The company's own business is not going well*

There is no doubt that the 2008 financial crisis hit Putzmeister is the most important reason why he can't wait to sell himself. In 2007, Putzmeister has just experienced the most brilliant year in the 50 years since its establishment, with an annual operating income of one billion euros. In 2008, the income was only 4.5 billion euros, and the company's first loss in 50 years. After 2008, under the influence of the global debt crisis, the performance of Putzmeister rebounded slowly to their highest point of 57%, and net profits of about one-tenth. At this point, Putzmeister's cash flow issues began to emerge, so Sany can fulfil the acquisition with 324 million euros, in cash. Putzmeister had no choice but to lay off employees. In addition, as the global heavy machinery industry shifted focus eastward, Chinese companies such as Sany Heavy Industry, Xugong, and Zoomlion exerted strong pressure on Putzmeister, which has made it impossible to break through the 10% market share in China. In order to continue the life of the company, Schlecht decided to sell.

Table 9.2 Ownership structure of Putzmeister before the acquisition

Shareholder name	*Shareholding ratio (%)*
Karl Schlecht Stiftung	99
Karl Schlecht Familienstiftung	1
Total	100

(2) *No Family-owned business successors*

In 1998, when Putzmeister was celebrating its 40th anniversary, the founder, Mr. Schlecht, officially announced his withdrawal from the day-to-day management of the company and was appointed as the chairman of the board of supervisors. Moreover, Schlecht donated his shares to a charitable foundation named after him. Putzmeister's shareholding structure was that about 99% of the shares are owned by family foundation and Schlecht himself, and less than 1% by Mrs. Schlecht. After being hit by the financial crisis, investment funds holding a majority stake in Putzmeister also suffered heavy losses, causing problems in their own operations, which put considerable pressure on all parties. As the founder of the company, Schlecht has shifted his energy to charity and ethics research. He did not want to continue to struggle in the business world in his twilight years. Schlecht's children did not intend to continue operating in the concrete machinery industry, which made the founder sad. Selling up was his only choice, that is, the proceeds of the sale can be invested in charity, and the Chinese construction machinery giants could use their capital flow to revitalize the company.

The shareholding structure of Putzmeister in Germany is shown in Table 9.2.

9.2.2 *The Process of Sany Heavy Industry's Acquisition of Putzmeister*

Sany established a German subsidiary before the merger, so the acquisition process would be relatively simple. Therefore, the entire acquisition period for Putzmeister began on December 20, 2011, when Norbert Scheuch, CEO of Putzmeister, visited Liang Wengen in Changsha. On January 21, 2012, the two parties signed a contract in Germany. It lasted only 33 days (as shown in Table 9.3). On January 31, 2012, Sany Heavy Industry announced that its subsidiary, Sany Germany Co., Ltd.

Table 9.3 Timetable of Sany Heavy Industry's acquisition of Putzmeister

Time	*Event*
December 20, 2011	Putzmeister visited Sany Heavy Industry and expressed his willingness to participate in the bidding
December 21, 2011	Putzmeister visited to Zoomlion, which also expressed interest in participating in bidding
December 22, 2011	Zoomlion submitted an official document to the Hunan Provincial Development and Reform Commission for declaration [1]
December 23, 2011	Putzmeister issued a formal invitation letter to all qualified companies
December 30, 2011	Zoomlion received approval of the National Development and Reform Commission for the acquisition of Putzmeister
January 2012	Liang Wengen, chairman of Sany Heavy Industry, sent a letter of intent to Karl Schlecht, the founder of Putzmeister. The letter expressed his willingness to cooperate and then set a preliminary intention for the acquisition
January 21, 2012	Sany Heavy Industry signed a contract with Putzmeister in Germany
January 26, 2012	Putzmeister issued a letter of termination to all bidders
January 31, 2012	Sany Heavy Industry announced that it would jointly invest EUR 600 million in buying 100% equity of Putzmeister with CITIC Industrial Investment Fund

(hereinafter referred to as Sany Germany) will jointly invest in CITIC Industrial Investment Fund (Hong Kong) Consulting Co., Ltd. (hereinafter referred to as CITIC Fund). The company acquired a 100% stake in Putzmeister in Germany for 360 million euros, of which 30% was acquired by Sany Germany and 324 million euros was invested. With such a short period of time, Liang Wengen has made huge investments in the former mergers and acquisitions. In recent years, it was indeed a rare "flash purchase" in cross-border mergers and acquisitions of Chinese companies. The transaction was the first merger of a famous German mid-sized company and a Chinese company. The founder of Putzmeister called it "a Sino-German acquisition test case."

Sany Heavy Industry did not have a smooth ride during the short-term mergers and acquisitions. On the second day of Putzmeister's visit to Sany Heavy Industry's bidding offer, Sany Heavy Industry's competitor, Zoomlion, also received a bidding offer, after which Putzmeister said that he would hold a bidding meeting to decide on the final partner. On December 30, 2011, Zoomlion received the "Road of the National Development and Reform Commission" on the acquisition of Putzmeister before Sany Heavy Industry. Zoomlion, which has a state-owned background, has become a roadblock for Sany's acquisition of Putzmeister. Afterwards, Putzmeister was impressed by the constant pursuit and sincerity of Sany Heavy Industry, canceled the original bidding meeting and announced cooperation with Sany Heavy Industry. However, after this, Zhonglian Heavy Industry accused Sany of acting first and reporting afterwards, and did not get approval to take the lead in mergers and acquisitions.

On January 21, 2012, Sany Germany Co., Ltd., an overseas subsidiary of Sany Heavy Industry Co., Ltd., together with CITIC Industrial Investment Fund (Hong Kong) Consulting Co., Ltd., signed the Transfer and Purchase Agreement with two shareholders of Putzmeister. And the purchase agreement, confirms that Sany Germany Co., Ltd. will jointly acquire a 100% stake in Putzmeister with CITIC Fund, of which 90% is acquired by Sany Germany and 10% by CITIC Fund. Sany Germany's capital contribution is EUR 324 million (equivalent to RMB 2.654 billion). The shareholding structure of Putzmeister changed a lot before and after the merger. The German family business owned by two natural persons has evolved into an overseas subsidiary of a Chinese multinational company with a 90% stake in China Sany Heavy Industry (see Table 9.4).

At 11:00 a.m. local time on April 17, 2012 in Germany, Sany Heavy Industry Co., Ltd. ("SANY") and Germany Putzmeister Holdings Co., Ltd. ("PutzMeister") held a press conference in Aichtal, Germany, officially announced the completion of the acquisition. This meant that Putzmeister officially became a member company of a Chinese construction machinery company.

The entire acquisition period of Sany's acquisition of Putzmeister was calculated from December 20, 2011 when Norbert Scheuch visited Liang Wengen in Changsha. On January 21, 2012, the two parties signed a

Table 9.4 Ownership structure of the German Putzmeister Company after the acquisition

Shareholder name	*Shareholding ratio (%)*
Sany Germany Co., Ltd. (Sany Heavy Industry Subsidiary)	90
CITIC PE Advisors (Hong Kong) Limited	10
Total	100

contract in Germany, just 33 later. On January 30, Sany Heavy Industry released an "Announcement on the Resolutions of the 16th Meeting of the Fourth Board of Directors of Sany Heavy Industry," which showed that the board of directors of the company reviewed and approved the "Proposal on the Acquisition of the German Putzmeister Company." Sany Heavy Industry announced that the company's holding subsidiary, Sany Germany Co., Ltd. and CITIC Industrial Investment Fund (Hong Kong) Consulting Co., Ltd. signed the Transfer and Purchase Agreement with Putzmeister on January 20, 2012. The acquisition was a joint venture between Sany Germany and CITIC Industrial Investment Fund (Hong Kong) Consultancy Co., Ltd. to jointly invest 360 million euros to acquire 100% of the German Putzmeister. Among them, Sany Germany acquired 90% of its shares, and CITIC Fund acquired 10%. According to the interim announcement in the 2012 annual report of Sany Heavy Industry Co., Ltd., in the acquisition, Sany Heavy Industry contributed a total of 324 million euros (equivalent to RMB 2.654 billion), and the German Putzmeister became the work of Sany Heavy Industry Holding subsidiaries as shown in Table 9.5.

9.3 Analysis of Transnational Governance Evolution

9.3.1 *Stakeholder Governance of Multinational Corporation Parent Company (SANY Heavy Industry)*

9.3.1.1 *Chinese Government*

In order to regulate the management of overseas investment projects, the National Development and Reform Commission issued the "Roads" regulations in 2009, requiring overseas investment projects to obtain foreign M&A licenses. In April 2012, around the German Putzmeister Company, the battle between Sany Heavy Industry and Zoomlion was once again ignited. As a result, Zoomlion took the lead in getting the "roads" of the National Development and Reform Commission, but Sany Heavy Industry negotiated with Putzmeister and finally reached a deal. Zoomlion began to attack Sany for making an illegal acquisition without the "roads."

Table 9.5 Interim announcement of Sany Heavy Industry's acquisition of Putzmeister

Counterparty or ultimate controller	*Acquired stock assets*	*Purchase date*	*Asset purchase price*	*Net profit contributed to listed companies from the date of acquisition to the end of the year (in thousands)*	*Whether it is a connected transaction*	*Asset purchase pricing principle*	*Whether the property rights of the assets involved have been transferred*	*Whether the bond debt involved has been transferred*	*The net profit contributed by the asset to the listed company as a percentage of total profit*	*Connection relation*
Sany Heavy Industry	Putzmeister	2012 April	324 million EUR	83,160	no	Protocol pricing	Yes	Yes	1.46%	Holding subsidiary

Source Sany Heavy Industry 2012 annual report

9.3.1.2 Putzmeister Employees

At the same time, learned that the company is about to be merged by Chinese companies, the hundreds of employees of Putzmeister are strongly opposed to the merger and acquisition of the company due to the impact of layoffs and corporate changes, and hold demonstrations in front of the General Department of Putzmeister. Meanwhile, the employees protest that they have been kept in the dark, and there is no knowledge of the acquisition of Putzmeister by Sany Heavy Industry. These episodes have cast a shadow over Sany Heavy Industry's acquisition of Putzmeister, Germany. The president of Sany advised Wenbo not to lay off employees after the merger, and gave certain compensation to the Putzmeister staff.

9.3.1.3 Financial Institutions

The Hunan Branch of the China Development Bank and the Hunan Branch of the Export-Import Bank of China issued a US$290 million M&A loan to the Sany Group on April 19, 2012 to support the Sany M&A Putzmeister to complete the fund delivery. The success of Sany cannot be separated from the support of the government.

The acquisition of Sany Heavy Industry also relies on PE company, CITIC Industrial Investment Fund Management Co., Ltd. The company is professionally engaged in investment business by China's CITIC Group Corporation and CITIC Securities Co., Ltd. In mergers and acquisitions, fund companies can play a role in the merger. The preliminary negotiations for investment and mergers and acquisitions are very complicated. There is a professional organization in which to carry out the merger, which can play a very important role in promoting and coordinating, CITIC Industrial Investment Fund played an important role in the long and complicated acquisition negotiation process.

9.4 Impact of Transnational Governance Evolution

Sany hopes that China's construction machinery enterprises will go abroad and compete in a global scale. They can turn their former strongest competitors into their "allies" and defend their foreign enemies. Although the cross-border M&A of the snake swallow has been successful and has become a milestone in the internationalization of the "Sany," Aichtal, the headquarters of Putzmeister, Germany, has become the new headquarters of "Sany" overseas concrete machinery, but after the merger Subsidiary corporate governance and parent–subsidiary relationship governance are still urgent issues to be resolved.

9.4.1 Putzmeister's Governance Structure Adjustment

Entrusted to the current CEO of Putzmeister: Norbert Scheuch as the sole authority, the board of directors only sent a senior assistant to the chairman of the board as a special liaison. Through a high degree of trust in the original CEO and executive team, Sany achieved a smooth transition of management to avoid cultural traps in integration.

Maintaining an independent management team: In order to maintain the stable operation of Putzmeister in the short term, Sany Heavy Industry announced that Putzmeister will remain an independent brand and have its own management team in Sany Heavy Industry.

9.4.2 Sany Heavy Industry Governance Structure Adjustment

9.4.2.1 Internationalization of Sany Heavy Industry Executives

Invited Putzmeister personnel as the executives of Sany Heavy Industry can improve the international team of Sany Heavy Industry. With the rapid expansion of overseas distribution and the acceleration of internationalization, Sany needs to be familiar with the investment environment and legal environment of each country. At the same time as overseas rapid expansion, Sany has always insisted on the localization of overseas executives.

- Upgraded Putzmeister's then CEO, Norbert Scheuch, to Senior Vice President of Sany Heavy Industry, and entered the board of directors to become the executive director of Sany Heavy Industry. On the evening of September 10, 2013, Sany Heavy Industry announced that Norbert Scheuch, senior vice president of the company, resigned for personal reasons. At the same time, he also resigned as CEO of Putzmeister Holdings Co., Ltd. The CEO of Putzmeister is served by Dr. Gerald Karch, Senior Vice President of the company.
- In July 2013, the Managing Director and Chief Technology Officer of the Putzmeister Group (since in 2008) Dr. Gerald Karch (male, born in 1964) began to serve as Vice President of Sany and Putzmeister Holdings Managing Director and Chief Technology Officer of the company (2013-07-10 to 2016-06-27).

9.4.2.2 Board of Directors and Board of Supervisors of Sany Heavy Industry

The parent company's 2011 board of directors consisted of 12 members, including one chairman, one vice-chairman and president, three executive directors, two non-executive directors and five independent directors. The 2011 Supervisory Committee consisted of three members, including one chairman of the Board of Supervisors and two supervisors. The specific board members and supervisory board members are shown in Table 9.6.

From the list of members of the 2011 Board of Directors and the Board of Supervisors of Sany Heavy Industry, we can see that there are two non-executive directors and five independent directors in the board of directors. The number is excellent, and it can play a good role of supervision and checks and balances on the management of Sany. In addition to the former Senior Vice President Zhao Xiangzhang becoming a non-executive director, the board of directors and other members of the board of supervisors did not change.

Table 9.6 Composition of the members of the 2011 board of directors and board of supervisors of Sany Heavy Industry Co., Ltd.—before the merger

Name	*Position*
Liang Wengen	Chairman
Xiang Wenbo	Vice-Chairman and President
Yi Xiaogang	Executive Director
Huang Jianlong	Executive Director
Zhao Xiangzhang	Executive Director
Tang Guoxiu	Non-Executive Director
Liang Zhongzhong	Non-Executive Director
Wang Shanping	Independent Non-Executive Director
Jiang Minsheng	Independent Non-Executive Director
Xie Zhihua	Independent Non-Executive Director
Feng Baoshan	Independent Non-Executive Director
Yan Jun	Independent Non-Executive Director
Yu Xian	Chairman of the Supervisory Committee
Yao Chuanda	Supervisor
Li Daocheng	Supervisor

It can be seen that for Sany Heavy Industry, after the acquisition of Putzmeister in 2012, the company's shareholding structure, board of directors, and supervisory board were basically stable, and no major changes occurred.

9.4.2.3 Sany Heavy Industry—Qiandu Beijing

After 2013, Sany Group implemented dual headquarters, that is, some departments and employees of the decision-making level, some in Changsha and some in Beijing. If "double headquarters" becomes the norm, it means that Beijing becomes the "nominal headquarters" where the registration is located, and Changsha is still the "actual headquarters." Including Liang Wengen, Xiang Wenbo, deputy general manager of Sany Heavy Industry Finance Headquarters Liu Hua, and director of Sany Group Yuan Jinhua, in an interview with the media, revealed that the main reason for the headquarters to move to Beijing is to avoid vicious competition, accelerate the promotion of the company, and realize the industrial ideals of "quality changes the world" and "achieve a world-class Sany." Some people in the industry have also suggested that Sany moved to Beijing to gain political resources. On the one hand, through the migration of the registered place, Sany can realize the convenience of internationalization and examination and approval, get rid of the restrictions of Zhonglian Heavy Industry on local government resources, and at the same time obtain some preferential policies of Zhongguancun Science & Technology Zone; on the other hand, maintain Changsha's "actual headquarters" status is conducive to business decision-making.

On November 21, 2012, Liang Wengen suddenly announced the decision of Sany to move to Beijing at the internal breakfast meeting. The functional headquarters of the Sany Group and the core business units will all be moved to Changping district of Beijing. The Changsha base will only be retained as a concrete pump division.

On November 30, 2012, Sany Heavy Industry issued a "clarification announcement" stating that the relocation of Sany Headquarters has nothing to do with the investment environment of Hunan Province, and the development of Sany fully proves that Hunan has a good investment environment. Changsha has everything to build the world; prerequisites for a class enterprise.

On December 4, 2012, at the staff meeting of the Sany Function Headquarters, Liang Wengen announced the move to Beijing. Liang Wengen has repeatedly stressed that the relocation of Sany is not for a bad investment environment in Hunan, nor is it that the Hunan government leaders favor its competitors. It is not the so-called anger at not being elected to the Committee, Sany's relocation is just to avoid the viciousness between his peers, while seek for better development.

9.4.3 *The Relationship Between Sany Heavy Industry and Putzmeister Governance*

The acquisition of three pairs of Putzmeister allows the two sides to complement each other by docking their respective superior resources. (1) At present, Sany has provided Putzmeister with many Chinese-made parts to reduce the production cost of Putzmeister for higher profits. (2) Putzmeister's manufacturing technology is mostly versatile. Sany acquires know-how through mergers and acquisitions. The manufacturing technology pays attention to edges, holes, seams, welding, and surfaces.

> We want to enter the Sany system, because Sany has a lot of resources in the manufacturing industry, and there are many suppliers in China. We have to eliminate potential competitors, we have done this, and have achieved the merger.—Norbert Scheuch

Putzmeister is a typical market segment that specializes in concrete pumping equipment. The leadership is convinced that this is the reason for his success and that he should stick to the strategic direction in the future. Sany Heavy Industry emphasizes customer orientation and gives customers a total solution. Therefore, there are differences in their business strategy. Sany repeatedly invited them, asked them, and even persuaded them to do concrete mixing, for the devices are highly correlated. After a long period of communication, Sany finally convinced them, agreed to increase the product line of concrete mixer trucks, and acquired the third largest mixer truck company in Germany. Later, all the data on the number of employees employed, performance, and profits increased. Now, we do more component synergy and synergy in the global market.

Driven by domestic transportation network construction, water conservancy and hydropower development projects, various key infrastructure projects have entered the intensive construction phase. Putzmeister's high-quality concrete construction equipment will be used in tunnels, slope protection, diversion tunnels, etc. Concrete spraying equipment will play an important role in ensuring the quality of the project, improving construction efficiency, and ensuring construction safety. Sany and Putzmeister (Spain) organized special training in sales and service of concrete injection equipment, and sales director of Putzmeister (Spain), MAX as training instructor, from product performance, use, construction technology, after-sales service skills, and other aspects, conducted comprehensive and meticulous training on marketing personnel at all levels in the country.

Contradictions and conflicts: (1) Market share: The biggest contradiction between Putzmeister and Sany is still concentrated in market share. Sany had promised to give up the entire concrete machinery market outside of China to Putzmeister. However, the cruel competition made Putzmeister still face other strong opponents even if Sany was withdrawn. (2) Degree of internationalization: Norbert Scheuch suggests that the team's degree of internationalization is different and one of the contradictions. He said that in addition to him, the seven executives of Putzmeister have members from five countries including Brazil, Spain, China, India, and Turkey. In the management team of Sany, "there is only one foreigner: me."

9.5 Discussion

Sany will focus on the Chinese market, while Putzmeister will continue to be an independent high-end brand. Retaining the original brand, Putzmeister will work together to create a new global leader in the concrete pump equipment industry.

After the successful acquisition of Putzmeister in 2013, Sany Heavy Industry's overseas operating income soared from 3.425 billion yuan in 2011 to 8.74 billion yuan, an increase of 155% year-on-year, and overseas business accounted for more than 19% of operating income. Compared with the delay in the general overseas acquisition, Putzmeister achieved strong growth in the year of its merger and acquisition. Xiaoyou Liang, the director of Sany Heavy Industry, declared a revenue of RMB 8.74 billion in the first year of financial consolidation. "In 2012, Putzmeister's operating income increased by 30% year-on-year, and profits increased substantially."

With the acquisition of the German Putzmeister, five years ahead of the international road, Sany shook up original global competition to become the new leader in the global machinery industry. Due to the disparity between the merger and the acquired party, it was referred to as "snake swallow." Sany and Putzmeister are the world's leading suppliers of concrete pumps in China and overseas. The merger is in line with Sany's strategic and industrial goals: to create a global leader in the concrete pump industry. Through the integration of brand, channel, and financial strength, Sany Heavy Industry can exploit emerging markets with the brand advantage of Putzmeister.

9.5.1 Broadening of Sales Channels

First of all, Putzmeister is now the world's best concrete technology company, its sales system established through 52 years cannot be measured by money, while its global sales and service network for 53 years, sales worldwide in 154 countries. Putzmeister has its own factories and sales systems in the United States, Brazil, India, France, Spain, and Portugal. Through the acquisition of the two companies, the market share can be complemented. Sany Heavy Industry has a 50–60% share in the concrete market in China, 90% of the total sales in China, and 10% in the international market. The sales of Putzmeister account for 10% in the country and 90% in the international market. Sany Heavy Industry is complementary to the Putzmeister sales network, which can achieve the highest market share in China and internationally after the acquisition.

Second, the status of competitors has changed. A month before the merger, Sany Heavy Industry and Putzmeister also played the role of a competitor in an Indian procurement case. In fact, Sany and Putzmeister have always regarded each other as the most strong competitor. Through this merger, Sany Heavy Industry has turned its competitors into a part of itself, and at the same time transformed the competitive advantage of its competitors into its own advantages.

Finally, Putzmeister and Sany's business are highly geographically complementary. As the leading supplier of concrete pump industry in China and a leading supplier of overseas concrete pumps, the two companies have met a clear strategic and industrial goal: to create a global leader in the concrete pump industry. Through the integration of brand, channel, and financial strength, Sany Heavy Industry can fully exploit emerging markets with the brand advantage of Putzmeister. Putzmeister's market share ranked first in the three emerging markets besides China (i.e., Turkey, Saudi Arabia, and India) Putzmeister constructed factories in India in 1958, after decades of market cultivation, it had a 60% market share of the concrete market in India. Sany Heavy Industry has invested in India to build a factory, gradually establish the Sany brand, and sales accounted for only 10% of the Indian concrete market in 2011. In fact, in the face of the increasingly saturated domestic market and the already mature developed markets, various machinery giants have a deeper understanding of the market potential of these regions. Therefore, emerging markets with great development potential have become the most coveted "cakes" for enterprises in various machinery industries.

9.5.2 *Reduction of Product Cost and Upgrade of Product Structure*

On the one hand, the acquisition is beneficial to the Putzmeister extended concrete equipment product line, including mixing stations, mixer trucks, etc., which quickly penetrates into the blank market and increases market share and sales. On the other hand, it is conducive to Sany Heavy Industry's extension of the industrial chain, which brings not only the integrity of the industrial structure, but also the cost reduction. Sany Heavy Industry's main person in charge of the acquisition said that the application of Putz Three technologies, such as Meister Smart Boom Technology and EBC Boom Vibration Reduction Technology, simplify the structural design and reduce the main product cost of Sany Heavy Industry—steel consumption by 10%. China's domestic low-cost advantage can enhance the profitability of Putzmeister. The successful international experience of Putzmeister can enhance Sany's overall efficiency, brand, international influence, financing platform and accelerate the internationalization process.

9.5.3 *Enterprise Scale and R&D Capability Upgrade*

Through this merger, Sany Heavy Industry's business volume will increase by about 10%. As the company's scale is further improved, Sany Heavy Industry will also receive 100% of German technology patents (Putzmeister owns pump-related patents around 200 pieces worldwide). Putzmeister is a high-end product line in the market segment. Its technical advantage is its guarantee in the concrete industry for decades. Its talents and good research and development capabilities make its products possess good reputation, Putzmeister's products can be used continuously for 100 hours without failure, but Chinese products can't reach this level of technology. After the merger, Sany will receive the world's top quality control and production from Putzmeister. Process, manufacturing technology and process, which will be the most important "assets" acquired by Sany, and M&A helps Sany Heavy Industry improve the technical manufacturing, stability, and reliability of its own brand products.

On April 17, 2012, Sany and Putzmeister officially announced the completion of the acquisition. On the one hand, the acquisition is beneficial to the Putzmeister extended concrete equipment product line, including mixing stations, mixer trucks, etc., which quickly penetrates into the blank market and increases market share and sales. On the other hand, it is conducive to Sany Heavy Industry's extension of the industrial chain, which brings not only the integrity of the industrial structure, but also the cost reduction. China's domestic low-cost advantage can enhance the profitability of Putzmeister. The successful international experience of Putzmeister can enhance Sany's overall efficiency, brand, international influence, financing platform and accelerate the internationalization process. Coupled with the overseas sales network of Sany forward-looking and vigorously deployed, this acquisition will surely become a watershed in the internationalization process of Sany.

From the perspective of operating income, according to the 2011 Sany Heavy Industry Annual Financial Report and the 2012 Sany Heavy Industry Half-Year Financial Report, the main business of Putzmeister's concrete machinery business: 2011 Sany Heavy Industry Concrete Machinery Business Revenue 26.01 billion yuan, operating profit of 10.9 billion yuan, gross profit margin of 41.83%, accounting for 51.30% of the main business income. From January to June 2012, Sany Heavy Industry Concrete Machinery business revenue was 17.1 billion yuan, operating profit was 720,000 yuan, gross profit margin was 42.21%, accounting for 53.98% of the main business income. Through the above comparison, we can clearly see that in 2012, during the overall sluggish domestic machinery industry, Sany Heavy Industry's concrete machinery business revenue, operating profit and gross profit margin increased year-on-year, and its proportion of main business income also increased. In addition, in 2011, Sany Heavy Industry's domestic (regional) revenue was 45.6 billion yuan, accounting for 89.89% of the total income, and international (regional) income was 3.4 billion yuan, accounting for 6.75% of the total income. From January to June 2012, Sany Heavy Industry's domestic (regional) revenue was 27.4 billion yuan, accounting for 86.17% of the total income, and international (regional) revenue was 3.3 billion yuan, accounting for 10.29% of the total income. Through the above ratios, we can see that after the merger of Sany Heavy Industry and Putzmeister officially on April 28, Sany Heavy Industry's overseas market revenue has improved significantly, which is attributed to the strong overseas market. Development, on the other hand, is the impact of the merger with the Putzmeister business. Through the cooperation with Sany Heavy Industry, Putzmeister has achieved excellent performance in sales growth of 10–15% year-on-year in the first half of the year in the context of the global economy is not very prosperous. The effect is initially revealed. In 2012, Sany Heavy Industry's concrete machinery sales exceeded 30 billion yuan, ranking first in the world.

9.5.4 *Merger and Acquisition Follow-Up*

According to the report of the board of directors of Sany Heavy Industry in 2012, the business indicators such as sales and profits of Putzmeister have improved significantly, and a good start after mergers and acquisitions has been achieved. With its first-class brand status and developed international market, the company achieved sales revenue of 8.7 billion yuan in overseas business in 2012, which was close to 10 billion yuan for the first time. Compared with the sales revenue of 3.4 billion yuan in overseas business in 2011, the growth rate was as high as 155.18%. The company's internationalization process has been greatly improved. In July 2013, Sany International Development Co., Ltd., a wholly owned subsidiary of Sany Heavy Industry Co., Ltd., invested US$548.77 million to acquire 100% equity of CP Machinery Limited, a company established and registered in Luxembourg under CITIC Industrial Investment Fund Management Co., Ltd. The remaining 10% stake in Meister. Upon completion of the transaction, Sany Heavy Industry holds a 100% stake in Putzmeister, Germany. Sany Heavy Industry said that the acquisition will help further enhance the company's R&D and innovation capabilities, international operation management experience and international development level, and consolidate the leading position of "the world's largest concrete machinery manufacturer."

9.6 Summary and Conclusions

Through the study of this case, we can see that the process of Sany Heavy Industry's acquisition of Putzmeister is relatively simple and fast. This is mainly due to the following two reasons: (1) Sany Heavy Industry is a typical private enterprise. The overseas mergers and acquisitions plans of Chinese enterprises have mostly failed. The main reason is that the "state-owned" background of most transnational M&A enterprises in China has made overseas entrepreneurs and politicians unable to agree. The strategic intention of Chinese companies to conduct overseas mergers and acquisitions has always been misinterpreted, and some countries always exaggerated political risks. As a private enterprise, Sany is less hindered by this aspect from the host country. With the advent of the financial crisis and the intensified European debt crisis, European and American companies and relevant government departments have relatively relaxed supervision and review of Chinese enterprises, thereby reducing the political obstacles and hidden costs of cross-border mergers and acquisitions have promoted Sany's acquisition of Putzmeister. (2) Sany Heavy Industry and Putzmeister are private enterprises with a simple shareholding structure and controlling shareholders. The largest shareholder of Sany Heavy Industry and Putzmeister is the actual controller of the company, who is able to make decisions on the company's and mergers and acquisitions decisions. Sany Heavy Industry has a large shareholder of more than 50% of the shares of Sany Group and the largest holding natural person shareholder Liang Wengen, and the chairman of the Sany Group is also Liang Wengen, so Liang Wengen became the actual controller of Sany Heavy Industry, the acquisition of Sany Heavy Industry Putzmeister has an absolute right to speak. Similarly, Karl Schlecht owns a 90% stake in Putzmeister and has an absolute say in the acquisition. (3) Fully consider the interests of the stakeholders of the acquired company. Hundreds of employees of Putzmeister are strongly opposed to the merger and acquisition of companies due to the impact of layoffs and corporate changes. They also staged demonstrations in front of the Putzmeister General Department. After the merger, there will be no layoffs and certain compensation will be given to the Putzmeister staff. (4) Co-investor selection in the process of cross-border mergers and acquisitions. The Hunan Branch of the China Development Bank and the Hunan Branch of the Export-Import Bank of China issued a US$290 million M&A loan to the Sany Group on April 19, 2012 to support the Sany M&A of Putzmeister to complete fund delivery. The acquisition of Sany Heavy Industry also relies on PE company, CITIC Industrial Investment Fund Management Co., Ltd.

CHAPTER 10

Conclusions

In the past 10 years, Chinese FDI has experienced rapid expansion. However, they have also encountered many difficulties, particularly with respect to institutional barriers and corporate governance. In response to the call for strengthening transnational governance and facilitating the high-quality of transnational operations, this book systematically sorts out the transnational governance, investment, and operations of Chinese companies by selecting eight typical Chinese MNCs across various industries. The eight cases include (1) "Alibaba Group – The Evolution of Transnational Governance"; (2) "Transnational Governance at Geely Auto During Its Acquisition of Volvo"; (3) "Transnational governance of Jinjiang Group's acquisition of Interstate Hotels and Resorts"; (4) "The Construction and Evolution of Lenovo Group's Transnational Governance Capability"; (5) "The equity governance model of the WISCO's overseas investment"; (6) "Transnational governance of Ping An Group's Cross-border Acquisition of Belgium's Fortis"; (7) "Transnational governance of Zoomlion's acquisition of Italian CIFA"; and (8) "Transnational governance of SANY Heavy Industry's acquisition of Putzmeister."

These case studies provide not only a systematic review of the successful and failed cases of corporate cross-border mergers and acquisitions, but also an analysis of the construction and evolution of corporate transnational governance capabilities (such as selection strategies of corporate overseas investment and equity governance models for entry into overseas markets), an analysis of corporate overseas investment governance

© The Author(s), under exclusive license to Springer Nature Singapore Pte Ltd. 2020
R. Lin et al. *Corporate Governance of Chinese Multinational Corporations*,
https://doi.org/10.1007/978-981-15-7405-4_10

selection strategies, and an analysis of the setting of equity governance models for overseas market entry. This book identifies and summarizes the construction and development of transnational governance capabilities of Chinese MNCs.

Specifically, this book identifies three important governance mechanisms. The first is stakeholder governance in the light of Geely's acquisition of Volvo, which indicates that multinational corporations must face domestic stakeholders (such as the Chinese government, local governments, and banks), host country stakeholders (such as host governments, trade union organizations, etc.), and the governance issues between their relationships. The second is the board of director's governance based on the case of Zoomlion's acquisition of Italian CIFA, which mainly focuses the structure and governance mechanisms of the board of directors and the board's decision-making process, particularly before and after cross-border mergers and acquisitions. The third is so-called executive governance based on the case of Jinjiang Group's acquisition of Interstate Hotels and Resorts, which mainly focuses on the governance strategies of the top management team, changes in personnel structure, and incentive mechanisms, particularly when dealing with cross-border M&A transactions.

The contribution of this book is multi-faceted. First, based on the selected typical cases on overseas investment and international business of Chinese MNCs, the book focuses on the transnational governance practices in these selected cases and explores their process of internationalization. Doing so can provide important theoretical and practical implications for the improvement of transnational governance capabilities of multinational corporations in emerging markets, which applies to China in this context.

Second, our eight cases represent typical examples across various industries, which include the high-tech industry, the hotel industry, the financial services industry, and the manufacturing industry. They also include both state-owned companies and private companies. By identifying and discussing both successful and failed cases of multinational governance and overseas investment, this book advances our knowledge and understanding of how efficient and appropriate governance should be structured and how mechanisms of multinational corporations should be used. Such knowledge and understanding can be the starting point of formal construction and theories or serve as a theoretical framework to further explore China's multinational corporations.

All in all, globalization is an inevitable trend of development of world economy, and this book employs case study analysis to summarize the characteristics and experiences of current transnational governance and business operations of Chinese MNCs, which provides a compilation of significant research and references for current and future multinational corporations in China.

This book has important implications. First, it explores the governance issues and challenges faced by Chinese multinational corporations in their process of internationalization, from the perspective of transnational governance and management. Our selected typical cases from various industries have suggested that some governance mechanisms (such as stakeholder governance, the board of director's governance, and executive governance) are very important for Chinese MNCs to enhance their capabilities of transnational governance and management. These governance mechanisms highlight that institutional differences and complex stakeholder relationship are important factors influencing the activities of international business operations and transnational governance of Chinese MNCs. Thus, existing Chinese MNCs and Chinese corporations that intend to be "going out" should be aware of the importance of these factors when they implement overseas investment and cross-border M&A transactions.

Second, this book also suggests a typical evolution process of corporate transnational governance. For example, in the light of the case of Lenovo Group's transnational governance, there are four suggested stages of the evolution process. Specifically, the first is the basic stage (i.e., the equity reform as the foundation for Lenovo's internationalization), which includes the reform of the property rights system, the development of business and organizational structure, and the proposal of the company's internationalization strategy. The second is the transition stage (i.e., the formation of Lenovo's transnational governance structure), which includes carrying out cross-border investment (e.g., M&A), and establishing a unified new organizational structure and developing appropriate governance mechanisms.

The third is the conflict stage (the formation of Lenovo's transnational governance mechanism), in which Lenovo's governance capabilities were enhanced by "personnel adjustment of senior management team," "reengineering business processes, reducing costs, and building a global supply chain," and "setting a chief diversity officer." The last is the formation stage (i.e., the synergy between Lenovo's transnational governance structure and governance mechanism), in which the company has formed a relatively stable transnational governance structure, achieved good integration of governance mechanisms, and gradually made itself as a global multinational company. Therefore, as a successful case of "going out," other Chinese companies could learn from and develop these four stages when they operate multinational business and transnational governance and management.

The publication of this book is particularly significant in its promotion of research of corporate transnational governance and the construction of transnational governance capabilities. It will also help facilitate the high-quality transnational investment and management of Chinese enterprises. For example, identification and analyze of these eight selected cases will provide a base and opportunity for development of theories of MNCs' corporate governance. Thus, one of the important future research directions is to formally develop new theories and/or theoretical frameworks for corporate governance of MNCs. Doing so will enhance both understanding of and explanatory power of current practices of Chinese MNCs.

The manufacturer's authorised representative in the EU is Springer Nature Customer Service Centre GmbH, Europaplatz 3, 69115 Heidelberg, Germany. If you have any concerns regarding our products, please contact ProductSafety@springernature.com

Printed and bound by CPI Group (UK) Ltd, Croydon, CR0 4YY

30/09/2026

02225326-0001